Contents

Acknowledgements

This book could not have been written without a great deal of help and advice from City institutions as well as from colleagues in the financial press. A full list of those who have assisted would be impossibly long, but I would like to thank first the *Financial Times*, *The Independent* and the *Investors Chronicle* for permission to reproduce material from their respective publications and Datastream International for the use of its charts.

Detailed comments and advice on the text from John Plender and Danny O'Shea were invaluable and I am also very grateful to Liisa Springham for casting a fresh eye over the typescript. I had the benefit of information and advice on individual sections from, among others, Adrienne Gleeson, Andrew Goodrick-Clarke, Helen Fearnley and Peter Wilson-Smith and considerable help from Prudential Assurance, The Takeover Panel and the press offices of The Stock Exchange and the Securities and Investments Board. I am also grateful to Hugh Partridge and Brian Roy for technical help with the second and third editions. The views expressed — and the mistakes — are my own.

Preface

Money is not complicated. The principles behind financial transactions are simple enough. It is usually the detail that confuses by obscuring the principles.

The money world, like many others, develops its own practices and jargon, which are usually incomprehensible to the layman. Even an intelligent watcher of the financial scene is at a natural disadvantage. Sometimes the financial world likes to keep it that way, because an aura of mystique can enhance the value of its services.

The financial press, at its best, attempts to bridge this comprehension gap, but it is often forced to satisfy two different markets. It is writing both for those in the money business and for the outsiders who like to follow the financial and economic scene and who, in their personal or business lives, have to choose among many financial services and investment products. A first-time reader of the *Financial Times* or the business pages of the national dailies or Sunday papers may still feel he is faced with a foreign language.

This book sets out to explain the language of money. It does so by explaining the principles and practices behind the markets and financial institutions which deal with money and investments. Understand the principles, and the jargon falls quickly into place. The book consists of two parts. The narrative chapters provide a guide to the workings of the financial system and its main components. This is suitable for the newcomer to the financial scene, though will also serve as an *aide-memoire* for those with existing knowledge. A new Chapter 23 in this third edition updates for events up to mid-1991. It should be read in conjunction with the earlier chapters. At the end of the book comes a combined glossary and index, which either provides explanations of financial terms or points to where they are explained in the text. References to latest developments described in the update chapter are picked out in bold type.

The approach is intended to be practical. The explanations of financial terms are not aimed at the professional economist or banker and should not be taken as legal definitions. They explain the sense in which these terms are most likely to be encountered in the financial press.

The book follows the pattern of financial press coverage. Much of what is written concerns companies and the stockmarket, which therefore require explanation in detail. The sections on company accounts help to explain the background to the main investment yardsticks in use — they can be skipped if you are familiar with the concepts. Other areas such as the eurodollar market warrant less space. Though far larger than the domestic stockmarket, the eurodollar market does not so frequently involve the general public in Britain and attracts far less press coverage.

A final word of warning. In times of boom, investment markets become infected by their own enthusiasm. The money men forget the existence of the word 'bust'.

Journalists who write about the City are not immune to this enthusiasm. It sometimes colours their judgement, as it colours that of the City's professionals. The way to read the financial pages during a stockmarket boom is with a modicum of caution. Booms do not go on for ever and some journalists, like brokers, are better at advising when to buy than when to sell.

Introduction

For those who first came into contact with the financial world in the early 1980s, life falls into two parts. A period of boom in financial markets up to 1987, when stockmarket investment seemed to provide a recipe for instant and effortless profit. And, after the stockmarket crash of 19 October 1987, a considerably bleaker world in which many of the illusions of the boom days were exposed to the cold light of reality. But perhaps less has changed than might have appeared in the immediate aftermath of the crash. As with the original edition of this book — written shortly before the crash — our starting point is the fundamental developments affecting the financial scene worldwide.

The British financial system is in a state of change. The changes mean we have to rethink our definition of traditional financial institutions and learn to accept new words to describe the practices of new markets or the new practices of existing ones.

A few years ago you could safely assume that a life assurance company sold life assurance and pensions, a bank took deposits and lent money and a building society provided mortgages for homebuyers. They still do, but they do a lot of other things as well. The life assurance company may manage unit trusts, provide mortgages for homebuyers and perhaps even own estate agents. The bank probably markets mortgages, unit trusts and insurance, and is deeply involved in the stockmarkets. The building society is chasing the banks by offering cheque accounts, personal loans and maybe even pensions.

The changes are part of a **deregulation** process known as the **financial services revolution**. This revolution means that the traditional demarcation lines between different types of financial institution are breaking down. Some of these were the result of legal restraints. Some had grown up over many years following custom and practice. Where the restraints were legal ones the government may have relaxed them, as in the case of the building societies. Where they were merely traditional, the institutions themselves have changed.

Deregulation at its simplest stands for competition in the domestic savings market. The financial community is vying for the privilege — and the profit — that derives from managing the nation's savings.

Another aspect of the financial services revolution in Britain is what came to be known as the **Big Bang** on The Stock Exchange. Traditionally The Stock Exchange had been a club, deciding its own rules, working practices and the very hefty charges clients paid for its services. The government forced a change towards a more competitive trading system and a breakdown of traditional demarcation lines. It became known as the Big Bang because the most important changes took place on one explosive day: 27 October 1986.

But deregulation means more than a few changes to the domestic financial system. What is happening in Britain is one aspect of changes taking place across the world's financial markets. Changes in the way money is borrowed and lent, changes in the way investments are traded. On the global scale deregulation means the breakdown of restrictions on different types of financial institution in the main financial centres, but also a breakdown of the barriers between the centres themselves. The abandonment of foreign exchange controls — Britain's were suspended in 1979 — is one part of the process.

Opening up domestic stock exchanges to foreign members is another. Widening the range of investments that can be traded in each financial centre is a third, opening the way for round-the-clock trading in investments and currencies. The time zones are such that British markets are opening around the time Tokyo markets close and New York opens while London is still going strong. The main **securities houses** which deal in investments are of necessity international, with representation in each of the main financial centres.

Why is the world suddenly obsessed with financial markets and the ability to trade round-the-clock? It comes back to another aspect of deregulation — the changing role of traditional banking institutions combined with the need to handle massive cross-frontier flows of money seeking investments, notably from Japan to the United States.

Traditionally, if someone had spare cash he lent it to the bank and the bank in turn lent it to someone needing to borrow money. Today, the name of the game is to cut out the middleman: the bank. Would-be lenders seek out would-be borrowers direct, and they need markets to bring them together.

Moreover, the way investors put up the money has changed. Instead of simply making a loan they prefer to exchange their money for pieces of paper they can later sell if they want their money back. And the markets in which the pieces of paper are bought and sold have blossomed. The banks have had to take on a new role: arranging the issues of these pieces of paper, putting the buyers and sellers together, organizing and participating in the markets where the pieces of paper change hands. It is a different business from simply borrowing and lending money.

A vigorous expansion of financial markets and the rapid introduction of new techniques thus characterize the second half of the 1980s. In Britain the climate was further influenced — up to October 1987 — by a period of unprecedented boom in share prices, accompanied by the arrival of many new individual investors on the stockmarket as they were persuaded to buy shares in the previously nationalized industries at bargain prices.

To complete the picture, a new **investor protection** framework — designed to remedy some of the shortcomings of the old systems and adapt to the changes in the financial environment — has gradually been installed. It was not fully in place before, in late 1986 and early 1987, a series of City scandals erupted.

This is the background against which financial journalists were writing in the second half of the 1980s: innovation, financial boom and the first whiffs of those particular forms of corruption that surface in the financial world when money-making seems easy and raw greed overrides enlightened self-interest. It was an invigorating but possibly an unstable climate.

***

This was the point where the introduction to the original edition ended, written in the early summer of 1987. Within a few months we had experienced a dramatic demonstration of the instability of the financial climate, when the British stockmarket fell 20 per cent in two days towards the end of October, and other markets worldwide suffered comparable falls. The events and some of the lessons of those days are described in a new section on the crash in Chapter 7. Far from overturning core financial principles, they serve to demonstrate how the fundamental rules of financial markets will reassert themselves in due course.

The post-crash world is a quieter world. Stockmarket activity has been lower. The high-earning stars of the City's dealing rooms are wondering whether they will keep their jobs rather than calculating the size of their bonuses. Some of the recent changes in the financial system are being called into question. Competition in financial markets has brought higher rather than lower charges for small investors in shares and unit trusts. They now also know from personal experience what the 'health warnings' in investment advertisements have always told them: share prices can go down as well as up.

Institutional investors have learned that competitive markets may offer **liquidity** — ease of dealing in large volumes at firm prices — when markets are rising but that liquidity disappears when prices turn down. They have seen that the new trading system introduced by Big Bang is highly volatile and that the internationalization of securities trading can spread panic from one financial centre to the rest of the world in the course of a day. The integrated securities house — offering one-stop shopping for the whole range of financial services — is less in vogue now, because it is clear that there is not the business to support more than a few such conglomerates. Many users of financial services prefer smaller, more specialist institutions. The new regulatory regime for the City was being revised and amended even before it was fully in place.

But just as some earlier innovations are being rethought in the light of experience, so new trends are emerging. The Chancellor's dramatic tax reductions for the rich in his 1988 Budget went a long way towards making it worthwhile to invest for income and not merely for capital gain. In the companies arena managements are — for better or worse — being shaken by the threat of mega-bids, financed with borrowed money, as the principle of the American leveraged buy-out crosses the Atlantic (see Chapter 11).

And as an antidote to these and other weighty developments in the financial markets, this edition ends with a light-hearted look at some of the more oblique terms and techniques financial journalists use in putting their message across. *June 1989*

***

If the 1980s were a period of revolutionary change in the financial world, the 1990s are the decade in which the financial world must learn to live with the consequences of change and to adapt some of the new structures in the light of experience. Aside from Britain's entry into into the **Exchange Rate Mechanism** of the **European Monetary System**, there have been relatively few structural changes since the second edition went to press in mid-1989. In this third edition, the changes in detail and in the market background up to mid-1991 are set out in a new update chapter that begins on page 253. *July 1991*

1

First principles

Write about money, and you cannot entirely avoid technical terms. The simplest terms and concepts need to be dealt with at the outset. They will crop up time and again.

Fundamental to all financial markets is the idea of earning a **return** on money. Money has to work for its owner. Here — ignoring for the moment some of the tax complications that crop up in practice — are some of the ways it can do so:

- You deposit £1,000 with a bank which pays you, say, 10 per cent a year interest. In other words, your £1,000 of **capital** earns you £100 a year, which is the **return** on your money. When you want your £1,000 back you get £1,000, plus any accumulated interest, not more or less. Provided your bank or building society does not go bust, your £1,000 of **capital** is not at risk, except from **inflation** which may reduce its **purchasing power** each year.

- You buy gold bullion to a value of £1,000 because you think the price of gold will rise. If, say, the price of gold has risen by 20 per cent after a year, you can sell your gold for £1,200. You have made a **profit** or a **capital gain** of £200 on your capital outlay of £1,000. In other words you have a **return** of 20 per cent on your money. If the price of gold fails to move, you've earned nothing because commodities like gold do not pay interest.

- You use your £1,000 to buy **securities** that are traded on a stockmarket. Usually these will be **government bonds** (known as **gilt-edged securities** or **gilts** in the UK) or **ordinary shares** in a company. The first always provide an **income**; the second normally do. Traditional gilt-edged securities pay a fixed rate of interest. Ordinary shares in companies normally pay a **dividend** from the profits the company earns. If the company's profits rise, the dividend is likely to be increased. But there is no guarantee that there will be a dividend at all. If the company makes losses, it may have to cease paying a dividend.

But when you buy securities that are traded on a stockmarket, the **return** on your £1,000 is not limited to the interest or dividends you receive. The prices of these securities in the stockmarket will also rise and fall, and your original £1,000 investment accordingly becomes worth more or less. So you are taking the risk of **capital gains** or **capital losses**.

Suppose you buy £1,000 worth of ordinary shares which pay you a gross dividend of £40 a year. You are getting a return or **dividend yield** of 4 per cent a year on your investment (£40 as a percentage of £1,000). If after a year the market value of your £1,000 of shares has risen to £1,100, you can sell them for a **capital gain** of £100 (or a 10 per cent profit on your original outlay). Thus your **overall return** over the year (before tax) consisted of the £40 income and the £100 capital gain: a total of £140, or a 14 per cent overall return on your original £1,000 investment.

Investors are generally prepared to accept much lower initial **yields** on shares than on fixed-interest stocks because they expect the income (and, in consequence, the **capital value** of the shares) to rise in the future. Most investors in ordinary shares are seeking capital gains at least as much as income. Note that if you are buying a security, you are taking the risk that the price may fall whether it is a government bond or a share. But with the government bond the income is at least guaranteed by the government. With the share there is a second layer of risk: the company may not earn sufficient profits to pay a dividend.

- Finally, you can put the £1,000 directly to work in a business you run. Since this option does not initially involve the financial markets, we'll ignore it.

To summarize: money can be deposited to produce an income, it can be used to buy commodities or goods which are expected to rise in value (including your own home) or it can be invested in stockmarket securities which normally produce an income but show capital gains or losses as well. There are many variations on each of these themes. But keep the principles in mind and the variations fall into place.

Markets and interest rates

For each type of investment and for many of their derivatives there is a **market**. There is a market in money in London. It is not a physical marketplace: dealings take place over the telephone, and the price a borrower pays for the use of money is the interest rate. There are markets in **commodities**. And there is a market in **government bonds** and company **shares**: The Stock Exchange. Much of what you read in the financial press concerns these markets, their movements and the investments that are dealt on them.

The important point is that no market is entirely independent of the others. The linking factor is the **cost of money** (or the **return** an investor can get on money, which is the other side of the same coin). If interest rates rise or fall there is likely to be a ripple of movement through all the financial markets.

This is the most important single mechanism in the financial sphere and it lies behind a great deal of what is written in the financial press: from discussion of mortgage rates to reasons for movements in the gilt-edged securities market. Money will gravitate to where it earns the best return, commensurate with the risk the investor is prepared to take and the length of time for which he can tie up his money. As a general rule:

● The more money you have to invest, the higher the return you can expect.
● The longer you are prepared to tie your money up, the higher the return you can expect.
● The more risk you are prepared to take, the higher the return you can expect if all goes well.

Different returns on different investments

To match investors' different needs, there is a whole range of different returns available across the financial system. An investor might, say, be prepared to accept a return of 7 per cent or less on money he deposited with a bank for a short time and might need in a hurry. The low interest rate is the price of safety and convenience. At the same time he might expect to get 10 per cent if he were prepared to lock up his money by lending it for a year. And if he were prepared to take the chance of capital gain or loss by buying a gilt-edged security in the stockmarket, he might expect a return of, say, 11 per cent.

But these and other returns available to investors will rise and fall with changes in the cost of money in Britain and abroad. What causes these changes is a different matter. Sufficient for the moment that there are times when money is cheap (interest rates are low) and times when it is expensive (interest rates are high).

Suppose interest rates rise. The investor who was content with 7 per cent for money he could put his hands on quickly will expect a higher return to match the interest rates being offered elsewhere. So the rate for short-term deposits might rise to 8 per cent. Likewise, the investor who considers tucking his money away for a year will no longer be content with 10 per cent. He'll only be prepared to lend his money for a year if he's offered, say, 11.5 per cent. So anyone wanting to borrow money for a year has to offer the higher rate to lenders.

The precise rates are not important to the argument. The essential fact is that when one interest rate moves significantly, most other rates will move in the same direction. There will still be a differential between the rate the investor gets if he deposits his money for a few weeks and the rate he gets for locking it up for a year, though the size of the differential may change. But both rates will usually move up if interest rates generally are rising.

Interest rates and bond prices

The change in interest rates has important implications for the stockmarket prices of bonds which pay a fixed rate of interest: **fixed-interest securities**, of which the traditional **gilt-edged securities** issued by the government are the most familiar though companies also issue fixed-interest bonds. It works like this.

Gilt-edged securities are a form of **IOU** (I owe you) or **promissory note** issued by the government when it needs to borrow money. The government undertakes to pay so much a year in interest to the people who put up the money and who get the IOU in exchange. Normally the government agrees to repay (**redeem**) the stock at some date in the future, but to illustrate the interest rate mechanism it is easiest initially to take an **irredeemable** or **undated** stock which does not have to be repaid.

The original investors who lend the money to the government do not have to hold on to the IOUs. They can sell them to other investors, who then become entitled to receive the interest from the government. Suppose the government needs to borrow money at a time when investors would expect an 11 per cent yield on a gilt-edged security. It offers £11 a year interest for every £100 it borrows. The investor is prepared to pay £100 for the right to receive £11 a year interest, because this represents an 11 per cent return on his outlay.

Then suppose that interest rates rise to the point where an investor would expect a 12.5 per cent return if he bought a gilt-edged security. He will no longer pay £100 for the right to £11 a year in income. He will only be prepared to pay a price that gives him a 12.5 per cent return on his outlay. The 'right' price in this case is £88, because if he pays only £88 for the right to receive £11 a year in income, he is getting a 12.5 per cent return on his investment (11 as a percentage of 88). So in the stockmarket the price of the gilt-edged security that pays £11 a year interest would have to fall to £88 before investors would be prepared to buy it. The original investor who payed £100 thus sees the value of his investment fall because of the rise in interest rates. Conversely, the value of his investment would have risen if interest rates had fallen.

This is why there is so much comment in the financial press on the outlook for interest rates. Higher interest rates mean higher borrowing costs for companies and individuals. They also mean losses for existing investors in fixed-interest bonds.

Markets discount future events

In practice, the movement in stockmarket prices is slightly more complex than this would suggest and there is another vital principle to grasp. Stockmarkets always look ahead and **discount** future events, or what investors expect these events to be. Prices of stocks in the bond markets don't fall or rise simply in response to actual changes in interest rates. If investors think interest rates are going to rise in the near future, they will probably start selling fixed-interest stocks. So there will be more sellers than buyers and the market price will begin to fall before the adjustment in general interest rates actually takes place. Likewise, investors will begin buying fixed-interest stocks if they think interest rates are going to come down, so that they have a profit by the time the interest rate cut has taken place and market prices have adjusted upwards to reflect the new lower interest rates. Making profits in the stockmarkets is all about guessing better (or faster) than the next man.

What is the market?

Reports in the press tend to say 'the market did this' or 'the market expected good news on the economic front', as if the market were a single living entity with a single conscious mind. This is not, of course, the case. To understand reports of market behaviour you have to bear in mind the way the market works.

A market is simply a mechanism which allows individuals or organizations to trade with each other. It may be a physical marketplace — a trading floor — where buyers and sellers or their representatives can meet and buy and sell face to face. Or it may simply be a network of buyers and sellers who deal with each other over the telephone or computer screen. The principle is much the same.

In either type of market, the buyers and sellers may deal direct with each other or they may deal through a middleman known as a **marketmaker**. If they deal direct, each would-be buyer has to find a corrresponding would-be seller. John Smith who wants to sell must locate Tom Jones who wants to buy. If there is a marketmaker, John Smith will sell instead to the marketmaker, who buys on his own account (acts as a **principal**) in the hope that he will later be able to find a Tom Jones to whom he can sell at a profit. Marketmakers **make a book** in shares or bonds. They are prepared to buy shares in the hope of finding somebody to sell to or sell shares (which they may not even have) in the expectation of finding somebody from whom they can buy to **balance their books**. Either way, they make their living on the difference between the prices at which they buy and sell. Marketmakers (in practice there will normally be a number of them competing with each other) lend **liquidity** — fluidity — to a market. A potential buyer can always buy without needing to wait until he can find a potential seller; securities can readily be turned into cash.

The market price of a security (or anything else) reflects a balance between the views of all the possible buyers and sellers in the particular market. This is what commentators really mean when they say 'the market thought ....' They are describing the dominant view among those operating in the market. An example helps to show how this operates on security prices.

How prices rise or fall

Suppose a security (it could be the government bond we looked at earlier) **stands in the market** at a price of £90. This is the last price at which it changed hands. Suppose there are only ten such securities in existence. But the price has been moving down, and even at £90 there are seven investors who think it is too expensive and would like to sell, and only three who would be prepared to buy. If £90 remained the price, only three sellers could find buyers and there would be an unsatisfied desire to sell.

Suppose the price is £89 instead. At this level one of the previous sellers decides the security is no longer expensive and he may as well hold on, while another investor decides it would be worth buying at this lower price. There are now only six sellers and four buyers. Still no balance.

Now suppose the price is £88. Another potential seller changes his mind if he can only get £88, while another investor reckons it is now attractive and emerges as a potential buyer at this lower price. There are now five sellers and five buyers. Thus at £88 the price has reached an equilibrium which holds good until something happens to persuade some of the investors to change their view again.

If there are marketmakers operating in the market, they will have moved their quoted price down from £90 to £88 — the price at which they can balance their books by matching buyers and sellers. Though their operations are in practice more complex (see Chapter 7) and they also quote a **spread** between the price at which they are prepared to sell and the one at which they will buy, the principle holds good. Prices will move towards the point where there is equilibrium between buyers and sellers.

This principle operates in all markets, not just the markets in securities. In the **money markets** banks will need to adjust the interest rates they offer and charge until they have the right balance between those who are prepared to lend to them and those who want to borrow. In the **foreign exchange markets** the value of the pound will need to find a level at which there is a balance between those who want to buy pounds and those who want to sell. Free markets in commodities, in gold bullion and in office accommodation in the City of London are affected by the same interaction of sellers and takers.

Primary and secondary markets

Fixed-interest securities and ordinary shares are the main stock-in-trade of the **securities markets** and The Stock Exchange is the main domestic securities market. By buying one or the other, investors are helping — directly or indirectly — to provide the finance that government or industry needs. Why do we say 'directly or indirectly'? Because the stockmarket is two markets in one: a **primary market** and a **secondary market**.

A **primary market** is one in which the government, companies or other bodies can sell new securities to investors to raise cash. A **secondary market** is a market in which the investors can buy and sell these securities to each other, and one market serves both functions. The buying and selling in the secondary market does not directly affect the finances of government or companies. But if investors did not know they could buy and sell securities in the secondary market they might well be reluctant to put up cash for the government or companies by buying securities in the primary market when they were first issued. And the prices established by the buying and selling by investors in the secondary market help to determine the price that government and companies will have to pay next time they need to issue further securities for cash in the primary market. A reasonably **liquid** secondary market is normally considered vital for a healthy primary market.

Interest rates and currencies

Another facet of interest rates: at a time of volatile **exchange rates** between different currencies, the interaction between interest rates and the value of currencies (or **parities**) dominates much financial comment. Investment is increasingly international, and in their search for the best returns investors look not simply at the different options available in their own country but at the relative attractiveness of different countries as a haven for funds.

16

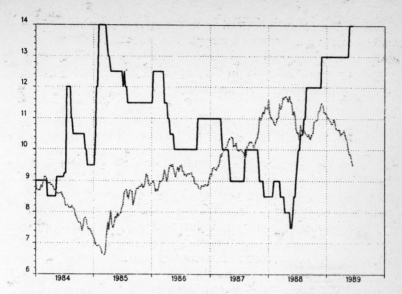

Figure 1.1 Interest rates have generally been high to support sterling when the value of the pound was slipping. The top line shows the London clearing banks' base rate and the bottom (dotted) line shows the movement in the value of sterling against the dollar. Source: *Datastream International.*

If Britain offers higher interest rates than, say, the United States or West Germany, international investors may be tempted to invest in Britain. This means they will need to exchange whatever currency they hold into pounds sterling in order to make deposits or buy securities in Britain. They will therefore be buying pounds on the foreign exchange market. If the buying of pounds exceeds any selling taking place, the **value of the pound** (the price of the pound in terms of other currencies) is likely to rise.

Interest rates are by no means the only factor affecting the value of a currency. And the **overall return** a foreign investor receives when he invests in Britain depends not only on the yield his money can earn but on the movement in the pound itself. If the pound rises against his own currency he makes a profit on the movement in the pound. If it falls, he makes a loss. So his total return is a combination of the **yield** he can get by investing in Britain and the profit or loss he makes on the currency.

Whatever the level of interest rates in Britain, overseas investors will not invest if they expect the currency itself will fall sharply for other reasons. But interest rates are still an important weapon the government can use in defending the currency by attracting investors to buy pounds to invest in Britain.

Effects of rising interest rates

Now look at some of the effects of a rise in interest rates across the financial system. In describing these effects different papers will highlight different aspects, according to where their readers' interests lie:

Higher interest rates probably mean:

- An increase in **borrowing costs** for industry, meaning that profits for many companies will be lower than they would otherwise have been and that companies may be less keen to borrow money to invest in new projects.
- A rise in the **opportunity cost** of holding non-yielding assets such as gold or commodities (it becomes theoretically more expensive to own them because, at higher interest rates, you lose more by not taking the opportunity of earning interest on your money).
- Higher monthly **mortgage payments** for homebuyers.
- More expensive **overdrafts** and **personal loans,** and higher **credit card** interest rates, possibly causing consumers to spend less.
- A fall in the value of **gilt-edged securities** on the stockmarket, unless investors think the rise in interest rates is very temporary or unless prices have already fallen in anticipation.
- A possible fall in the value of **ordinary shares** on the stockmarket (though the mechanism here is more complicated than with the gilt-edged market — see below).
- An increase in the returns that **investors** and **savers** can expect to earn on their money.
- A strengthening (all else being equal) in the **value of the pound sterling,** as overseas investors buy pounds to invest in Britain and get the advantage of the higher returns from depositing money in Britain or buying British bonds.

In the popular press it is the effects on the individual, and particularly the homebuyer, that are likely to make the headlines:

'Mortgage costs to rocket'. The quality press will probably mention the effect on mortgages, too. In a country where many people derive their main sense of economic security from selling their houses to each other at ever-rising prices, nobody is going to ignore the housebuyer. But the more serious papers will also be analysing the effects on sterling, industry, the stockmarket and on the outlook for economic growth. In the *Financial Times*, which regularly covers virtually every financial market, the ripple effects will spread to most corners of the paper.

Debt and equity

Much of the day-to-day comment in the financial press is concerned with the securities markets and the investments that are traded in them. And so far we have talked mainly of the bond market (the market in long-term debt: particularly the gilt-edged market in which the government's own debt is traded). But this leads to another fundamental concept: the difference between **debt** and **equity**.

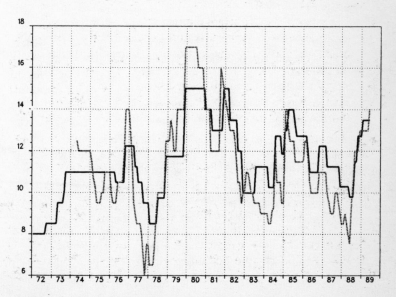

Figure 1.2   Mortgage interest rates (solid line) and bank base rates (dotted line). Mortgage interest rates do not stray far away from commercial rates for very long nowadays. Source: *Datastream International*.

A company can raise money in a number of different ways. These are the main ones.

First, it can simply borrow money from a bank or elsewhere. Normally the money has to be paid back in due course, and meantime interest has to be paid to the original lender. The interest may be at a **variable** or **floating rate**: it rises or falls with changes in the general level of interest rates in the country. Or it may be at a **fixed rate**, in which case the interest rate remains the same for the life of the loan.

Secondly, it can **issue a loan** in the form of a security. In other words, it creates an IOU and offers it to investors in return for cash, in the same way as the government does in the gilt-edged market. Normally the company agrees to repay — **redeem** — this loan at some future point. But the loan can usually be traded in the stockmarket in the same way as a gilt-edged security. The investor who originally put up the money does not have to hold on to his IOU until it is repaid. If he wants the money sooner, he sells the IOU to somebody else. He may get less for it than he paid, or he may sell it at a profit. The company simply pays interest to whomever owns the IOU when interest is due, and eventually repays the money it originally borrowed to the person who owns the IOU on the **redemption date**.

These loans may pay a fixed rate of interest or a floating rate. If they pay a fixed rate, they are very similar to a fixed-rate government bond. The rate of interest is known as the **coupon** and for convenience it is expressed as a percentage of the **nominal**, **par** or **face** value, which in Britain is taken to be a unit of £100, as with a government stock. The loans issued by companies go under various names such as **loan stock, industrial debenture** or **bond**. The value of fixed-interest loans is affected by movements in interest rates, but the health and standing of the company also plays a part. The company has to earn the profits to pay the interest and repay the capital, whereas with a gilt-edged security these payments are guaranteed by the government.

Thirdly, a company may raise money by creating new **ordinary shares** and selling them for cash. This is quite different in principle from issuing a loan, because ordinary shares — also known as **equity** — are not a debt of the company. They do not normally have to be repaid. The owner of a share becomes part-owner of the company. In return for putting up his money, he shares in the risks and rewards of the company's operations:

hence the term **risk capital**. He is entitled to a share of everything the company owns, after allowing for its debts, and to a share of the profits it earns. If its profits increase he can normally expect higher **dividends** — income payments — on his shares.

A share is also a **security** of the company and can normally be bought and sold in the same way as a loan stock. In the same way, its price in the market depends on the interplay of buyers and sellers, not on the price at which it was originally issued. An investor who wants his money back simply sells the share to somebody else; whether he gets more or less than he paid originally depends on what the market price has done in the interim. If profits of the company rise, it will probably pay higher dividends and — all else being equal — the value of the shares will normally rise. If the company gets into trouble, the owners of the shares or **shareholders** are the last people to get any money back. All of the loans and other debts have to be repaid first.

Interest rate effects on ordinary shares

Investors will generally accept a lower initial **yield** on shares than on fixed-interest securities because they expect their income and the capital value of the shares to rise. Take the earlier example of shares that could be bought at a price that offered a 4 per cent yield but which rose in value by 10 per cent over the year. The overall return to a buyer would have been 14 per cent. This is attractive relative to the 11 per cent return on gilt-edged securities. The additional three **percentage points** allow for the risk element in the ordinary shares.

But investors do not know in advance what return they will get from ordinary shares. Even the 4 per cent dividend yield could fall if the company had to cut its dividend. And if it cut its dividend, the value of the shares in the stockmarket would almost certainly fall too. Hence investing in shares involves a judgement about a company's prospects and its ability to earn the profits out of which the dividends will be paid.

However, share values may be affected by movements in interest rates as well. If yields on gilt-edged stocks rose to 14 per cent, investors would almost certainly want a higher overall return than 14 per cent on ordinary shares to allow for the risk element. In the short run share prices would have to fall in the market to provide the higher return. But the prices of shares in

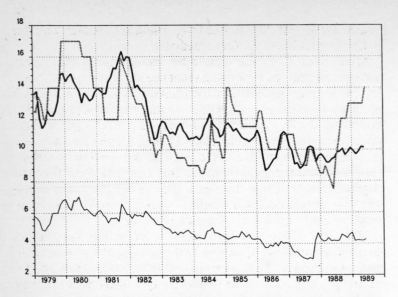

Figure 1.3 Note how yields on different types of investment respond to each other. The two lines at the top show the redemption yield on medium-dated gilt-edged stocks (solid line) and banks' base rate (dotted line). The thinner solid line at the bottom shows the average yield on equities. However, in 1988 and 1989 the very sharp rise in short-term interest rates was not fully reflected in rates on longer-term investments. Source: *Datastream International.*

individual companies are also affected by the profits outlook for the company. In the very long run the return from shares will depend on the profits the company earns or is capable of earning. A large proportion of the press's financial coverage concerns the profits companies earn and the profits they are likely to earn in the future.

Don't expect markets to be rational

One final word about markets. We can describe dispassionately how they operate and the main forces at work. This is not always how they present themselves in the short run to those who operate in them or those who comment on their day-to-day behaviour. Markets are moved by tips and rumours, by frenetic temporary enthusiasms and by devastating panics. They are creatures of mood and can sometimes be manipulated. Their enthusiasms and panics are frequently self-feeding, losing all contact with the underlying realities: the **fundamentals**.

Markets are a vital mechanism between investors with money and governments and companies that need money to put to work. But the average dealer in a marketmaking firm may rarely think about his function as a cog in this essential economic process. His business is dealing in shares and he has a gut feeling that share prices are due to rise, so he buys. He will usually find a reason afterwards for what he did. Do not take too seriously all of the reasons for market behaviour you find reported in the financial pages. Market professionals earn their bread from movements one way or another. If no logical reason for movement exists, they are quite capable of inventing one.

The City of London provides the main mechanisms for distributing the flows of money. In the next chapter we look at the sources of money, the markets that distribute the money and the people you will meet in the financial pages who operate in these markets.

2

Money flows and the money men

When a financial journalist describes somebody as 'an eminent City figure', he probably means what he says. The man is perhaps a senior member of the banking establishment. If a journalist describes somebody as 'the controversial City financier', he's probably coming as close as he dares within the libel laws to calling him a financial spiv.

But what exactly is this 'City' which harbours these characters and many more? 'The City' is a convenient blanket term for the commercial institutions at the heart of Britain's financial system. They do not necessarily operate within the square mile of the City of London, though a surprising number of them do. They provide the financial services that oil the wheels of industry and trade. They are not, however, concerned only with serving Britain's domestic economy. Much of the City's activity relates to international finance and trade, and one of the more common criticisms of the City is that it is too remote from Britain's own productive industries.

The City is a major source of **invisible earnings** for Britain's **balance of payments**, contributing a net £7.35 billion in 1988. Of this total, by far the largest amount is normally contributed by insurance and banking.

To put into context what we read about the City, we need some idea of the sums of money involved and the relative importance of different institutions. What follows in this chapter is an outline of the main investment flows and the bodies which handle them. Other markets are described in more detail in the chapters devoted to them.

The savings institutions

The City provides the mechanisms which channel money to where it can be put to work. The main external source of new long-term investment funds for business and government is the **savings** of private individuals, and in Britain these savings are channelled mainly through the large **financial institutions**: primarily the **pension funds** and **insurance companies**. With some £21 billion a year of new money, they invest funds in companies by buying shares. By buying gilt-edged securities they supply much of the money the government normally needs to borrow — though in 1988 and 1989 the government was in the unusual position of repaying debts rather than borrowing afresh. **The Stock Exchange** allows these institutional funds to find their way into company securities, and the financial institutions are The Stock Exchange's largest clients.

The financial institutions also invest in **commercial property** and in **overseas securities and property**, and put money to work short term in the **money markets**.

A third type of investment institution is significant in the equity market: the **unit trust**. Unit trusts pool the money of individual investors to provide a spread of risk by investing in a range of shares, mainly via the stockmarket (see Chapter 20).

The **building societies** also act as a funnel for the savings of individuals but the money they take goes primarily into providing **mortgages** for home buyers. However, a proportion of their funds is invested in government securities via the stockmarket, where it can readily be turned into cash if needed.

Banking and money markets

The other major source of external funds for business is the **banking system** and the **money markets** (see Chapter 14). The banks' main sources of funds are shorter-term — the money of individuals and companies deposited with them (**retail deposits**) plus the **wholesale funds** they borrow in the money markets. The banks lend money in one form or another. They do not, as in some other countries, invest in company shares to any significant extent. But increasingly they act as arrangers of finance as well as lenders by organizing and guaranteeing issues of various types of short-term IOU by companies. The banks also invest in government securities via The Stock Exchange. And they are the main participants in the **foreign exchange** or **forex** markets.

Euromarkets

A third source of finance for business and governments is the **eurocurrency** market or **euromarket**. Here the sources of funds are the deposits of currencies held outside their country of origin — in banks round the world — and the users are borrowers round the world (in spite of the name, this market does not deal solely with deposits held in Europe). London is the main centre of this market, but Britain is neither the main supplier nor the main user of eurocurrency funds (see Chapter 16).

The market mechanisms

The Stock Exchange, the banking and money markets and the euromarkets are main markets for investment funds. But the City contains many other markets which provide services for business.

There is a range of markets concerned with the **management of risk**, in which investors or businesses can either **hedge** (protect themselves) against the risks inherent in their operations or opt for high risks and high rewards by betting on movements in prices and interest rates. These include the **traded options market** (part of The Stock Exchange), the **financial futures market** and a range of **commodities futures markets**. The **foreign exchange** market also comes within this category as a medium for hedging currency risks.

There is another aspect of risk management: a market in **insurance**. This divides into two parts: insurance provided by insurance companies (the **company market**) and the international insurance market operated under the aegis of **Lloyd's of London**.

Savings institutions and intermediaries

Occupational pension schemes — pension schemes provided by companies or industries for their employees — have (in 1989) investments valued at some £250 billion and invest some £9 billion of new money each year. The contributions companies and individuals pay into these schemes are invested in a fund to provide the pensions at the end of the day. Some pension funds manage their own investments — the biggest run into many billions of pounds. Others farm out the investment management, often to merchant banks (see Chapter 6). Others are **insured** schemes where payments are made to an insurance company which contracts to provide the pensions.

Life assurance companies provide life assurance and pensions, but the larger ones are also becoming more diversified investment management groups, offering unit trusts and other financial services. Life assurance is mainly a savings business as opposed to **general insurance** which provides cover against fire, theft and similar risks. The life assurance companies have (in 1989) existing investments of about £230 billion and invest some £12 billion of new money each year.

Both the pension funds and life assurance companies are vehicles for **contractual savings**: money coming in under long-term savings schemes which can safely be invested for the long term because the savers have contracted to make regular payments.

Unit trusts grew rapidly up to the stockmarket crash of October 1987, at which point they had investments of some £50 billion; by the end of that month their investments were worth £37 billion. They have recovered subsequently but the bull market euphoria that enticed the small investor has gone for the time being. They are often operated by large **investment management groups** which market a range of savings products and services.

The pension funds, life assurance companies and unit trusts between them own two-thirds to three-quarters of all listed shares in British companies and the first two own close to half the gilt-edged securities in issue.

Life assurance and unit trusts are sold direct by the organizations that provide them, but are also extensively marketed through **financial intermediaries** who operate on commission. These include **insurance brokers** and **independent investment advisers. Accountants, solicitors, bank managers** and **stockbrokers** may also sell these investment products.

The **building societies** at end-1988 had shares and deposits of some £160 billion, plus other borrowings and their own reserves. They had lent a total of £157 billion to homebuyers and had around £9 billion invested in gilt-edged securities. Under recent legislation their possible range of activities has been widened and some of the larger ones are providing or planning a range of

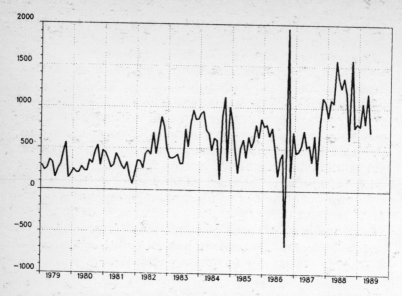

Figure 2.1 The net inflow of funds to the building societies. Normally they can rely on a fairly regular flow of new money. But see what happened in 1986 when investors temporarily withdrew funds to play the stockmarket by subscribing for shares in the TSB issue (subsequently a disappointing investment, as it turned out). Source: *Datastream International.*

services including cheque accounts, personal loans, estate agency services and a variety of financial and savings products. Hitherto they have been **mutual** organizations — owned in theory by the people who deposit money with them — but they will have the option to become companies owned by shareholders. One of the biggest, the Abbey National, has already embarked on this course.

The banks

At end-1988 **banks** in Britain had sterling deposits of £369 billion and outstanding sterling loans of £251 billion apart from money market loans. The bulk of this money is with the major **clearing banks** such as Barclays and Lloyds, whose traditional deposit-taking and lending services are familiar enough. But a major recent change for some of the clearing banks has been their involvement in Stock Exchange business via the acquisition of broking or, in some cases, marketmaking businesses. These changes have not always brought success to the banks concerned.

The **merchant banks** — the Warburgs and the Kleinworts — do not have such large-scale funds of their own. Their expertise lies in arranging finance, not necessarily in providing it. They are very active in the **investment management business** — particularly for pension funds — and their **corporate finance** arms advise companies on capital raising and on takeover attacks and defences. They have also become prime players in the stockmarket by acquiring broking and jobbing firms. Each of the major clearing banks has a merchant banking arm.

London is also host to a wide range of **foreign banks** — over 500 at the last count — many of which were attracted by London's position as centre of the euromarkets though some of the larger ones also do significant domestic banking business in Britain and may be involved in Stock Exchange business.

The Stock Exchange

Britain's domestic **Stock Exchange** is the third largest stockmarket after those of Japan and the United States. At end 1988 the total market value of shares in UK companies was £392 billion, while UK government securities listed on the exchange had a value of £140 billion. In 1988 some £10 billion was raised by the first-time sale of shares in new and existing companies on the stockmarket.

In October 1986, dealing methods on the London market changed radically in the course of what came to be known as the **Big Bang**. Stock Exchange members are now divided between **marketmakers** and **broker-dealers**. The first make a continuous market as principals and the second supply shares from their own stocks or simply act as agents for investors. Marketmaking in gilt-edged securities is undertaken by **primary dealers** known as **gilt-edged marketmakers**.

Most of the major London marketmakers and brokers are now owned by banks or other financial institutions and in some cases several firms have been brought together to form major **securities houses** which undertake all kinds of securities business. A number of major American securities houses are now also active in the British market, with the Japanese entering slightly more cautiously. Many smaller brokers and **country brokers** remain independent, though some have got together into larger groupings. Most of the larger Stock Exchange businesses employ numbers of **investment analysts** who produce research into companies and other investment topics as a service to clients.

The professional back-up

The components of the other markets are described in the chapters devoted to them. But among the City figures encountered in the financial pages there is also a range of professional firms without which the City could not function: notably, accountants, actuaries, lawyers and chartered surveyors.

Accountants are a vital link in the financial chain, if only because they **audit** the accounts of companies (see Chapter 3). Their services are particularly vital in the preparation of a **prospectus** when shares are **marketed** (sold to a range of investors) for the first time. **Audit** and **tax** work is the traditional mainstay of the accountant, with **liquidation** work — **winding up** companies that have gone to the wall — as a specialist sideline for some of them.

But the major international firms which number their employees in tens of thousands worldwide are pushing fast into areas which overlap with other established interests: **corporate finance** and all manner of **management advisory services**.

Consulting actuaries are the firms that advise on the highly complex business of **pension funding** and **pension fund performance** and they crop up with some regularity when pension topics are discussed. This is in addition to the actuary's original function of valuing life assurance assets and liabilities and deciding on bonuses.

Commercial lawyers. Few documents in the investment world can safely be prepared without the advice of a commercial lawyer, and the City boasts a dozen or so major firms specializing in commercial work.

Surveyors and **estate agents** act as intermediaries in the market in investment properties. But they do a great deal besides. **Valuations** of a company's properties may be needed in a new issue or takeover document. They will certainly be needed when finance is to be secured on properties. The chartered surveyor frequently helps to arrange finance for **development of properties**. He manages **property investment portfolios** for numerous institutions and is the main source of information on conditions in both the **property investment market** and the **letting market** (see Chapter 19).

Perhaps the **financial public relations** agencies should also rank as one of the City's back-up services. **Crawford's Directory of City Connections** — the financial journalist's *vade mecum* — lists around 120 of them and many have a significant client list among stockmarket-listed companies. The reader of the financial press is not necessarily aware of their presence, but much of the routine information from companies — profit announcements and the like — reaches the journalist in the form of a press release on the paper of one of these agencies. They perform a more active role in publicizing the virtues of companies coming to the stockmarket, in helping to present the case for an aggressor or a defendant in a takeover bid and generally in ensuring that information which could be good for the share price of a client company does not remain hidden under a bushel.

3

Companies and their accounts

Financial journalists write extensively about **companies**. Companies that are growing, companies that are contracting, companies that are taking over other companies, companies that are going bust. They tend to approach company affairs from one of two angles (or, most usefully, from both). Take two examples:

'Mark Hustler, the thirty-year-old accountant who took charge at Interpersonal Video Systems earlier this year, has not let the grass grow under his feet. Following the purchase of Insight Compact Discs in June he plans a further important acquisition in the interpersonal systems field to consolidate the company's lead in this fast growing business. The shares are acquiring a strong institutional following and at 180p — up from 60p earlier this year — look one of the best bets in the high technology sector'

What do we deduce from this? First, that the writer thinks Interpersonal Video Systems is a good thing, because he is advising you to buy the shares. Secondly, that he is suggesting the investing institutions are buying the shares, which should help the price to rise. Thirdly, that the shares have already risen strongly, presumably since Mark Hustler took charge. Fourthly, that Mark Hustler is expanding his company by buying other companies. Fifthly, that the company is a leader in interpersonal systems and that these are a high-technology area. Finally, we might suspect that the writer probably hasn't the faintest idea what an interpersonal video system is, whether it is a growth business, whether Mark Hustler is paying too much or too little for the companies he is acquiring or who the institutions are that are supposed to be following the company. In other words, the writer has clearly had a **tip**. It's not necessarily to be sneezed at. If enough people follow the tip and buy the shares because they think they are going up, they will go up. For a time at least.

Now take the following:

'Interpersonal Video Systems, the manufacturer of visual sales aids for the toothpaste industry, reports turnover up from £18m to £27m for the year to end-March. Pre-tax profits have risen from £2m to £4.3m, including a first-time contribution of £1.5m from Insight Compact Discs, acquired for shares last June, and earnings per share are up from 10p to 12.5p on the enlarged capital. If the company meets its target of 15 per cent a year internal growth, the 25p shares at 180p are on a prospective PE ratio of only 12.5, which is below the sector average. They look undervalued.'

In fact, the message from the second writer is essentially the same as that from the first: the shares should be bought. Not because Mark Hustler is a great guy, not because another important acquisition is planned, not because institutions are rushing to buy the shares. But because the conventional **investment arithmetic** says that they are cheap. We also learn roughly what Interpersonal Video Systems does and we have an indication that it probably didn't pay too much for Insight Compact Discs.

Neither approach is totally satisfactory on its own. It is useful to know who runs a company. It helps us to get a feel for the operation if we know it plans expansion via take-over. It is useful to know (if, in fact, it is true) that institutions are investing in the company. But it is also useful to know what it does, how much it earns and how it is rated on accepted investment criteria.

Phrases like 'PE ratio' and 'earnings per share' are part of the currency of the investment business. But what do they mean? This requires a gentle incursion into company accounts.

Limited liability

First, what is a company? It is a trading entity that belongs to its shareholders and the **Ltd** or **plc** after the name indicates that it has **limited liability**. The plc also indicates that the company is a **Public Limited Company**: one whose shares or other securities may be held by the investing public and traded on a market. In either case the liability of the owners is limited to the amount of money they have put into the business. Unless they give **personal**

guarantees for the debts of the business, the **owners** or **shareholders (members**, in the legal jargon) of a limited company cannot be called on to meet the company's debts where these exceed its assets. Only the money put into the company can be lost. Anybody who operates a business as a sole trader or as a partner in a **partnership**, on the other hand, is liable for all the debts of the business.

Voting and control

The owners of the **ordinary shares** in a company normally have the power to **control** the company if they act together, though the directors and managers — who may or may not be shareholders — run the company. Usually each ordinary share carries one **vote**. Owners of more that 50 per cent of the votes will thus — if they all vote the same way — control the company. In practice shareholders can influence the way a company is run primarly by voting on the appointment or dismissal of directors and on certain other major policy matters that have to be presented to shareholders at a formal meeting of the company. Certain major resolutions — to change the aims and objectives of a company, say — will require 75 per cent voting in favour.

Most of the time shareholders vote the way the directors advise them to, especially at the **annual general meeting** of the company, which is normally a non-contentious event where the required resolutions are duly passed. The press will generally pick up the occasions when there is dissent between different groups of shareholders or between shareholders and directors. This is where the question of voting power becomes interesting.

Content of the accounts

Ordinary shareholders are entitled to receive **accounts**. As a rough rule (it's not technically quite correct) companies are required to produce a set of accounts each year. This is a legal requirement. The Stock Exchange further requires that listed companies produce figures showing profits at the **half-year** stage (in America they produce them each **quarter**).

The best way to look on accounts is as a sort of shorthand for what is really going on in a company. The bare figures don't conjure up the smoking chimneys or the salesmen out on the road. But once you are reasonably familiar with the basic figurework you can begin to look at what lies behind it.

The main items in the accounts are a **profit and loss account** and a **balance sheet**. Various other bits of legally required information are usually contained in the **directors' report** or in the detailed **notes to the accounts**. And there is a **sources and application of funds** statement showing the different ways in which the company generated additional funds during the year and how these were used in the business.

Role of the auditors

With the accounts will come an **auditors' report**. **Auditors** are firms of accountants who hold a watching brief on behalf of the owners of the company (the shareholders). The directors of the company prepare and sign the accounts. It is the auditors' job to certify that these accounts present a **true and fair view** of the company's profits and financial position, or to point out any failings where they do not. The auditors are meant to be independent of the company's management, though obviously need to work quite closely with the managers in agreeing the form of the accounts. The managers appoint them, though the shareholders approve their fees. There is normally a certain amount of give and take when opinions vary on the presentation of different items. An auditors' report which says the accounts do not give a 'true and fair view' or that they do so only with important **qualifications** will normally be picked up by the press as a strong warning bell.

Company reporting

Companies which are quoted on The Stock Exchange need, we have seen, to provide their shareholders with more frequent information than that supplied by the legally required annual accounts. Some weeks after the end of the first half of the company's year it will normally produce an **interim profit statement** (or **interim**) giving unaudited first-half profit figures. The statement also normally gives the size of the **interim dividend** (see below) and includes some comment on trading and prospects from the company.

Some time after the end of the full year a **preliminary announcement** (**prelim**) will usually be published, giving the profits for the year and often a lot of background information. This appears some weeks before the full report and accounts are posted to shareholders. Most daily press comment on the company's figures is based on the interim and preliminary statements which have greater news value — though less depth of information — than the full accounts.

Profit and loss account

A **profit and loss account** shows the results of a company's trading over the last financial period. Usually this means a year, though the year can run to whatever date the company chooses. December 31 and March 31 year-ends are popular, though it could be April 1 or November 5. The profit and loss account thus shows the effect on the company's revenue account of all the transactions over the past year. If a company made profits of £20m in the first ten months of its year and losses of £22m in the last two months, the profit and loss account would show a loss of £2m: the final outcome. It would not by itself reveal that the company had been trading profitably for much of the period.

Balance sheet

The **balance sheet** is a totally different animal. It gives a snapshot of a company's financial position on one particular date: the last day of its financial year. Everything the company owned on this date and everything it owed on this date will be shown in the balance sheet, grouped under a number of different headings. The balance sheet is usually the best measure an investor has of a company's **financial health**. But it needs interpreting with caution. The position it shows on the last day of the company's year could be very different from what it would have shown if drawn up three months earlier or would show if prepared three months later. Where companies deliberately bring forward some items and delay others, so that the balance sheet gives a picture which is totally untypical of the company's position at any other time during the year, it amounts to excessive **window-dressing**. **Creative accounting** has a similar implication. It usually means figures have been twisted beyond the bounds of decency to present the picture the company wants.

Note the difference between a balance sheet or **parent company balance sheet** and a **consolidated balance sheet** or **group balance sheet**. Most companies listed on The Stock Exchange are not, in fact, single companies. Bloggs Engineering Plc may be a group of companies consisting of Bloggs Engineering Plc, Scraggs Scrap Ltd and Muppet Metalbashers Ltd. Bloggs Engineering is the **parent company** and controls the other two by owning all or a majority of their shares. They are therefore **subsidiary companies**. The head company of a group is also sometimes called the **holding company** because it holds the shares of the subsidiaries.

A parent company balance sheet shows the detail for Bloggs Engineering alone; its ownership of the other two companies is represented merely by the **book value** (value for accounting purposes) of its interest in these subsidiaries, which is generally pretty unhelpful. A consolidated balance sheet, on the other hand, treats the three companies as if they were a single entity. The assets and liabilities of all three are grouped together. Thus, if Bloggs owned buildings valued at £2m, Scraggs's buildings were worth £1m and Muppet's worth £1.5m, the figure for buildings (or 'properties') in the consolidated balance sheet of Bloggs Engineering Plc would be £4.5m.

Companies are normally required to present both a balance sheet and a consolidated or group balance sheet, unless there are no subsidiaries, in which case only parent company figures are given. The consolidated balance sheet is the important one. They are not required to produce a parent company profit and loss account, only a **consolidated** one which shows the aggregate of the profits and losses of all the different companies in the group.

Where the money comes from

In looking at a company's finances as shown by its balance sheet (and when talking of balance sheets from now on we'll be referring to consolidated balance sheets) it is vital to distinguish the different **sources of money** the company uses in its operations. There are three main sources. First, money put up as **permanent capital** by the owners (the shareholders) of the business. This is the company's own money, usually put up in the form of **ordinary share capital** when it is also known as **equity capital**. Then there is the part of the profit the company earns which it **ploughs back** into the business rather than paying out by way of dividend to shareholders. This also becomes part of the equity funds of the business, because it belongs to the shareholders and is shown as **reserves**. Third, there is the money the company borrows and which it will have to repay at some point. The general term for this is **debt** or **borrowings** but it can take a lot of different forms: **overdrafts, term loans** (bank borrowings which are not securities) or **debentures, loan stocks** and so on (which are securities of the company).

The main balance sheet items

The easiest way to understand the various accounting terms that crop up in press reports is to take a sample set of accounts. The accounts — for a mythical John Smith & Co Ltd — are slightly simplified to emphasize the main items: some of the complexities that will crop up are examined later in Chapter 5. First, the **balance sheet**. Assume that John Smith is a young company which makes, say, metal paperweights.

In fact, John Smith & Co was set up only a year ago by four friends who decided there was a future in paperweights. Each put £10,000 into the business by subscribing for 10,000 £1 ordinary shares and the company borrowed the rest of the money it required. Let us take the main balance sheet items in order.

Fixed and current assets

First come the **assets** of the business: what it owns. Assets are defined as **fixed assets** or **current assets**. Fixed assets are not necessarily fixed in a physical sense. A company operating oil tankers would show them as a fixed asset. They are 'fixed' because they are not something the company is buying and selling or processing in the course of its normal trade. They represent mainly the buildings and plant in which or with which the company produces its products and services. In this case John Smith's only fixed assets are £27,000 worth of paperweight-making machinery. Originally John Smith paid £30,000 for this machinery, but out of its profits it has set aside £3,000 to allow for a year's **depreciation** of the equipment and written down the **book value** by this amount. This recognizes that machinery will eventually wear out and need to be replaced.

Current assets are the assets which are constantly on the move. Stocks of raw materials that will be turned into products, stocks

John Smith & Co Ltd
Balance sheet for the year to 31 December

	£	£
FIXED ASSETS		
Plant and machinery		27,000
CURRENT ASSETS		
Stocks	50,000	
Debtors	35,000	
Cash at bank	5,000	
	90,000	
CURRENT LIABILITIES		
(Creditors: amounts due within one year)		
Trade creditors	20,000	
Tax payable	6,000	
Dividend proposed	4,000	
Bank overdrafts	8,000	
	38,000	
NET CURRENT ASSETS		52,000
TOTAL ASSETS		
LESS CURRENT LIABILITIES		79,000
CREDITORS		
(amounts due in more than one year)		
Term loans		30,000
NET ASSETS		49,000
Represented by:		
Share capital		
(£1 ordinary shares)	40,000	
Revenue reserves	9,000	
SHAREHOLDERS' FUNDS		49,000

of products that will be sold to customers, money owing to the company by customers, money temporarily held in the bank that will be withdrawn as it is needed in the business. If there were a company whose business was buying and selling oil tankers, the tankers would be shown under current assets as 'stocks', and not under fixed assets.

John Smith has **stocks** of £50,000. These comprise mainly stocks of raw metal from which the paperweights will be made and stocks of finished paperweights that have not yet been sold.

The **debtors** item shows the money that is owing to John Smith, probably by customers who have bought paperweights they have not yet paid for. In effect, John Smith is making a temporary loan of £35,000 to its customers, on which it receives no interest. **Trade credit** of this kind is a fact of business life, but it poses problems, particularly for younger companies. John Smith has had to bear the costs of producing the paperweights, which soaks up its available cash, and does not get paid by customers till some time later.

Finally, current assets include £5,000 of **cash** sitting in the bank until it has to be spent.

John Smith's total assets are therefore £117,000: the £27,000 of fixed assets and £90,000 of current assets. This figure is known as the **balance sheet total**. It represents everything John Smith & Co owns.

Current liabilities

Next we have to knock off everything the company owes. The short-term debts are shown as **current liabilities** or **creditors: amounts due within one year**. These are the counterpart of current assets and are therefore deducted from current assets in the balance sheet to give **net current assets** (or **net current liabilities** if current liabilities exceed current assets).

The first item under current liabilities is **trade creditors** of £20,000. This is the counterpart of debtors. It represents money the company owes for goods and services it has received but not yet paid for. In other words, it is much like an interest-free loan to the company: **trade credit** from which the company benefits.

Each year a company has to make provision from its profits for the **corporation tax** it must pay on these profits. But corporation tax is payable by instalments and at any time there is likely to be some tax which the company knows it will have to pay but which has not yet been handed over. This therefore appears as a liability of £6,000 under the heading **tax payable**.

Next comes the **dividend** the company plans to pay. A company needs approval from its shareholders for the dividend it intends to pay, and until they have voted to approve the dividend at the **annual general meeting (AGM)** which takes place at least three weeks after they have received the accounts it remains a short-term liability: something that will need to be paid in the near future. A public company normally pays its dividend in two parts: an **interim dividend** in the course of the year and a **final dividend** (which has to be approved by shareholders) when the profits for the full year are known.

Finally, the company owes £8,000 it has borrowed by way of **overdraft**. Since an overdraft is technically repayable on demand, it has to be shown as a current liability.

Deducting the current liabilities of £38,000 from the current assets of £90,000 gives a figure of £52,000 for net current assets. This is sometimes referred to as **net working capital**: the net amount of money tied up in the day-to-day operations of the business.

Longer-term debt

Fixed assets plus net current assets give the figure described as **total assets less current liabilities**. From this figure of £79,000 we still have to knock off any **medium-** or **long-term debts** before arriving at a figure for net assets. In the event, John Smith has borrowed £30,000 in the form of a **term loan**. This is a bank loan, typically for a period of three to seven years, and normally repayable in instalments.

The net asset figure

After knocking off everything the company owes, we find John Smith is 'worth' £49,000: the **net asset** figure. This is the value of the **shareholders' interest** in the company. It equates to the £40,000 the four founder-shareholders provided by subscribing for 40,000 £1 shares at par, plus the £9,000 of profits the company has earned and **retained** in the business rather than paying out as dividends. The two items together constitute the **shareholders' funds** of £49,000.

After looking at the individual items, translate them into a picture of the company's financial position. It has assets of £117,000 (fixed assets plus current assets). Where did the money come from to acquire these assets? It has effectively borrowed (partly as trade credit) the £38,000 shown as current liabilities. It has a longer-term borrowing of £30,000: the term loan. Knock these two items off the assets figure and you are left with £49,000. Where did the money come from for this remaining £49,000 of assets? The answer: £40,000 was put up as share capital by the original shareholders and £9,000 was 'saved' out of the profits of the year's operations.

Gearing

The relationship between **borrowed money (debt)** and **shareholders' money (equity)** in a business is important. Borrowed money has to be repaid at some point, though it might be a long way off. More important in the short run, interest has to be paid on borrowed money, and it has to be paid whether the company is earning good profits or not. A company that existed largely on borrowed money could be in be in bad trouble if it ran into losses for a year or so. If it was unable to pay the interest, the lenders could ask for their money back, which would usually result in the business folding up.

Equity finance does not carry this risk. In the good times the shareholders reap the rewards of the company's success, usually in the form of rising dividends. But if the company should run into trouble and make losses, it does not have to pay any dividend at all on the ordinary shares. Equity capital is also called **risk capital** for this reason.

The relationship between borrowed money and equity money in a business is referred to as **gearing** (or **leverage** in the United States). It is a term that crops up in other contexts as well. A **high-geared company** is one which has a large amount of borrowed money in relation to its equity or its shareholders' funds. A **low-geared company** has a large equity and few borrowings. The appropriate mix of borrowings and equity depends on the type of business (see Chapter 4). If a journalist points out that a company is high-geared, he is probably suggesting that this is a good thing for shareholders if the company is doing well. If the company is doing badly, he is probably sounding a warning.

The main profit and loss account items

Next, look at the record of the company's profits for the past year, as shown in the profit and loss (P&L) account.

John Smith & Co Ltd
Profit and loss account for the year ended December 31

	£
TURNOVER	200,000
TRADING PROFIT	24,000
Less	
INTEREST PAID	4,000
Leaving	
PROFIT ON ORIDINARY ACTIVITIES BEFORE TAX	20,000
Less	
CORPORATION TAX	7,000
Leaving	
PROFIT AFTER TAX ATTRIBUTABLE TO MEMBERS OF JOHN SMITH LTD	13,000
Less	
DIVIDENDS	4,000
Leaving	
RETAINED PROFIT	9,000

Turnover and profit

Most of these terms are pretty much self-explanatory. They don't all have a precise legal or accountancy significance and some can be used in slightly different ways. The **turnover** of £200,000 is the total value of all goods and services sold by the company to third parties in the normal course of trade — it is sometimes called **sales** instead. It does not usually include any taxes (like VAT) charged on these goods or services.

The difference between turnover and the **trading profit** of £24,000 is the costs incurred by the company in its operations during the year: wages, rent, raw materials, distribution costs and so on. These will be broken down to a greater or lesser extent in the notes. They also in this case include the **directors' salaries**, the **auditors' fees** and the amount set aside to provide for **depreciation of plant and equipment**. The trading profit is what remains after these costs have been deducted.

The next deduction is the **interest** the company pays on its borrowings of all kinds (for convenience we've ignored the fact that it may also have received a little interest on its temporary bank balances). In the notes this interest should be broken down between interest on **short-term borrowings** and interest on **long-term borrowings**. An overdraft is technically a very short-term borrowing.

After deducting the interest paid we are left with a figure of £20,000 for **profit on ordinary activities before tax**. Mercifully this can be abbreviated to **pre-tax profit** and is the most frequently quoted measure of a company's profit, in the press and elsewhere.

The tax take

Next, the tax man has his cut. Companies pay **corporation tax** on their profits, after all other costs except dividends have been deducted. Under the **imputation tax system** in force, the corporation tax tax rate was 35 per cent in 1989 (we will ignore the fact that small companies like John Smith actually pay a somewhat lower rate). But there is a complication. The tax the company pays includes **basic rate income tax** (25p in the pound or 25 per cent for 1989-90) paid on behalf of shareholders on the dividends they receive. If the shareholders are not liable for tax — pension funds or pensioners on a very small income, say — they can claim it back. If they are liable for tax at the higher rate, then they have to pay the extra on top. But the dividend cheque the shareholder receives is for an amount from which basic rate tax is deemed to have been deducted. And it includes a **voucher** for the tax that has been paid, which the shareholder uses to claim it back if he is not liable.

This income tax paid on behalf of the shareholders is known as **advance corporation tax (ACT)** and because it forms part of the company's corporation tax bill, the system means that the total tax paid by the company is not normally affected by the amount of its profits it pays out as dividends. If it pays out nothing, the 35

44

per cent tax on its profits will all be **mainstream corporation tax**. If it pays dividends, the tax charge on profits will still be 35 per cent, but part of this tax is ACT: basic rate income tax paid on behalf of shareholders and then offset against the company's corporation tax charge.

Equity earnings, dividends and retentions

The **profit after tax attributable to members** or **net profit** is much what it says. Provided there are no further deductions, it belongs to the shareholders or owners of the company and may be referred to as **equity earnings**. But it is up to the company to decide, with the approval of its shareholders, how much of this profit is to be paid out as dividends and how much should be kept in the business to help finance its expansion. Most companies in their early stages need all the money they can get and tend to keep most of the profit in the business. In the case of John Smith & Co the company has decided to pay out just under a third of its profits — £4,000 — as dividends and to 'plough back' the remaining £9,000 which is therefore described as **retained earnings** or **retentions**.

Remember, the £9,000 of retained earnings belongs to the shareholders just as much as the £4,000 they actually receive as dividends which is why it was shown in the balance sheet as part of shareholders' funds, under the heading of **revenue reserves**.

The £4,000 paid as dividends is divided equally among the 40,000 £1 shares in issue. Normally, the dividend is expressed as an amount (in pence) per share. In this case the dividends are equal to 10p net per ordinary share. But this 10p is the equivalent of 13.3p before tax, since basic rate income tax of 25 per cent is already deemed to have been deducted. So 13.3p is the **gross dividend per share** and 10p is the **net dividend per share**. **Gross** normally means 'before deductions' and **net** means 'after deductions'. It is important to remember the distinction, because most yields or returns on investments are expressed as a gross amount — before tax — to provide a way of comparing them with each other. What different investors actually get from the payments after tax depends on the tax rates they are paying.

Minor complexities

The figures shown for John Smith & Co are obviously simplified. They illustrate the main figures on which the investment ratios explained later are based. But a few technicalities must be mentioned briefly.

If John Smith has **interests in associated companies** (companies which are not subsidiaries, but where it has a significant shareholding — see Chapter 5) it will show as a separate item its proportionate share of the profits of these companies and include them in the pre-tax profit figure.

The profit after tax will not always be the same thing as the **profit attributable to ordinary shareholders** or equity earnings. First, the company may have to make a deduction for **minority interests** or **outside shareholders' interests**. These arise where a company controls other subsidiary companies but does not own all the shares of all of them. Suppose John Smith had a subsidiary called Super Stampings. Smith holds 70 per cent of the Stampings shares, and the original founders of Stampings have held on to the other 30 per cent. So 30 per cent of the profits of Stampings belongs to these **minority shareholders**. Smith includes the whole of the Stampings profits in its own trading profit figure, but makes a deduction after tax for the amount of the net profit of Stampings belonging to the minority holders.

Secondly, the company may have **preference shares** in issue (see Chapter 5). In this case the dividends on the preference shares must be deducted from the net profits. Both minority interests and preference dividends must be allowed for before arriving at the net profits or earnings that belong to Smith's ordinary shareholders.

Thirdly, the aim of any investment commentator is to assess a company's earning power, present and future. This means he may need to adjust the published profit figures to exclude 'one-off' items that distort the profits in a particular year. These items usually appear under the heading of **exceptional items** or **extraordinary items**. They can include items such as costs incurred in closing down a subsidiary business or windfall profits on the sale of a surplus factory. Neither item is a normal feature of the company's trading.

Exceptional items are added or subtracted in the published accounts **above the line**: before reaching a pre-tax profit figure. Extraordinary items do not affect the published pre-tax profits but are deducted **below the line** from net profits after tax. What is 'exceptional' and what is 'extraordinary' is a matter for some debate. Extraordinary items are generally the larger and very unusual items. In reaching his own version of profits and earnings from the point of view of the investment ratios, the analyst or commentator will usually **adjust** the published figures for anything that does not reflect the company's normal trading. This means that profits and earnings shown in the newspapers (and hence the ratios derived from them) will not always correspond with those published by the company — often a point of friction between company directors and financial journalists.

Inflation accounting

The accounts we have looked at are prepared according to the **historic cost convention**. This is the traditional way accounts are prepared and is the form required for most taxation and legal purposes. It means that most items — particularly fixed assets and stocks — are normally shown at what they originally cost, less provisions for depreciation or other necessary write-offs. The main exception is that properties are sometimes revalued, with the new values included in the accounts.

In a period of high inflation, historic cost accounting may be misleading. Plant and equipment will cost more to replace than was paid for it originally. Stocks of raw materials will cost more when they have to be replaced.

To overcome this problem, various forms of **inflation accounting**, including **replacement cost accounting**, have been developed to supplement or replace historic cost accounts. Before reaching a profit figure, deductions will be made for the higher costs of replacing fixed assets and stocks (there are other adjustments, but these are usually the most important). The result for most companies is that profits will be lower than those shown under the historic cost convention. You will see references in the press to inflation accounting. But with the lower rates of inflation prevailing in the second half of the 1980s, the steam has gone out of the debate on the merits of different accounting systems, though the rise in the inflation rate in 1989 caused some resurgence of interest.

4

The investment ratios

After a first look at the main accounting items, we can see how they translate into comment on a company's standing and prospects. The figures are used in two main ways to produce the ratios on which investment judgement is often based. Take an example:

'Following the rights issue in July last year, Super Silicon has £4m in cash or near-cash form to see it through the planned expansion programme, and borrowings as a percentage of shareholders' funds are down to 14 per cent.'

This makes it clear that Super Silicon is unlikely to run out of cash (which is a good thing) and that its gearing is low (which is probably also a good thing). What it does not do is to tell you whether the shares look cheap or expensive at their current level. Next take this:

'With the benefit of interest on the proceeds of last year's rights issue, Super Silicon should achieve earnings of 12p per share on the enlarged capital. With the shares at 120p this suggests a prospective price earnings ratio of 10, which is well below the sector average'.

The difference is that the second piece does not merely comment on Super Silicon's prospects. It relates these prospects to the market price of the shares so that readers can form a view on whether the shares are cheap or expensive.

Two types of financial ratio

An investment is only a good investment if you buy it at the right price. Super Silicon may be a superb company. Marks & Spencer and Sainsbury both are superb companies and have proved it over many years. This does not mean, however, that their shares are always a good buy. As with anything else, there are times when you could pay too much even for the best — though it is obviously better to pay too much for something that is intrinsically good than for a load of rubbish.

So there are two layers of **financial ratios** applied to companies: the ones which tell us something about the operations and health of the company itself and the ones which relate the company's performance to the price you would have to pay for the shares.

Profit margins

First, let's look at the company itself. Look again at the profit and loss account for John Smith & Co. It is making a profit, but how can that profit be quantified in such a way that it could be compared with the profit performances of other companies? One of the more common measures is the **profit margin**. If we take the pre-tax profits of £20,000 and the turnover of £200,000, it is clear that 10 per cent of what the company gets for its products after all costs and overheads have been paid is profit. So the **pre-tax profit margin** is 10 per cent. This figure does not mean a great deal by itself. But if we compared it with other companies in the same field, it could be informative.

Assuming there is another paperweight manufacturer, and that it earns a pre-tax margin of only 6 per cent, we might reckon that John Smith & Co is the more successful company. If the following year's accounts show that John Smith's profit margin has increased to 11.5 per cent, we might deduce that it is strengthening its competitive position still further. If, on the other hand, turnover has doubled to £400,000 but the profit margin is down to 9 per cent, it might seem that John Smith has decided to sacrifice a bit of profitability in order to increase its turnover — possibly by reducing prices or offering bigger bulk discounts. If turnover had dropped to £180,000 and profits were down to £9,000 (a pre-tax margin of only 5 per cent) it would be clear that something had gone wrong: possibly the competitors had hit back with lower prices themselves and made a big dent in John Smith's business.

No ratio on its own is going to give the full picture, and it can be dangerous to jump to conclusions. But taken together with other indicators from the accounts, and with whatever else we can learn about the company, they can provide valuable clues.

Income gearing

The next ratio to look at is the **gearing** or in this case **income gearing**. How much of the company's trading profit goes to pay interest charges? John Smith produces a trading profit of £24,000, and £4,000 of this goes in interest charges. This is important because the company has to pay the interest whatever profits it makes. Income gearing is normally calculated by expressing the interest charge as a proportion of the profit before interest is deducted: in this case, £4,000 as a proportion of £24,000 or 16.7 per cent. It can be expressed in slightly different ways, but the principle is the same.

At all events, John Smith's income gearing is fairly low, and to see the full significance of gearing we need a more extreme example. Take a company whose profit and loss account looks like this:

	£
TRADING PROFIT	100,000
less:	
INTEREST PAID	50,000
leaving:	
PRE-TAX PROFIT	50,000

Assume that the company does not increase or reduce its borrowings and that interest rates remain unchanged. Assume also that the company increases its trading profit by 50 per cent to £150,000. The profit & loss account then looks like this:

	£
TRADING PROFIT	150,000
less:	
INTEREST PAID	50,000
leaving:	
PRE-TAX PROFIT	100,000

So for an increase of only 50 per cent in trading profit, pre-tax profits have risen by 100 per cent. Since the profits, after tax has been deducted, will belong to the owners of the company, the gearing is working very much in favour of the shareholders. But do the same sum assuming a 50 per cent fall in trading profits:

	£
TRADING PROFIT	50,000
less:	
INTEREST PAID	50,000
leaving:	
PRE-TAX PROFIT	NIL

It has only taken a 50 per cent fall in trading profit to wipe out completely the profits that belong to the shareholders. If trading profits fell by more than 50 per cent, the company would be making losses.

The appropriate level of gearing will vary between companies in different fields. But as a general rule, high gearing might be appropriate for a company whose income is very stable and on a rising trend: a property company deriving its income from rents on good commercial buildings, for example. It would not be appropriate for a company whose profits are liable to shoot up one year and down the next.

Effect of changing interest rates

One final point about income gearing. It is not simply that a company's trading profits can shoot up or down. The interest charge could vary up or down as the general level of **interest rates** changes. This is why you have to look more closely at a company's borrowings. Has it borrrowed its money long-term at a **fixed rate of interest** (in which case the interest charge will not be affected if interest rates rise or fall)? Or are its borrowings at **variable** or **floating** rates of interest, which will change with general movements in interest rates?

In the example we have taken, a doubling of the rate of interest the company has to pay would be just as serious as a halving of its trading profits. So **high income gearing** based on variable-rate loans can be dangerous in a period of sharply rising interest rates.

When interest rates do change dramatically, investment analysts and the press tend to comb the gearing statistics for companies that will suffer badly from a rise in interest rates or benefit from a reduction. But nowadays they need to be a little careful. The company might have bought a **cap** which sets a top limit on the interest rate it pays (see Chapter 14).

Earnings per share

The next calculation concerns the **profit after tax** or **net profit**. In the case of John Smith & Co., this is the same thing as **net profit after tax attributable to members** or **available for ordinary shareholders** or **equity earnings**. Again, it is not very useful in isolation, though in subsequent years we can chart its rise or fall. But the key information is the amount of profit the company is making for each share in issue. And to get at this we simply divide the net profit by the number of shares in issue; the result is normally expressed in pence. John Smith has 40,000 shares, for which it earns £13,000 or 1,300,000 pence. This works out at 32.5p for each share.

This 32.5p is the company's **earnings per share** or **eps** and its rise or fall from year to year is an important measure (perhaps the most important measure) of how good a job the company is doing for its shareholders. Why is it more important than the simple profits figure? Again, an example helps.

Suppose John Smith & Co decided to take over another company exactly similar to itself, in exchange for shares. It creates 40,000 new shares and swaps them for shares in the company it is taking over. The enlarged John Smith now has combined net profits of £26,000 (its own £13,000, plus £13,000 from its acquisition). Its net profits have therefore doubled, which looks impressive. But the number of John Smith shares in issue has also doubled to 80,000. Divide the £26,000 net profits by the 80,000 shares and you get earnings per share of 32.5p. In the short run at least, a John Smith shareholder is no better off.

When looking back over a company's profit record it is easy to miss the fact that much of the growth might have come from **acquisitions** or issues of additional shares for cash. But look at the record of earnings per share and you have a far better picture of whether the company is really increasing the amount of profit it earns for shareholders.

Writers tend to talk of **internal growth** or **organic growth** for the profits growth the company generates from its existing activities and **growth by acquisition** or **external growth** for increases in profit resulting from the purchase of other businesses.

Dividends per share

The figure for the cost of dividends — £4,000 in the case of John Smith — is also normally expressed as an amount per share. Divide it by the 40,000 shares in issue and you get a figure of 10p per share. This, remember, is the **net dividend per share**, because income tax at the basic rate of (in 1989-90) 25p in the pound has been paid. To find the **gross dividend** you **gross up** the net dividend. In other words, you calculate what figure before tax would give you 10p after tax. Since 10p is seventy-five hundredths of the figure you are looking for, you multiple the 10p by a hundred and divide the result by 75 (or alternatively you simply divide 10p by 0.75). The result, in any case, is 13.3p. This gross dividend is the one on which yield calculations will be based.

Dividend cover

Remember, too, that it is up to the directors to decide what proportion of profit is paid out as dividend, though shareholders have to approve the decision. In this case £4,000 has been paid out of a net profit of £13,000 available for the ordinary shareholders. **Dividend cover** is thus 3.25 times — this is the result of dividing the £13,000 available profit by the £4,000 paid out. There are other more complex and strictly more accurate ways of calculating it, but this will suffice to illustrate the principle. Dividend cover is an important measure of the safety of the dividend — the more strongly it is covered, the less chance that the company will have to reduce or **pass** (drop altogether) its payment if profits fall. In practice, companies do sometimes continue to pay a dividend even if they are temporarily making losses — it then comes out of **reserves** (see below). But they cannot do so indefinitely. The figure for dividend cover also gives an indication of the maximum dividend a company could have paid if it had distributed all of its profits.

Retained profit and cash flow

The final item is **retained profit** of £9,000. This is money **ploughed back** into the business. But the **depreciation** (£3,000 in the case of John Smith) is also money ploughed back into the business, though it is ploughed back to allow for the gradual wearing-out of plant and equipment. The term **cash flow** is used for the combination of depreciation and retained profits, since both represent money that is retained in the company out of its profits and can be used for any of its various needs. If you know John Smith will need to spend £10,000 on new plant and equipment over the next year, you might look at its cash flow to see if the company can cover this **capital expenditure** from the money it is generating internally. With a cash flow of £12,000, it can — though it will probably need further money for additional **working capital** (to finance higher levels of stocks, and so on).

Stockmarket ratings

The next stage is to take some of the figures we have worked out and relate them to the price of the company's shares in the stockmarket. Assume, for this purpose, that John Smith's shares are quoted on the stockmarket and that the current market price is around 300p. This market price is determined by the balance of buyers and sellers in the stockmarket and has nothing to do with the nominal or par value of the shares, nor with the amount of money subscribed for them originally by the founding shareholders — more of this later.

Yield

An investor who bought a share for 300p would stand to get a dividend equivalent to 13.3p gross or an initial return of 4.4 per cent on his outlay (13.3 as a percentage of 300). This is the current **yield** on the shares and it will change slightly each time the share price changes on the stockmarket, which will be frequently. It will also change when the other component of the equation — the dividend — changes, though this will obviously not happen so often. The formula to calculate a dividend yield is simply:

$$\frac{\text{Gross dividend per share}}{\text{Share price}} \times 100$$

What is the significance of the yield? Clearly, it gives the investor an indication of the income return he might expect on his shares. An investor mainly concerned with income might select **high-yielding** shares. And it is one of the characteristics on which one company can be compared with another. But as such it is an imperfect instrument.

In theory, a **low yield** should suggest a fast-growing company and a **high yield** would indicate a company that is probably not going to increase its profits very fast or a company that carries an above-average risk. Investors are prepared to accept a low income today if they think the income will rise rapidly in the future as the company earns larger profits and pays higher dividends. If the dividends are not going to rise much, they will want a higher yield today.

The theory holds good up to a point. Unfortunately, it is completely arbitrary how much of its profit a company pays out as dividend. One somewhat cynical financial journalist habitually defines a dividend yield as 'five clowns sitting round a boardroom table'. And because the dividend is arbitrary, the dividend yield is an imperfect way of comparing two companies. Look at John Smith again. At 300p the shares yield 4.4 per cent on the 13.3p gross dividend. But out of its profits John Smith might quite easily decide to pay a dividend of twice as much: 26.6p gross. In this case the yield would be 8.9 per cent if the share price were still 300p. Yet it is the same company, earning the same profits.

Price-earnings ratio

To overcome this problem when comparing one company with another, there is another measure which is not affected by the dividend decision. It is the **price-earnings ratio** or **PE ratio**. Whereas a dividend yield is a fact, though an imperfect comparison tool, a PE ratio is a theoretical concept but much more useful for comparisons. In essence, it is a way of measuring how highly investors value the earnings a company produces. It is derived by dividing the **earnings per share** or **eps** figure into the market price of the shares. If John Smith has earnings per share of 32.5p and the market price is 300p, the shares are on a PE ratio of 9.2 (300 divided by 32.5). Other common ways of saying the same thing are: 'the shares sell at 9.2 **times earnings**' or 'the shares are on a **multiple of** 9.2'.

Why is this relevant? The thinking goes something like this. The amount a company earns determines ultimately what dividend it will be able to pay. If its earnings are growing, there's a good chance that dividends will rise in step. Earnings which are likely to grow fairly fast are therefore more valuable than static earnings, because they point to higher income in the future. Thus, in relation to what a company currently earns, investors will pay more for the shares if they think the earnings will rise rapidly. The investor is buying the right to a future flow of income and what he is prepared to pay today depends on what income he thinks he will get in the future. The way of quantifying this is by relating the earnings per share to the share price.

High and low PE ratios

All else being equal, a **high PE ratio** suggests a growth company and a **low PE ratio** suggests a company with a more static profits outlook or a company in a high risk area. It is not quite as simple as this, because a high PE ratio could indicate a company which had suffered a sharp temporary profits fall (reducing the 'E' element of the PE ratio) whereas the share price (the 'P' element) had not fallen in step because investors expected earnings to recover the following year. But the principle holds good.

Nil and net PE ratios

When we come down to detail, there are several slightly different ways of calculating a PE ratio, though for practical purposes a reader of the financial columns does not have to bother too much with the variations. A **nil PE ratio** calculation ignores how much of its profit a company pays out as dividend. A **net PE ratio** takes account of the dividend distribution. Normally they both give the same answer, but in the case of a company paying large amounts of tax on profits earned overseas there can be a significant difference. It is not worth worrying about: where the difference is significant, any comment will normally make this clear.

Share price tables

Most 'serious' papers and magazines which quote share prices will show a yield and PE ratio as well. The *Financial Times* also shows the amount of the net dividend (in pence) and the dividend

56

Figure 4.1 The top line gives a long-term picture of the FT 30-share index, emphasising the extent of the Thatcher boom. But the long-term performance does not look so impressive when adjusted for inflation (bottom line). Source: *Datastream International*.

cover. These figures will not always be worked out in exactly the same way. For example, the dividend used could be the total dividend the company paid for its last financial year (the **historic dividend**). It could be the sum of the last two half-yearly payments (perhaps the last year's final and the current year's interim). Or it could be the dividend the company has forecast for its current year (the **forecast** or **prospective dividend**). Hence the terms **historic dividend yield** and **prospective dividend yield**. Be a bit wary of some prospective dividend yields, because they might also be based on the writer's own estimate of what the company is likely to pay, though possibly with a nod and a wink from the company itself; the context normally makes this clear.

You will also come across **historic PE ratios** and **prospective PE ratios**. The principle is the same. The first is based on actual earnings, the second on forecast or estimated earnings for a year for which the figures are not yet available.

Remember that yields and PE ratios move in opposite directions. A low yield and a high PE ratio probably indicate considerable expectations of growth. If the share price rises, the yield will fall further and the PE ratio will rise further. If the share price falls, the yield will rise and the PE ratio will fall. If a share price in a newspaper has **xd** after it, this stands for **ex-dividend**, and means that the buyer does not acquire the right to the recently-announced dividend. **Cum dividend** means the buyer gets the dividend.

Yield and PE ratio yardsticks

For an idea of typical levels of yield and PE ratio, look at the table headed **FT-Actuaries Indexes** in the *Financial Times*. It probably comes near the end of the 'Companies & Markets' section of the paper, before the pages of unit trust prices.

In May 1989, the estimated average dividend yield for electronics companies was a low 3.1 per cent and the average PE ratio was a relatively high 14.9. This high rating makes it clear that electronics was regarded as a strong growth sector. At the same time the average yield for companies in the textiles industry was 5.3 per cent and the PE ratio 10.4, reflecting the very much lower stockmarket rating of companies in one of the traditional and somewhat depressed sectors of British manufacturing industry.

These are only averages, and within each sector there will be a wide variation in the ratings of individual companies. Don't be thrown, incidentally, by an occasional rating that looks way outside the normal range. It could be, as we have seen, that profits have suffered a very temporary setback. It could also be that the market thinks the company might be taken over and has chased the share price up way beyond the levels it could sustain on its own merits.

Share price indexes

We have mentioned the **FT-Actuaries Indexes,** but the question of share price measurement for the stockmarket as a whole needs a little more explanation. In the past the index that newspaper readers would have been most familiar with was the **FT 30-Share Index**, also known as the **Financial Times Ordinary Share Index**. The index, started in 1935 with a base of 100, is compiled from the share prices of 30 leading British companies and calculated as a geometric mean. It is biased towards major industrial and retailing companies — the traditional **blue chips** of the stockmarket — though now includes financial and oil stocks which have assumed greater importance. Its ups and downs reflect the mood of the market, but it would not be a good index against which to measure the performance of a typical investment **portfolio** ('portfolio' is simply the collective term for the shares an investor or a fund owns).

For this purpose the **FT-Actuaries Indexes** are a great deal better. First, they reflect the movements of over 700 shares, accounting for more than 80 per cent of the value of all listed shares. Second, each company in the index is weighted according to its market value. A movement in the share price of a large company has more effect on the index than movement in a small one.

The **FT-Actuaries All-Share Index** (the **All-Share**) is the most representative of all, reflecting the full 700-plus companies. The **500-Share Index** includes all except financial and property companies and the **Industrial Group Index** further excludes oil companies. These indexes are in turn further broken down by **industrial sector**, so that there is a yardstick for, say, electronics companies, textiles or property concerns. Not only do the indexes give a measure of price movements but they also show average

TEXTILES

1989 High	Low	Stock	Price	+ or −	Div Net	C'vr	Y'ld Gr's	P/E
°36	24	Aitch Hldgs. 20p...y	26	......	—	—	—	—
383	313	Allied Textile..... β	380	......	10.6	2.8	3.7	12.9
336	223	Atkins Bros......y	223xd	−3	11.0	2.2	6.6	9.3
260	228	Beales (J.) 20p.....y	255	......	t6.3	4.0	3.3	9.7
90	82	Beckman A 10p ... y	86	......	h4.78	1.5	7.4	11.8
219	195	Brit. Mohair........y	200	......	8.0	3.2	5.3	7.7
358½	263	Courtaulds.......α	356	+6	13.0	2.3	4.9	10.2
237	196	Dawson Intl........β	219	......	8.6	2.0	5.4	11.8
107	80	Drummond Group..y	80	......	3.7	φ	6.4	φ
172	129	Early's Witney 10p..y	159	......	1.32	0.5	1.1	—
°170	128	Foster (John).......y	165	−1	5.5	3.6	4.6	7.9
275	185	Gaskell 20p.......y	238	+1	7.5	4.0	4.2	7.9
112	84	Haggas (John) 10p..y	92	......	4.0	3.1	5.8	7.3
119	78	Hicking Pentecost..y	118	+2	2.0	φ	2.3	φ
160	137	Ill'gworth M. 20p..y	145	......	4.5	3.2	4.1	10.0
125	100	Ingham(G) 10p	103	......	3.0	φ	3.9	φ
242	180	Jerome (Hldgs.)....y	180	−1	7.8	2.9	5.8	7.2
341	240	Kynoch (G & G) ....y	245	......	5.5	4.4	3.0	(7.2)
281	210	Lamont Hldgs 10p...β	258	......	9.5	3.4	4.9	8.0
317	210	Leeds Grp...........y	217	......	8.0	3.8	4.9	7.2
152	130	Lister............y	134	−1	4.0	2.5	4.0	11.2
°144	88	Lowe (Robert H.)...y	88	......	φ3.5	4.5	5.3	4.6
72	58	Lyles (S.) 20p.......y	58	......	3.5	2.4	8.0	6.9
250	213	Mackay Hugh......y	215	+2	7.0	1.7	4.3	16.0
139	77	Palma Group.......y	78	......	3.7	2.7	6.3	7.8
189	155	Parkland 'A'.......y	183	......	6.3	3.9	4.6	7.3
°69	55½	Readicut 5p ....β	60	......	3.16	φ	7.0	φ

Table 4.1　Share price information. Source: *Financial Times.*

**These indices are the joint compilation of the Financial Times,
the Institute of Actuaries and the Faculty of Actuaries**

EQUITY GROUPS & SUB-SECTIONS Figures in parentheses show number of stocks per section	Index No.	Day's Change %	Est Earnings Yield% (Max.)	Gross Div Yield% (Act at 25%)	Est P/E Ratio (Net)	xd adj. 1989 to date	Tue Jun 27 Index No.	Mon Jun 26 Index No.	Fri Jun 23 Index No.	Year ago (approx) Index No.
1 CAPITAL GOODS (206)	969.66	+0.5	10.80	4.05	11.38	14.74	965.25	960.61	959.88	788.35
2 Building Materials (29)	1197.80	+0.3	11.86	4.32	10.41	22.32	1194.73	1184.59	1190.75	1008.48
3 Contracting, Construction (37)	1628.73	......	14.48	4.31	9.06	30.72	1629.66	1638.91	1640.82	1592.81
4 Electricals (9)	2851.34	-0.5	8.37	4.04	14.74	50.60	2866.13	2868.81	2867.43	2086.57
5 Electronics (31)	2227.67	+0.8	8.50	3.10	15.35	23.92	2208.93	2202.14	2190.91	1705.44
6 Mechanical Engineering (54)	535.04	+0.2	9.94	3.97	12.37	8.04	534.14	531.61	531.14	406.54
7 Metals and Metal Forming (7)	522.17	-0.7	19.18	5.73	5.74	3.02	518.48	517.21	519.93	473.93
9 Motors (17)	329.47	+0.2	11.28	4.61	10.41	6.83	328.98	328.07	327.58	278.69
10 Other Industrial Materials (22)	1659.48	+1.1	9.06	4.16	13.17	26.35	1641.79	1621.59	1614.24	1314.96
21 CONSUMER GROUP (187)	1250.48	......	8.85	3.61	14.13	17.90	1250.68	1240.60	1237.19	1093.44
22 Brewers and Distillers (22)	1368.40	+0.2	9.93	3.54	12.65	19.41	1365.73	1350.29	1351.85	1115.82
25 Food Manufacturing (20)	1105.25	-0.1	9.19	3.78	13.62	17.13	1106.41	1099.71	1098.64	989.45
26 Food Retailing (15)	2367.25	-0.7	8.53	3.22	15.39	25.59	2382.82	2389.37	2399.55	2023.57
27 Health and Household (14)	2297.53	-0.3	6.46	2.59	17.59	21.50	2305.37	2280.83	2245.00	1862.97
29 Leisure (33)	1669.74	+0.4	7.62	3.39	16.44	22.05	1663.78	1650.62	1651.07	1345.25
31 Packaging & Paper (15)	565.30	+0.4	10.28	4.34	12.31	8.15	562.96	561.74	563.46	520.93
32 Publishing & Printing (19)	3569.55	......	8.62	4.65	14.63	71.88	3568.65	3558.35	3577.30	3436.07
34 Stores (34)	829.89	+0.3	10.95	4.34	11.95	14.98	827.67	814.34	811.16	804.32
35 Textiles (15)	542.39	+0.6	10.92	5.35	10.96	13.42	539.35	539.51	536.71	601.92
40 OTHER GROUPS (93)	1143.65	-0.5	9.97	4.11	12.20	13.55	1149.32	1136.65	1127.55	910.35
41 Agencies (17)	1421.89	+0.1	7.07	2.29	17.50	14.91	1420.88	1423.63	1413.26	1162.86
42 Chemicals (22)	1317.46	-0.6	10.82	4.52	10.90	26.38	1325.86	1309.31	1296.39	1095.15
43 Conglomerates (12)	1669.61	+0.1	10.09	4.86	11.67	20.16	1667.77	1649.23	1641.71	1207.71
45 Transport (13)	2482.67	......	8.50	3.63	15.30	39.22	2481.62	2460.82	2440.68	1901.32
47 Telephone Networks (2)	1113.80	-1.6	11.20	4.46	11.58	2.76	1132.16	1109.02	1098.54	1001.86
48 Miscellaneous (27)	1672.02	+0.1	9.53	3.58	11.91	23.26	1672.31	1665.93	1652.92	1172.11
49 INDUSTRIAL GROUP (486)	1168.21	+0.2	9.71	3.87	12.71	16.18	1168.49	1159.11	1154.82	975.96
51 Oil & Gas (14)	2155.12	+1.4	9.86	5.19	13.48	51.14	2125.53	2092.44	2066.16	1847.66
59 500 SHARE INDEX (500)	1251.62	+0.2	9.73	4.05	12.81	19.04	1249.56	1238.29	1232.26	1049.76
61 FINANCIAL GROUP (124)	741.90	+0.3	–	5.30	–	17.62	739.63	731.38	731.10	710.31
62 Banks (8)	742.58	+0.6	24.00	6.44	5.47	21.71	737.82	724.43	724.40	682.60
65 Insurance (Life) (8)	1068.22	-0.3	–	5.59	–	29.86	1064.62	1058.31	1059.02	1060.62
66 Insurance (Composite) (7)	584.54	+0.4	–	6.16	–	16.75	582.14	572.05	567.09	546.98
67 Insurance (Brokers) (7)	980.35	+0.8	7.70	6.39	17.46	31.63	972.19	959.20	954.85	1008.73
68 Merchant Banks (11)	335.17	-0.8	–	4.63	–	5.93	332.60	328.72	328.75	359.90
69 Property (52)	1314.99	-0.4	6.33	2.91	20.13	15.98	1320.39	1316.20	1318.73	1225.41
70 Other Financial (31)	356.47	+0.5	11.52	6.05	11.05	8.02	354.69	353.95	356.37	387.69
71 Investment Trusts (70)	1167.84	+0.3	–	2.81	–	14.25	1164.79	1159.09	1152.68	907.88
81 Mining Finance (2)	664.02	-0.5	8.69	3.87	12.81	10.45	667.12	664.66	663.96	521.13
91 Overseas Traders (8)	1334.14	+0.4	11.29	5.56	10.08	35.07	1328.68	1321.28	1324.39	1159.16
99 ALL-SHARE INDEX (704)	1126.69	+0.2	–	4.20	–	18.53	1124.67	1114.48	1109.89	960.90

	Index No.	Day's Change	Day's High (a)	Day's Low (b)	Jun 27	Jun 26	Jun 23	Jun 22	Jun 21	Year ago
FT-SE 100 SHARE INDEX‡	2209.4	+3.0	2225.6	2206.2	2206.4	2179.6	2167.5	2180.0	2172.2	1855.1

Table 4.2 FT-Actuaries indexes. Source: *Financial Times.*

yields and PE ratios. On Saturdays additional information is
published on the **highs** and **lows** for each sector.

Most recent of the UK equity indexes is the **Financial Times-
Stock Exchange 100-Share Index (FT-SE** or **Footsie** index) which
started with a base of 1,000 at end-December 1983. It reflects

price movements of the 100 largest companies and because of the smaller number of companies it can be calculated more rapidly and frequently. It was introduced mainly as a basis for dealing in equity index options and futures (see Chapter 17). The *Financial Times* also publishes **FT-Actuaries World Indexes** of all major (and some minor) stockmarkets, expressed in terms of the local currency, of dollars and of sterling.

Journalists frequently refer to shares as cheap or expensive relative to their sector of the FT-Actuaries Indexes. Movements in an index are usually measured in **points**. If the FT 30-share index falls from 1,600 to 1,580, it has dropped 20 points and a point is also sometimes used to mean a 1p price movement in an individual share or a £1 movement for a gilt-edged stock. Why movements are not expressed more meaningfully as percentage changes is obscure.

Matching the index

Institutional investors attempt to **beat the index** most relevant to their portfolios of shares, but on balance have difficulty in doing so. They control such large volumes of money that they find it difficult to buy adequate numbers of shares in some of the smaller companies represented, whose shares often outperform those of their larger counterparts.

Some of them do run portfolios which seek merely to match a particular index by buying the stocks which constitute the index in the same proportions as they are represented in the index, or by otherwise trying to mimic the performance of the index. It is more difficult than it sounds. But these **indexed portfolios** mean that when a large company such as British Telecom launches on the stockmarket, many institutions are bound to buy its shares in large quantities simply to maintain the balance of their portfolios.

Balance sheet ratios

The balance sheet can tell you a great deal about the financial health of a company, but it doesn't throw up convenient investment ratios in quite the same way as a profit and loss account. There's one possible exception — the net asset value — which we'll come to later. But there are a number of items an investment analyst or a financial journalist will check.

Borrowings and balance sheet gearing

Back to John Smith & Co. One of the first things to look at is the company's **gearing**: the relationship between the **borrowed money** and the **shareholders' money** in the business. We've already touched on it briefly but now it can be reduced to a convenient formula.

The borrowings, in the case of John Smith, are the £8,000 bank overdraft and the £30,000 term loan, totalling £38,000. Trade creditors do not count as borrowings in this context, since they are not clocking up interest charges. The shareholders' money in the business is the £49,000 of **shareholders' funds**. The most common way of relating the two is to calculate **borrowings as a percentage of shareholders' funds** — a definition which can be a little confusing because it could suggest that borrowings are a part of shareholders' funds, which of course they are not.

In this case the £38,000 **gross borrowings** are equivalent to 77.6 per cent of the £49,000 figure for the shareholders' interest. This would be fairly high for an established stockmarket-listed company but by no means out of the ordinary for a private company. Sometimes the gearing is worked out on the **net borrowings** (borrowings less cash) instead. In this case the net borrowings are £33,000 after the £5,000 of cash in the bank is deducted and the ratio is 67.3 per cent.

The 'Borrowings as a percentage of shareholders' funds' ratio, whether worked out on the gross borrowings or the net borrowings, is referred to as the **balance sheet gearing** to distinguish it from the **income gearing**: the relationship between profits and interest charges that was discussed in the context of the profit and loss account. Both can be useful in estimating whether a company is **over-geared** or **over-borrowed**. High balance sheet gearing matters rather less if a company is exceptionally profitable or if the borrowings are at a very low fixed rate of interest. John Smith is, as it happens, quite highly profitable so interest charges only take a small proportion of profits despite fairly high balance sheet gearing.

Bankers and other lenders always look for a **cushion** for the money they advance. In income terms the cushion is the level of profit out of which the company pays the interest charges. John Smith's profit would have to fall a long way before it was unable to pay its interest, so there is a comfortable cushion for the lender. In balance sheet terms, the cushion is the shareholders' funds. If the company starts losing money, it is the shareholders' funds that will be depleted first, so in John Smith's case there is (on paper, at least) a reasonable margin before the lender might be at risk of losing his money.

Security for borrowings

The other thing a lender normally requires is **security** for his loan in the form of a **charge** over some or all of the assets of the company. The principle is similar to taking a mortgage on a home. If the borrower fails to keep up his interest and capital payments, the lender — the building society — can sell the house and recover its loan from the proceeds. With a company the charge may be a **fixed charge** on specific assets — its machinery or buildings — or may be a **floating charge** on all the assets of the business including the current assets. The lender has priority for repayment out of the proceeds of selling the assets over which he has a charge. The importance of this in practical terms is that a company, particularly a smaller company, may find it difficult to borrow further money when it does not have enough reasonably saleable assets to provide adequate security for the loan.

John Smith's financial position

From John Smith's gearing and from our knowledge of the business we might deduce the following. The company is likely to expand further in the current year, which means it will need yet more money to finance higher levels of stocks and debtors (see below), and it may need to install additional machinery to meet the demand for its paperweights. It generated a cash flow of £12,000 last year and, assuming profits continue rising, the cash flow ought to be higher in the current year. But it is unlikely to be enough to provide all the money John Smith will need. It could probably increase its borrowings a little. But if it were a stockmarket-listed company, it would almost certainly be thinking of raising further equity capital by issuing additional shares for cash. This would reduce the gearing by increasing the proportion of shareholders' money in the business. And quite apart from bringing in money for the immediate needs, by increasing the size of the equity 'cushion' it also prepares the way for bringing in additional borrowed money in the future.

Remember that fast-growing companies tend to use up cash faster than they can generate it from their profits. The expansion means that they are having to tie up more and more cash in higher and higher levels of stocks and debtors: their **working capital** need rises rapidly. A company that expands too fast may be described as **overtrading** (trading beyond its financial resources). It can go bust simply because it runs out of cash to pay its bills, even though it may have been operating at a profit.

Investment analysts therefore check the accounts to see if a company has adequate resources to finance its business and whether it would be able to raise any additional money needed. In the short run, a rights issue to raise further money from the sale of shares (see Chapter 9) often depresses the price of the shares because it increases the number in issue.

While looking at John Smith's borrowings, we would also check whether they are long-term or short-term and whether they are at fixed or variable rates of interest. The overdraft has to be counted as short-term and the interest rate will be variable. The term loan, we might learn from the notes, has to be repaid over seven years, which would normally be classed as 'medium-term'. The interest rate could be fixed or variable — the notes should say.

Net assets per share

Next, look at the £49,000 figure for shareholders' funds: the book value of the shareholders' interest in the company. Often this value is expressed as an amount per share or a **net asset value per share (NAV)**. Divide the ordinary shareholders' funds by the number of ordinary shares in issue (£49,000 divided by 40,000 shares) and you get £1.225 (or 122.5p as it is usually expressed). It corresponds, in this case though not always, with the £1 the original investors subscribed for each share plus the 22.5p of retained profits attributable to each share.

It is very important to grasp what this NAV figure means. The £49,000 of shareholders' funds on which it is based is very much an accounting figure and does not usually tell you anything much about the value investors are likely to put on the company in the stockmarket, which usually depends far more on the profits the company is capable of earning. First, John Smith & Co has no intention of closing down the business, selling the assets, paying the debts and returning what is left to shareholders. Even if it did,

CHURCH

| T | Shoe manufacturer and retailer |

Ord cap £2.69m (Market value £40.9m)
25p Ord price 380p (Net assets 279p)
(1988-9 high 478p: low 375p) PE ratio 13* (11†)
Dividend yield % 4.2
Net debt/shareholders' funds %: 25
*Based on 35% tax charge †Based on stated earnings

Year to 31 Dec	Turnover £m	Pre-tax profit £m	Stated earnings per share (p)	Gross dividend per share (p)
1984	51.8	4.72	31.0	10.7
1985	55.2	4.35	25.6	12.0
1986	58.4	4.96	29.1	13.1
1987	61.5	5.54	35.3	15.4
1988	65.3	4.86	33.4	16.0

Table 4.3   Investment yardsticks.
Source: *Investors Chronicle.*

what was left would be very unlikely to amount exactly to
£49,000. The paperweight-making machinery **stands in the books**
at £27,000, but would a buyer necessarily pay exactly £27,000 for
a used paperweight-making machine? It is highly unlikely.
Would stocks of raw materials and half-finished or finished
paperweights actually bring in £50,000? Again, unlikely.

When a long-term investor buys shares, what he is really buying
is the right to a certain flow of income (by way of dividend) in the
future, and generally he is buying shares in companies which he
hopes will provide a rising income. If the income rises there is a
good chance that the capital value — the market value — of the
shares he holds will rise too.

Some companies are capable of providing an increasing flow of
earnings without owning anything much in the way of assets. A
successful advertising agency, say, might rent the offices it
operates from and hire its photocopiers, typewriters and other
equipment. Apart from a few sticks of office furniture and
whatever cash it had accumulated from its profits, it might own
virtually nothing. Its 'assets' are the people who work for it, its
reputation in the business and its client connections — items
which do not normally appear in a balance sheet. Yet the
stockmarket might put a high value on the shares purely because
of the profit-earning potential. This is why a yardstick that relates
to earnings rather than assets — the price earnings ratio — is the
main one investors use.

Asset-rich companies

But there are certain types of company where the assets or a fair proportion of the assets can be reasonably accurately priced and easily sold. Companies whose main business is owning property, owning shares in other companies (**investment trusts** — see Chapter 20), or which have a lot of cash or investments in the balance sheet are the main examples. Others in this category are companies carrying on a trade which involves owning large amounts of property: stores groups like Kingfisher (which owns the Woolworth chain), hotel companies and breweries which own large numbers of pubs.

In these cases the **net asset value** can and does affect the price investors will pay for the shares in the stockmarket. The shares are commonly described as standing **at a premium to** (above) the net asset value, or **at a discount to** (below) the net asset value. The size of the premium or discount is expressed as a percentage. If XYZ Holdings has net assets per share (or an NAV) of 100p and the shares stand at 90p in the market, the shares are at a discount to assets of 10 per cent. If the market price is 108p, the shares stand at a premium to assets of 8 per cent. For taxation and other reasons, the shares of **property investment companies** and investment trusts normally stand at a discount to assets except at times of market euphoria.

Readily saleable assets are most important when takeovers are in the air. A company with high earnings but few assets may try to acquire an **asset-rich company** to give it more substance. And the company at the receiving end of the bid will argue (not always successfully) that the takeover price should be at least as high as the value of its assets.

Return on assets

This brings us to another commonly used ratio: a company's **return on assets**. It is a measure of the profits the company earns relative to the capital employed in the business. As such, it can be used as a measure of the efficiency of one company against another, though it needs using with care. And it is not specifically a stockmarket measure: it does not reveal anything about the return the company earns on shareholders' money. It measures the return on all money used, whether derived from loans or from the shareholders. A company such as our successful advertising agency, with very few assets, will be earning a very high return on capital employed, simply because very little capital is employed. The return on assets is used mainly to compare one company with another in the same or a similar business.

To calculate the return on assets you take the profit before tax and before the interest on longer-term debt and express it as a percentage of shareholders' funds (less goodwill) plus long-term loans, deferred tax and minorities (see Chapter 5).

The return on assets figure can sometimes provide useful clues for a **stockmarket predator**: a company on the look-out for other companies it might take over. Suppose a retail stores group which owns most of its shops is showing a return on assets of only five per cent. Clearly, it is not a very efficient trader: it could make this level of return simply by renting its shops to other retailers. It is earning very little profit from the trading operation. A predator might reckon he could take over the retail stores group and vastly improve the return it earned by supplying more retailing flair. And it might be possible to recoup part of the costs of the takeover by selling some of the properties or selling them and leasing them back (see Chapter 19).

5

Refining the figurework

There are a few more terms relating to company accounts that will crop up fairly frequently in the press commentary and the best way of illustrating what they mean is with another sample balance sheet.

This time we've taken a more mature company: call it Jones Manufacturing. Its assets are in the millions rather than the thousands. It owns the buildings from which it operates: note the £3m item for properties included under fixed assets. And, partly because it has been ploughing back a proportion of its profits over many years, its shareholders' funds are a substantial £11m.

Goodwill

The first item that may be unfamiliar is the £1m entry against the heading **goodwill** which might also appear as **intangible assets**. There are two main ways in which this is likely to have arisen and the notes to the accounts should make this clear. First, the company might own trade marks or patents which are not physical or **tangible** assets like plant and buildings, but which have a value nonetheless. These would usually be classed under the general heading of goodwill. Second, Jones Manufacturing might have purchased other businesses and paid more for them than the net value of the physical assets they owned. In this case, the difference between the price paid and the value of the net assets acquired might be accounted for as a **goodwill item**. The important point about goodwill is that investment analysts will normally exclude it when calculating a company's net asset value, which strictly ought to be expressed as **net tangible asset value**.

Jones Manufacturing
Consolidated balance sheet at 31 December

	£'000	£'000
FIXED ASSETS		
Land and buildings	3,000	
Plant and machinery	5,600	
		8,600
GOODWILL		1,000
INVESTMENTS IN ASSOCIATED COs		3,000
CURRENT ASSETS		
Stocks	5,000	
Debtors	3,500	
Cash at bank	500	
	9,000	
CURRENT LIABILITIES		
(Creditors: amounts due within one year		
Trade creditors	3,000	
Tax payable	600	
Dividend proposed	400	
Bank overdrafts	800	
	4,800	
NET CURRENT ASSETS		4,200
TOTAL ASSETS LESS CURRENT LIABILITIES		16,800
CREDITORS		
(amounts due in more than one year)		
Term loan	800	
5% Debenture stock 1998	2,800	
6% Convertible Loan Stock	1,500	
		5,100
PROVISIONS FOR LIABILITIES AND CHARGES		500
NET ASSETS		11,200
MINORITY SHAREHOLDERS' INTEREST		200
JONES MANUFACTURING SHAREHOLDERS' INTEREST		11,000
Represented by:		
Issued ordinary share capital		
(20p ordinary shares)	1,500	
Preference share capital		
(£1 shares)	500	
Revenue reserves	5,400	
Share premium account	1,650	
Capital reserves	1,950	
SHAREHOLDERS' FUNDS		11,000

And companies themselves tend to write off against their reserves the goodwill arising on acquisition. More of this later.

The next item is **investments in associated companies** or **interests in associates**; sometimes associates are also called **related companies**. The definition of an **associated company** is open to interpretation. But in general it would be a company which was not a subsidiary, but in which Jones Manufacturing had an interest amounting to between 20 per cent and 50 per cent of the share capital and over whose affairs it exerted some management influence. In other words, Jones Manufacturing does not hold the shares in the associate simply as an unrelated investment, as it might own a holding of government stock.

There is probably some trading relationship between Jones Manufacturing and its **associate**. The associated company might, say, be an important supplier of components to Jones, or it might be an important customer for Jones's products — in either case it could be of benefit to Jones to be able to exert some influence over the associate's affairs. In accounting terms, the interest in the associated company will normally appear in the balance sheet at a figure representing Jones Manufacturing's share of the net assets of the associate. If the associated company or companies had net assets of £10m and Jones Manufacturing owned a 30 per cent stake, the figure in Jones's balance sheet would be 30 per cent of £10m, or £3m. An interest in an associate is different from a mere **trade investment**: a shareholding in a company with which there is probably no particular management or trading relationship.

Varieties of debt

Jones Manufacturing's **sources of finance** are also more varied and a little more complex than those of Smith & Co. There is a bank overdraft, though small in relation to the company's size. But there are three types of medium-term or long-term debt under the heading of **creditors due in more than one year**. First comes the familiar term loan: again fairly small at £800,000.

The other two items — the **debenture stock** and the **convertible loan stock** — are in a different category of borrowings, because they are **securities** issued by the company rather than loans from a bank. Much as the government does when it borrows by issuing a gilt-edged stock, Jones Manufacturing has raised money by creating different forms of loan stock and selling them to investors: the familiar principle of issuing an IOU note in return for cash. These stocks, once issued, will normally be traded in the stockmarket. Investors who paid cash to the company for them when first issued can either wait till the date they are due to be repaid by the company, or can sell them to other investors in the stockmarket. Both in this case pay a fixed rate of interest.

The **debenture stock** will probably be secured on specific assets of the company. Provided the assets are of good quality, it should thus be a safe form of investment for buyers. It is a long-term borrowing. It is not due for repayment until 1998, and when first issued it probably had a **life** of 25 or 30 years — possibly more. It was also presumably issued at a time when interest rates were considerably lower than in the 1980s. Thus the company has the use of some **cheap long-term money**.

The convertible loan stock is almost certainly an **unsecured loan stock**. It is not secured on the assets of the company, and to this extent it is a little less safe than the debenture. But its most important feature is that it is **convertible**. At some stage of its life, it can be exchanged for ordinary shares according to a pre-arranged formula. This gives it some of the attributes of a loan and some of the attributes of an ordinary share. Until it is converted, it pays a fixed rate of interest like the debenture stock. Once it is converted into ordinary shares, the shares are identical to the other shares in issue and receive the same dividend.

If the stock is not converted into shares during the **conversion period**, it normally reverts to being a simple unsecured loan stock, paying the fixed rate of interest until it is eventually repaid. Whether or not holders of the stock exercise the right to convert it will depend on how successful Jones Manufacturing is. The **conversion terms** were probably pitched originally at a level somewhat above Jones Manufacturing's share price at the time of issue (the **conversion premium**). If the share price at the time had been 80p, the terms of the loan might have stipulated that £1 nominal of the loan could be converted into one ordinary share, meaning that anyone who paid £100 for £100 nominal of the loan would be paying £1 for a share if he exercised his conversion rights. Five years later, if Jones had increased its profits and dividends at a good rate, the share price might have risen to, say, 180p. At this level there is clearly a value in the right to exchange £1 nominal of loan for a share worth 180p.

Because of this **conversion value**, the price of the convertible loan stock itself would have risen in the stockmarket. Investors would have been prepared to pay more than £100 for £100 nominal value of the loan, when they knew that each £1 nominal could be converted into a share worth 180p. The calculations that give the likely price of a convertible loan stock in the stockmarket, relative to the price of the ordinary shares, are quite complex. In general a convertible loan rises in value to reflect the rise in value of the ordinary shares, but rises at a slower percentage rate than the ordinary shares. On the other hand, it normally provides a higher and more secure yield than the ordinary shares, at least in the early years.

Typically, the Jones Manufacturing **convertible loan** might originally have been issued with a life of 20 years to **redemption** or **maturity**. Holders of the convertible might have had the right to convert it into ordinary shares at the 'one share for £1 nominal' rate in years six, seven, eight, nine and ten of its life (the conversion period). If the share price does not reach a level that makes conversion worthwhile by year ten, holders will not convert. Any stock remaining unconverted after year ten would become an ordinary unsecured loan stock until repaid at the end of year twenty. Convertible stocks with considerably more complex features are also commonplace nowadays, particularly in the case of issues made through euromarket mechanisms (see Chapter 16).

For the company the main advantage of the convertible loan is that the interest rate it needs to pay will probably be lower than for an ordinary unsecured loan stock. Investors will accept the lower interest rate because of the possibility of capital gains if the share price rises and the market value of the convertible stock follows it. The convertible also represents a form of **deferred equity**. If the company had issued ordinary shares instead, its earnings and dividends would immediately be spread over a larger number of shares: the earnings would be **diluted** over the larger capital immediately.

Diluting earnings and assets

By issuing the convertible loan, Jones Manufacturing can offset the interest cost (the cost of **servicing** the loan) against tax, whereas dividends on shares would have to be paid out of taxed income. By the time the loan can be converted, earnings should have risen significantly and the company's asset value should also have risen. Investment analysts and journalists sometimes refer to **fully-diluted earnings per share** and **fully-diluted assets per share**. This means they have calculated what the earnings per share would be on the assumption the stock was converted and current earnings (adjusted for the disappearance of the interest charge on the convertible) were spread over the larger number of shares. They have also done the same sums for the NAV (see below). Note that companies may issue convertible preference shares (see below) instead of convertible loan stocks. They convert into ordinary shares in much the same way, but the dividend on the convertible preference is not tax-deductible as the convertible loan stock interest is.

Provisions

There are two other unfamiliar items. The **provisions for liabilities and charges** of £500,000 has to be knocked off the assets figure before arriving at a net asset value. It normally consists of **deferred tax**, which is tax that might become payable in the future but is not yet a sufficiently certain liability to be provided for under current liabilities.

Minority shareholders

The second item, **minority shareholders' interest**, was mentioned in Chapter 4. Where Jones does not own all the shares of all of its subsidiaries, this figure represents the value of the shares in these subsidiaries held by other parties. Since this value does not belong to the shareholders in Jones it has to be deducted before reaching a net asset value.

Capital commitments

Two further items which could affect the balance sheet in the future appear in the notes to the accounts but not in the accounts themselves. One is **capital commitments**. This is expenditure on assets which the directors have authorized or contracted for but which has not yet taken place. It can be useful in giving an idea of the company's investment plans and whether these would be covered by the cash flow.

Contingent liabilities

The other is **contingent liabilities**. Jones Manufacturing might provide a **guarantee** for the bank borrowings of one of its associated companies. Or there might be a legal case pending against Jones, in which the other side is claiming £500,000 of damages, though Jones denies liability. In both cases Jones does not expect any liability to arise, but it might. So contingent liabilities such as this must be noted.

Preference shares

Back to the balance sheet itself. The make-up of shareholders' funds is also more complex than in the case of Smith & Co. First, Jones Manufacturing has two classes of share capital: **preference shares** as well as **ordinary shares**.

Companies with **preference share capital** often have it for historical reasons, though issues of preference shares (particularly convertible preference) have regained popularity in recent years. Various mutations of preference capital may also crop up in the financing of young businesses which are not quoted on a stockmarket and in the financing of management buy-outs (see Chapter 11). Preference shares usually pay a fixed dividend and in this respect are more like a loan stock than an ordinary share. But the dividend has to be paid out of profits which have borne tax, whereas interest on a loan stock is allowable against tax. Hence the tendency nowadays to issue loans rather than preference shares.

Preference shares are part of **shareholders' funds** but not part of **ordinary shareholders' funds**. They are **share capital**, but they are not **equity share capital**. They do not share in the rising prosperity of a company, because their dividend is fixed and does not increase with rising profits. But they are entitled to their dividend before the ordinary shareholders get anything, so the dividend is safer than that of an ordinary share. And if the company should be **wound up** (closed down), preference shareholders are normally entitled to be repaid the par value of their shares (usually but not necessarily £1) before the ordinary shareholders get anything. This is assuming there is something left after loans and all the other debts of the company — which

74

rank before preference shares — have been repaid. Preference shares do not normally carry votes unless the dividend is **in arrears** (the payments have not been kept up).

Less usual types of share

We have only shown preference shares and ordinary shares, but there are various other less common forms of share capital that companies may issue. These are variations on the theme of equity or preference. **Deferred ordinary shares** probably do not **rank for dividend** until converted into ordinary shares at some future date. **Preferred ordinary shares** will get a minimum dividend before the ordinary get anything, and probably share in ordinary dividends thereafter. **Participating preference shares** may be similar; they get a fixed dividend plus an extra dividend on top that depends on profits. **Convertible preference shares** convert into ordinary shares, and so on.

Par values

Look next at the **equity capital**. Note that Jones Manufacturing has **issued ordinary share capital** of £1.5m, but that this is divided into units of 20p each. In other words, each pound of nominal capital is divided into five shares, so there are 7.5m shares in issue, each with a **nominal** or **par** value of 20p. The meaning of the par value sometimes causes problems. It has nothing to do with the price at which the shares may be traded in the stockmarket and for most practical purposes you can forget it — American companies often have ordinary shares (known as **common stock**) with **no par value**.

However, if you look at the share prices in the *Financial Times* you will see that after the name of a company comes the par value of the shares. If no par value is given, you assume it is 25p, and the other common denominations are 5p, 10p, 20p, 50p, and £1. But this is relevant mainly for certain accounting purposes and for a technical **Companies Act** requirement that companies may not issue shares at prices below their par value. What interests investors is the price at which a share is quoted in the stockmarket, and it is perfectly possible to have a 5p share quoted at 400p or a £1 share quoted below its par value at 80p.

Authorized and issued capital

One other facet of a company's capital crops up in press reports, particularly of take-over offers. As well as the figure for **issued capital** (the nominal value of the shares in issue) you will see references to **authorized capital**. This is the maximum amount of capital that the company has authorization from its shareholders to issue. Jones Manufacturing might have an authorized capital of £3m, divided into £500,000 of preference capital (all of which is issued) and £2.5m of ordinary capital. Since only £1.5m of ordinary capital is so far issued, there is £1m of **authorized but unissued capital** in existence, equivalent to 5m 20p shares. The directors can thus issue a further 5m shares without needing to get shareholders' permission first. And, in fact, 1.5m of these unissued shares are already earmarked for the eventual conversion of the convertible loan stock.

If a company wants to issue more shares than it is authorized to do, it must call a meeting of shareholders and get them to vote in favour of an increase in the authorized amount. This might crop up if Jones Manufacturing wanted to take over another company by issuing 6m of its own shares in exchange for shares in the target company. Unless Jones's own shareholders agreed, the deal could not go through. It may also crop up when a company wants to make a **rights issue** or a **scrip issue** (see Chapter 9).

Because of the takeover possibilities many shareholders — particularly the big institutions — are unwilling to vote a company a big increase in authorized capital unless they know for what purpose the new unissued shares are required. Where the authorized capital exceeds the issued capital by a large amount, the directors of the company have considerable discretion. Shareholders may be happier if they know their permission would be required before the company could, say, radically change the balance of its business by issuing shares to take over another concern. This is one of a number of ways shareholders may exercise control over the companies they invest in.

Warrants

Apart from shares there is another type of quasi-security that a company may issue, which will be referred to in the notes to the accounts but not in the balance sheet itself. This is the **warrant**. A company may issue warrants which give the holder the right to

subscribe at a fixed price for shares in the company at some future date. The **subscription price** will usually be fixed above the current price of the shares when the warrant is issued, so at this stage any value in the warrant is simply hope value.

Suppose a warrant is issued which gives the right to subscribe for one share at 180p at some point in the future. The current share price is 150p and there is no **intrinsic value** in the warrant. But if the share price should rise to 250p, there is a clear value in the right to subscribe at 180p for a share that could immediately be sold for 250p, and the price of the warrant itself will reflect this value. The principle is much the same as for a **traded option** (see Chapter 17 for a fuller explanation). But a warrant gives the right to subscribe cash for a new share the company issues. An option gives the right to buy an existing share from its present owner and does not affect the finances of the company itself. Warrants are traded in the stockmarket much like shares themselves.

Warrants are sometimes issued to improve the attractions of a loan stock and are often referred to as an **equity sweetener** or **equity kicker**. Fixed interest loans are unpopular in periods of high inflation, but if subscribers to a loan are given, say, one warrant for every £3 of loan, they have an interest in the increasing prosperity of the company, as reflected in its share price. When warrants are issued in this way, they are afterwards normally traded separately from the loan. Valuing a warrant, relative to the price of the ordinary shares, is a pretty technical process and best left to the experts.

Revenue reserves

Jones Manufacturing's **revenue reserves** at £5.4m are considerably larger than its issued capital. This points to some years' worth of **ploughed-back profits (retained earnings)**. If the company went through a temporary bad patch in which it did not earn any profits it could, if it chose, use part of these ploughed-back profits of previous years to pay a dividend (always assuming it also had enough cash). And in a loss-making year the revenue reserves will be depleted by the amount of the net losses plus the cost of any dividends paid.

Share premium account

The **share premium account** is part of shareholders' funds, but needs rather more explanation. It arises when the company issues new shares at a price above their par value (and in the case of an established company, the shares almost always will be worth more than their par value and new shares will be priced accordingly). Assume that in the past Jones had decided to raise money by offering new ordinary shares to its existing shareholders (a **rights issue** — see Chapter 9). Its share price at the time was 110p and it issued the new shares at 80p. Since the shares have a par value of 20p, each new share was being sold at a **premium** of 60p to its par value. So for each new share sold the company added 20p to its nominal capital and accounted for the additional 60p by adding it to share premium account.

The share premium account has a special position in law in that it cannot be **written down** without the permission of the courts (it could not be used to cover **trading losses**, for example, without this permission). Since it arises from the issue of capital, it is treated rather as if it were part of the company's capital — part of the 'cushion' of equity that provides protection for creditors.

Capital reserves

Capital reserves will have arisen from transactions that are not part of the company's normal trading. If Jones Manufacturing had sold a surplus factory building at a **capital profit** of £1.95m after tax, this profit would be accounted for in capital reserves. The capital reserve need not even reflect a cash transaction. Suppose Jones had commissioned a professional **revaluation** of its buildings which showed them worth £1.95m more than their book value. It would have increased the value of properties in the accounts by £1.95m and added £1.95m to capital reserves to show that this extra value (the **surplus over book value**) belonged to the shareholders. Balance sheets must balance.

The revaluation of properties is often referred to in the context of takeover bids. If a company owns properties that were last revalued ten years ago (not Jones Manufacturing in this instance), a press report might say: 'the book net asset value is 250p per share against the offer of 275p per share. But if properties are now worth £3m more than the book value, the net asset value would rise to 310p and the offer would look to be on the low side'. Thus the writer is mentally adding £3m to the value of properties, increasing capital reserves (and therefore shareholders' funds) by a like amount, and working out his net asset value figure on the result. He would apply the same arithmetic if the company owned investments that were worth more than the figures at which they were **stated in the books**.

Adjusting the net asset value

Finally, the **net asset value** for Jones Manufacturing. There are two complications. First, goodwill is normally excluded to produce a figure for **net tangible asset value**. Second, the preference shares are not part of the ordinary shareholders' funds, and also have to be excluded. So the sums go:

	£'000
Shareholders' funds (as stated in the accounts)	11,000
less:	
Goodwill	1,000
	10,000
less:	
Preference capital	500
Ordinary shareholders' funds	9,500
Divide by the 7.5 million shares in issue	
Net tangible asset value per ordinary share	126.7p

The whole question of the accounting treatment of goodwill is in a state of flux. Companies are encouraged to write off goodwill against reserves when they incur it via a takeover. But this has the effect of reducing shareholders' funds, which can cause problems. Some companies have attempted to compensate by including as an asset the value of well-known **brand names** they own, though in effect this value is only another form of goodwill. Most investment analysts will exclude goodwill from net asset value calculations, however it is presented.

As an added sophistication, we can work out the **fully-diluted** net asset value per share for Jones. Take the £9.5m adjusted

79

ordinary shareholders' funds. Add in the nominal value of the convertible loan stock — £1.5m — since this will cease to exist as a liability when converted and therefore shareholders' funds will increase by £1.5m. Then divide the result by the enlarged number of ordinary shares: 7.5m plus the 1.5m arising on conversion. The result: £11m divided by 9m shares = £1.222 or 122.2p. So conversion of the loan stock will **dilute** assets per share from 126.7p to 122.2p. A fairly minor **dilution** as it happens, but worth bearing in mind.

6

Equities and the Big Bang

What is **The Stock Exchange**? It is the sole stock exchange in Britain, with its headquarters in Throgmorton Street in the City of London.

Major regional cities used to have their own trading floors. But all of the **regional exchanges** are now merely branches of The Stock Exchange, and trading floors where market members dealt with each other face to face — even the London trading floor — are now largely obsolete. **Dealing** in shares and bonds takes place over the telephone between dealers' offices. The London floor no longer operates for gilt or equity trading, except on rare special occasions.

What was the **Big Bang**? It was a term coined to describe this and other major changes to the operating methods of The Stock Exchange and its member firms. The most significant changes were introduced on **27 October 1986**. Much of what was written about Stock Exchange trading methods prior to 1986 has now been overtaken by events. And strictly we should no longer even speak of The Stock Exchange. At the end of 1986 it merged with **ISRO**, a body representing London dealers in international bonds, to become The International Stock Exchange of the UK and the Republic of Ireland Ltd. It will probably continue to be known as The Stock Exchange or The International Stock Exchange. We will stick with the former.

Securities traded on The Stock Exchange

What has not changed is the types of security traded on The Stock Exchange, though the range has expanded a little. It is the main market in which **ordinary shares** in companies (**equities**) and **government bonds (gilt-edged securities** or **gilts**) are bought and sold. These are not the only types of security traded. Various types of bond issued by companies (usually known as **industrial debentures** or **industrial loans**), **convertible loan stocks, preference shares** and more esoteric pieces of paper such as **options** and **warrants** are also traded. And the term **fixed-interest market**, used mainly to cover gilt-edged securities, also embraces loans issued by local government in the UK and by certain overseas governments as well as fixed-interest industrial debentures.

The total value of shares listed in the market — £392 billion at end-1988 for UK companies listed in London — is known as the **market capitalization**. The **turnover** figure — £266 billion for equities in 1988 — needs treating with care. In London each transaction counts twice. Mr Smith sells shares which initially go to a marketmaker and are ultimately bought by Mr Jones. The value of the sale and of the purchase will be counted as separate items under turnover. The same applies to the measurement of **bargains**. (a Stock Exchange transaction is called a 'bargain', whatever price you pay). In 1988 a total of 6.7m equity bargains was recorded. London ranks third to Tokyo and New York in terms of market capitalization.

The Stock Exchange is both a **primary market** and a **secondary market**: a market where new securities are issued for cash and a market where existing securities are sold by one investor to another. In 1988 £10 billion was raised by the first-time sale of shares by new or existing companies — little more than half the figure for 1987, reflecting the decrease in activity following the stockmarket crash of October 1987.

The Stock Exchange's three tiers

More than one market comes under the aegis of The Stock Exchange, and the terminology can become confusing. Until 1980 The Stock Exchange was the sole market. Companies whose shares or other securities were traded there were **listed** on The Stock Exchange, and still are. The 'listing' refers to a **Listing Agreement** that companies have to sign, which governs some aspects of their behaviour and their reporting to shareholders. At end-1988 there were around 2,000 UK listed companies. In addition, the shares of many overseas companies are listed on the London exchange as well as in their country of origin.

In 1980 The Stock Exchange introduced a **second-tier market** called the **Unlisted Securities Market** or **USM**. It was designed to provide a nursery for smaller or more recently established companies, which might eventually aspire to a listing on The Stock Exchange itself. The costs of entry were somewhat lower, and the criteria a little less strict: normally a three-year profit record would be required before entry as against five years for The Stock Exchange, which now began to be referred to as the **main market**. The USM was successful in attracting new entrants. By end-1988 it embraced over 450 companies, but the number changes rapidly as USM companies move up to the main market and new companies join the USM.

Companies whose shares are traded on the USM are not 'listed', though they have to sign a very similar agreement. Their shares are usually described as being **quoted** on the USM, though the term 'quoted' is loosely used to cover listed companies as well. The USM is run by Stock Exchange member firms and for most purposes is treated as being part of The Stock Exchange: USM stocks are traded in exactly the same way as listed companies. In the *Financial Times* share price pages a Maltese cross symbol is used to denote USM stocks.

In 1987 The Stock Exchange introduced yet another market layer known as the **Third Market**. This is a fairly loosely-regulated market, aimed at still smaller companies of the type sometimes previously traded on the freewheeling **Over-The-Counter** or **OTC** markets (see below). It has not been an unqualified success.

Over-The-Counter markets

The OTC markets were never part of The Stock Exchange. They were 'unofficial' and The Stock Exchange did not like them. Dealing in the OTC markets used to be conducted over the telephone by **licensed dealers in securities**, who had satisfied the minimal requirements of the Department of Trade and Industry to be allowed to deal in securities with the public. There was no central marketplace and no very effective supervision or regulation; safeguards for investors were minimal. Each firm operated a market in the shares of a restricted list of (generally small and little-known) companies. Sometimes the dealer simply operated on a **matched bargain** basis. He put would-be buyers and sellers together but did not take a position in the shares himself. Dealers sometimes also provided an 'unofficial' market in shares listed on The Stock Exchange.

Some former licensed dealers have applied for Stock Exchange membership and a few former OTC stocks are now traded on the Third Market. But effectively the Financial Services Act has put paid to the OTC market in its previous form. The new rules make life very difficult for a marketmaker who is not a member of a recognized investment exchange.

Why trading systems changed

To understand how The Stock Exchange works today it is easiest to look briefly at the largely defunct system that was replaced in the course of the Big Bang.

Before October 1986, there were two classes of Stock Exchange member and members were generally grouped into firms or partnerships. There were the **jobbers** who operated as **marketmakers**. They operated a **book**, buying and selling shares on their own behalf **(taking positions in shares)** and hoping to make a profit on the difference between their buying and selling price. This difference was known as the **jobber's turn**. Jobbers were not allowed to deal with the public. They could deal only with stockbrokers or with each other. They operated during trading hours from **pitches** (stalls) on the Stock Exchange floor.

The **stockbroker** was the agent who executed the public's buying and selling instructions and was remunerated via a **commission** calculated on the value of the deal. Mr Smith (or a major institution) wanted to buy 500 ICI shares. He contacted his broker with the instruction. The broker or one of his trading staff went to the jobbers on the trading floor and bought the shares from the firm which offered the most favourable price. The theory was that this **single-capacity** system (single-capacity because a jobber could act only as principal and a broker only as agent) provided a valuable safeguard for investors. Competition between jobbers prevented their overcharging. And the broker as agent had only his client's interests at heart.

But the system was expensive. The Stock Exchange imposed a scale of **minimum commissions**, which all brokers had to observe and was pitched at a level to provide a living for the least efficient. On equity transactions it ranged on a sliding scale from 1.65 per cent on transactions or parts of a transaction under £7,000 to

0.125 per cent on the portion of a transaction above £2m. In addition, the investor was meeting the cost of the jobber's turn.

The system had other drawbacks. The market was **undercapitalized**, because it was difficult under a partnership structure for jobbers to raise the finance required to take large **positions** in stock and provide **liquidity** for the market by always being ready to buy or sell in large quantities. The big investing institutions could not deal easily in the quantities of stock they required. The supposed competition between jobbers was often illusory. And dealing in the shares of some major British companies was moving towards the more liquid New York market.

Trigger for change

The impetus for change came eventually from the government. The Stock Exchange had been served notice that it would have to justify its **restrictive practices** (notably the fixed commission structure and the jobber/broker distinction) or abandon them. Then, in 1983, a deal was struck between Stock Exchange Chairman Sir Nicholas Goodison and the then Trade and Industry Secretary, Cecil Parkinson. The action in the **Restrictive Practices Court** against The Stock Exchange would be dropped if The Stock Exchange voluntarily agreed to abandon its fixed commission structure.

The New York Stock Exchange had abandoned fixed commissions in 1975. From that year commissions on large deals were by negotiation, and the level of commission on large deals dropped sharply. British brokers realized they would see their income slashed under **negotiated commissions** and the larger ones demanded the right to operate as **marketmakers**, hoping to recoup the loss on commissions from the profits on making a book in shares. Thus the old **jobber/broker distinction** broke down. The Stock Exchange also announced that its rule against outside ownership of Stock Exchange member firms would be abandoned. This opened the way for banks and other cash-rich institutions to acquire broking and jobbing businesses and provide them with the finance they would need.

Takeover of Stock Exchange firms

Between 1983 and 1986 most of the major firms of jobbers and brokers (with the notable exception of brokers Cazenove) arranged to sell out — generally at very inflated prices. Sometimes the new bank or merchant bank owners put together several Stock Exchange firms to form a powerful **securities house**. Most of the larger groupings planned to operate as **marketmakers in equities** as well as **agency brokers**. At the same time it became clear that a number of large American securities houses (and Japanese houses in due course) would be applying for membership of The Stock Exchange. Changes in the pattern of trading in gilt-edged stocks were being planned at the same time (see Chapter 12).

Computers and the new trading system

With as many as 35 **equity marketmakers** immediately after the Big Bang, it was clear the new market would have to rely heavily on **computerized systems**. The plan was that the **Stock Exchange floor** would continue to function. But most marketmakers would operate from their firm's **dealing floors**, possibly some way from The Stock Exchange, feeding the prices at which they would deal into a computerized system that would provide in all brokerage offices a screen display of prices quoted by different marketmakers.

Drawing heavily on an established American system, The Stock Exchange developed the necessary computer network called **SEAQ (Stock Exchange Automated Quotation system)**. This was grafted onto its existing **TOPIC** screen-based price and market news display system. Meanwhile, individual securities houses were developing their own computer systems to interface with SEAQ and provide the services they needed to operate a book in shares. SEAQ itself was planned initially as a **price information system** rather than an **automated dealing system**. The dealer uses the SEAQ screen to see who is offering the best price in the stock that interests him. He then phones the chosen market-maker and negotiates the deal. Later, in 1989, a fully automatic system for executing small transactions was introduced under the name of **SAEF (SEAQ Automatic Execution Facility)**.

For Stock Exchange purposes, shares were classified after the Big Bang into four groupings. First come the **alpha shares**, which are shares in very large companies in which a high proportion of the dealing takes place; there are about 160 of them. Next come the considerably more numerous **beta** stocks: usually somewhat smaller and less active. The **gamma** stocks form the next tier, with fewer marketmakers in each, and finally come the very inactive **delta** stocks whose prices are not shown on the SEAQ screen systems. The classification is shown in the *Financial Times* share price pages after the name of the company. However, by the spring of 1989 there were already plans to replace this classification with a new system based on the liquidity of the individual stocks.

Commission deals or net prices

Under the new system, major investing institutions have a choice. They can continue to use a broker as an agent, in which case the broker executes the purchase or sale with the marketmaker offering the best price (possibly his own firm's market-making arm). In this case the institution is liable for commission, though at a negotiated rate, as well as bearing the cost of the marketmaker's turn. Or the institution can have its own SEAQ screen and deal direct at a **net price** with the marketmakers, in which case it avoids commission costs. Immediately after the Big Bang a high proportion of institutional business was being undertaken direct with marketmakers at net prices, but subsequently there was a swing back to the agency system.

However, the changes brought about by the Big Bang were more fundamental than a mere switch in trading methods. For most institutional investors, the investor/broker relationship has entirely changed. Previously, the broker's job as an agent was to get the best deal for his client. But the relationship between an investor and a marketmaker is **adversarial**. The marketmaker wants to sell at the highest price possible. The investor wants to buy at the lowest price possible. They are on opposite sides of the fence. And once marketmakers and brokers have been brought under one roof there will be an inevitable temptation — doubtless honourably resisted in many cases — for the securities house to recommend purchases of shares which it has on its books. It is one of the invitable **conflicts of interest** under the new system.

Marketmakers, brokers and securities houses

With the Big Bang, existing Stock Exchange firms had a choice. They could become **marketmakers** or **broker-dealers**. Marketmakers had a duty to make a continuous market in the shares in which they had opted to deal. Broker-dealers could supply clients with shares they held on their own books, but they had no obligation to make a continuous market. Both types could also act as **agency brokers** (like the old-style stockbrokers) executing clients' buy and sell orders with the marketmakers and charging a commission on the deal.

But it is not just the brokers' functions that have changed. The bigger ones are now parts of large financial groups which offer a wide range of banking and financial services. Barclays de Zoete Wedd (BZW) combines brokers de Zoete & Bevan and former jobbers Wedd Durlacher. But the new **securities house** is owned by Barclays Bank, which is both a clearing bank and has a merchant banking arm. Another large securities house was brought together by merchant bank Warburg which combined two existing brokers and a jobber. Other groupings started with a broker as a base and built up their marketmaking know-how from scratch.

The change has brought some problems with terminology. Financial journalists often tend to talk of **brokers** and refer to them by their original names even when they are part of a larger grouping. But the term **securities house** is gaining ground when referring to the large concerns. **Marketmaker** is normally used when referring to the specific function of making a book in shares.

The new financial conglomerates

The terminology becomes clearer if you look at the services the new integrated financial groups can provide. Clearing banks offer virtually every form of financial service, though prior to the Big Bang their share dealing had to go through an independent broker. Merchant banks offer many of the same services, except for **retail banking**: dealing with the public via a branch network. They undertake **foreign exchange dealing, eurobond dealing, new issues** of shares on the stockmarket and **underwriting** of securities issues. Many have extensive **investment management** business: they manage investments on behalf of the pension funds in particular. Their **corporate finance** arms advise companies on capital raising and help to plan their takeovers and takeover defences.

Even before the Big Bang, the larger brokers had diversified some way beyond pure agency broking business and overlapped with the merchant banks in several areas: notably new issues, investment management and — up to a point — advice to companies. **Investment research** on industries, individual companies, interest rates and economic prospects had long been a vital service provided particularly to institutional investors to try to secure their business. The **investment analysts** who prepare it are a useful source of information for financial journalists as well, and much press comment is influenced by their views.

Conflicts of interest

Put all these functions together in a single group and it is clear that most types of financial service can be provided by a single organization. But paradoxically, several of these disciplines ought to be kept well clear of each other. The investment management arm must not know if the corporate advice arm is counselling ABC Industries on a planned takeover of XYZ Holdings. If it knew, it could make large profits by buying the shares of XYZ before the bid became public. The marketmaking arm must not know if Myopic Mutual Assurance has approached the agency brokerage arm to acquire a couple of million pounds' worth of shares in ABC, though the information would assist the marketmaker considerably in adjusting the price it quoted. The marketmaking arm must not learn of the intentions of the fund management arm, nor of ABC's plan to take over XYZ. And so on.

To deal with the possible **conflicts of interest** and to convince the outside world that no improper use is being made of information available in different parts of the organization, techniques had to be found. Securities houses have **compliance departments** or **compliance officers** with a brief to ensure the confidentiality rules are observed. Within the organization there are **Chinese Walls**: barriers that are supposed to exist between different arms of a securities house to prevent information from passing between them. Sometimes they are invisible walls. Sometimes the different arms are physically separated. Cynics claim they've never met a Chinese Wall that did not have a grapevine growing over it. Or, more succinctly, that there's no Chinese Wall without a chink.

The proliferation of marketmakers after the Big Bang resulted in greatly increased competition and initially in a reduction in **spreads** between buying and selling prices for shares. The abolition of fixed commissions brought a reduction of 50 per cent or more in commission rates on large deals. Both factors made dealing cheaper so investors — in true market fashion — initially dealt more actively so that they paid as much in the long run. Equity turnover in March 1987 was £32 billion against £16 billion in March 1986, though part of the increase resulted from more frenetic dealing between the marketmakers themselves. The market undoubtedly had greater liquidity and its main constituents had the improved financial backing essential for active marketmaking. But small investors often paid more than previously, as the minimum commission charged on small bargains often rose sharply.

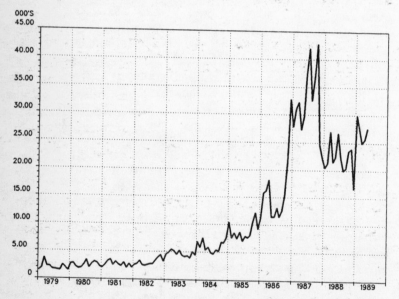

Figure 6.1   How they learned to love Big Bang. Stock Exchange turnover in ordinary shares soared in 1986, though dealing between marketmakers accounted for a significant part of the growth. After the October 1987 crash the picture was a lot less buoyant, with insufficient business to allow many marketmakers to operate at a profit. Source: *Datastream International.*

Even with improved turnover immediately after Big Bang, however, it was clear that not all of the new marketmakers could survive. The first public casualty was the Greenwell stockmarket arm of Midland Bank which early in 1987 dropped out of equity marketmaking to confine itself to agency broking. Other firms later drew in their horns, with merchant bank Morgan Grenfell withdrawing totally from equity and gilt marketmaking at the end of 1988 with a loss of over 400 jobs.

Six-figure salaries and Porsche cars offered to top investment analysts and dealers did not help. The stakes were high and in pitching for the business the securities houses competed strongly for the staff who would attract it: the costs might be justified for the survivors but they increased the pressure on those who were not making the grade. In the process a new terminology was coined: **golden hallos** for the lump sum cash inducements paid to attract top staff and **golden handcuffs** for the financial arrangements made to lock them in their jobs.

As it emerged, the securities houses had been kidding themselves as to the volume of business in the new competitive market place. After the stockmarket crash of October 1987, activity settled back to a much lower level and even by March 1989 was well below March 1987 levels (see Chapter 7).

Despite the changes to the dealing system, many aspects of Stock Exchange organization, and the terminology that goes with them, remained virtually unchanged from the investor's viewpoint, though further developments are now in the air. Here are some of the more important aspects, as the system operated midway through 1989:

Stockmarket technicalities

Equity trading is organized on an **account** system, whereas trading in gilts is for **cash settlement** (in practice this means payment the day after you buy the stock).

The account system works as follows. The year is divided into two-week Stock Exchange accounts, plus four three-week accounts which usually cover the Bank holidays. The normal account thus runs from the Monday of one week to the Friday of the following week. A buyer of shares does not have to pay (and a seller will not get the proceeds of the sale) until **settlement day** or **account day**, which is ten days after the end of the relevant account. There are proposals to shorten or change the nature of the account, but these are not yet agreed.

When an investor buys or sells a share, he is sent a **contract note** which gives details of the transaction. By settlement day the investor must pay his broker or should receive a cheque from him in the case of a sale.

Once the contract note has been sent, the broker deals with the subsequent paperwork. Purchases and sales have to be registered with the company whose shares are involved and the company eventually issues a **share certificate** to the new owner. British company shares are thus **registered securities** (though the identity of the real owner is sometimes cloaked in a **nominee name**). It is a Companies Act requirement that a company keep a **register of shareholders**, and the public has the right to inspect the register on payment of a fee. In some countries shares in **bearer** form are more common. The certificate alone is proof of ownership.

Dealing for the account

The account dealing system provides scope for speculative dealing activity in the equity market at reduced cost. An investor who buys shares on the first Monday of an account can hold them till the following Friday week, then sell to realize a profit if the price has risen. He has not had to pay for the shares and on settlement day he simply receives a cheque for his profit (or has to stump up for any loss).

Likewise, if the investor expects the price of a share to fall, he can sell shares he does not own on the Monday in the hope he can buy them more cheaply by the following Friday week before he has to deliver. If all goes as he expects, he receives a cheque for the difference (less costs). This is known as a **bear sale** or a **short sale**. The investor is **short** of the shares — he does not own them — at the time he sells them. Because of the risks — the price might rise sharply instead of falling — brokers do not like short selling unless they know the client well.

The flexibility of the account system can sometimes be further extended — at a price. During the last two days of an account it is possible to buy for **new time**: the purchase will count as being made in the following account. Or a position taken in one account may be carried over to the next on payment of a fee known as **contango**.

It is important to bear the account system in mind when reading market reports. In a rising market there may be a tendency for investors to buy strongly on the first day of the new account, hoping to sell at a profit by the following Friday week before they have to take delivery. The selling can cause prices to fall at the end of the account even in a generally rising market.

Bullish and bearish

The term **bear** (see Chapter 7) is used not only to cover a short seller but anyone who expects the market to go down. By extension, a **bear market** is a falling market and a **bearish** news item is one that might be expected to cause the market to fall. The opposite of a bear is a **bull**, who expects prices to rise. A **bull market** is a market on a long-term rising trend and **bullish** news is news that is likely to push prices up. **Long** is (self-evidently) the opposite of **short**. Somebody who is **long** of a particular share owns the share in question — possibly with the implication that he holds large quantities which he intends to sell rather than holding for the long term. A **stale bull** is somebody who bought shares in the hope of a price rise, has not seen the rise and is tired of holding on.

Bid and offered prices

Though the newspapers normally quote only a **middle price** for a share, we have seen that the marketmaker quotes a price at which he will sell and a price at which he will buy. The marketmaker's selling price is the **offered price** (the higher of the two, and the price at which the investor will buy). The marketmaker's buying price is the **bid price** (the price at which an investor can sell to him). The difference between the two is the **spread** or **turn**. Different marketmakers may quote a different range, depending on the state of their books and whether they want to encourage investors to buy from them or sell to them. Thus you might see:

	Marketmaker A	Marketmaker B
Offered	102p	103p
Bid	100p	101p

The spread is the same in both cases (though it need not be). The likelihood is that marketmaker A is long of the particular share.

He wants to encourage investors to buy from him so that he can square his book, so he is prepared to sell to investors at 102p. Marketmaker B is probably short of the share, so he will only sell at the higher price of 103p to discourage still more investors from buying from him shares that he does not have. But he is prepared to offer investors 101p if they will sell to him, thus hoping he can pick up the shares he needs to square his book. An investor who wanted to buy would naturally get the best price from marketmaker A and one who wanted to sell from marketmaker B. The difference between the lowest offered price and the highest bid price (in this case 1p) is known as the **touch**.

The Stock Exchange publishes a **Daily Official List** of prices of all shares traded on The Stock Exchange or the Unlisted Securities Market. But since it gives the highest price and the lowest price at which dealings took place during the day, the spread is unrealistically wide. In an adjusted form, however, these **official prices** are relevant for some tax purposes, particularly probate. Of more interest is the information in the Official List on prices at which deals actually took place. Details of price, size and time of transactions allow the day's performance to be tracked.

What moves share prices
In 'normal' times

'Observers attributed the lacklustre tone to the absence of any market-affecting news'.

Share prices had been slipping slightly, activity was very low, and the reason — we are told — was that there was no reason on this particular day for things to be otherwise.

The quotation comes from a report on the French stockmarket, but might have been written about other markets, too. News — good or bad — is what brings out the buyers and sellers. Without the buyers and sellers, there is no **activity**. Markets thrive on activity and for the professionals, the brokers and market-makers who derive their living from market activity, no news is very definitely bad news.

But in London, where shares of over 2,000 companies are traded, there is no such thing as a day without news. The daily **stockmarket reports** which feature in the financial pages record both the ups and downs of the markets and the movements of individual shares. At their best, when they give background information on reasons for price movements, they are essential reading. At their most turgid, they are simply a list of price movements in narrative form, stretching the writer's imagination to find synonyms for 'rose' and 'fell'. Most of what they contain is self-explanatory, but a few technical terms crop up. More serious, the general tenor may be difficult to grasp without some knowledge of the influences that move share prices.

The most dramatic example of movement in share prices in London was on 19 and 20 October 1987 when the equity market fell 20 per cent in two days. We will look in the second part of this chapter at the facts behind the stockmarket's fastest ever bust. But the events of Autumn 1987 will be easier to understand if we look first at the influences that operate on share prices in more normal times.

Bull and bear markets

In the summer of 1987 the London equity market had enjoyed a long **bull phase** — in other words, rising share prices had been the rule for a number of years. If you adjust share prices for inflation, they had been rising in **real terms** since 1982. If you ignore inflation, share values had been on a rising trend since 1975. There had been ups and downs along the way, but the trend had not been broken.

This was unusual. Previously, for most of the post-war period share prices had followed a regular cyclical pattern of **bull markets** (prices in a sustained rising trend) followed by **bear markets** (where prices were falling). The highs and lows of each cycle generally mirrored the **stop-go** pattern of the British economy itself. The stockmarket **peaks** and **troughs** normally preceded those in real economic activity, because stockmarket prices are always looking forward a step. In the depths of a recession, share prices begin to rise to reflect the coming upturn. At the height of a boom they tend to become weak in anticipation of the next downturn. But over the post-war period as a whole, the movement in prices was upwards until the 1973-75 financial crisis brought a horrendous stockmarket collapse with prices falling to scarcely a quarter of their previous peak.

While business cycles have not disappeared in the 1980s, the stockmarket has been less cyclical, helped for much of the time by a boom in the value of financial assets which sometimes seemed almost independent of underlying economic performance. But the influences on share prices have not entirely changed. And the crash of 1987, though it brought a sharp halt to the bull market of the 1980s, in practice wiped less than a year's growth off share prices. It was remarkable more for the speed with which it happened than for the size of the fall.

Stockmarket movements need to be seen on at least three levels. First, there is the long-term trend of the equity market, secondly the short-term fluctuations up and down within this trend, and thirdly, the movements of individual shares within the movement of the market as a whole.

96

Share prices reflect earnings growth

Investors buy **ordinary shares** mainly because they expect share values to increase. Over a long period, what causes share prices to increase is the increasing **earning power** of companies, and their ability to pay higher **dividends** out of these increased earnings. But in the short run a lot of other factors can distort the picture.

An example helps. Suppose that companies on average pay out half of their earnings as dividends and the average **yield** on ordinary shares is 4 per cent and the average **PE ratio** is around 17. Suppose also that on average companies are increasing their earnings and dividends by 10 per cent a year. Share prices might be expected to rise by 10 per cent a year to reflect the underlying growth in profits and dividends.

Different values put on earnings

Over a long period this may well happen. But the example assumes that investors always expect — again on average — that ordinary shares will yield 4 per cent and that they will be prepared to buy shares at a price equal to 17 times their current earnings. In practice there will be some times when they expect higher yields and others when they will accept lower yields. Some times when a PE ratio of 17 looks too high and others when it may seem on the low side.

Why is this the case? It is easier if we now come down to a single company. Call it ABC Holdings and assume it is totally typical of the market averages: the ABC shares at 100p offer a yield of 4 per cent and stand on a PE ratio of 17. If its earnings and dividends grow at 10 per cent a year, a buyer of the shares can expect a 14 per cent a year overall return: 4 per cent of income and 10 per cent of capital gain from the rise in the share price. But suppose something happens to alter the outlook for ABC's future profits: it comes up with a new product that should help raise the future growth rate from 10 to 12 per cent. Earnings will now rise faster in the future than had been expected. And, all else being equal, investors will be prepared to pay a higher price for the shares today because they are buying a more rapidly rising flow of future earnings. The share price might rise from 100p to 110p, where the yield drops to 3.7 per cent and the PE ratio rises to 18.7. The share has been **re-rated**.

When interest rates change

Now take a totally different aspect, which we touched on in Chapter 1. ABC Holdings at 100p yields 4 per cent and stands on a PE ratio of 17. With expectations of 10 per cent a year growth in earnings, the overall return is 14 per cent if the share price rises in line. An expected overall return of 14 per cent might look about right if, at this time, investors could get a redemption yield of 11 per cent on long-dated gilt-edged securities. It would not look nearly so good if interest rates rose so that gilt-edged stocks offered a risk-free 14 per cent. Investors would want a higher return on the ordinary share, so its price would have to fall. Nothing has necessarily happened to alter the outlook for ABC's profits. But the price falls because the returns available on other forms of investment have increased.

So the price of any individual company's shares — relative to others — will reflect the growth prospects of that company and therefore the **overall return** investors can expect. And the prices of ordinary shares as a whole will be affected by returns available on alternative forms of investment.

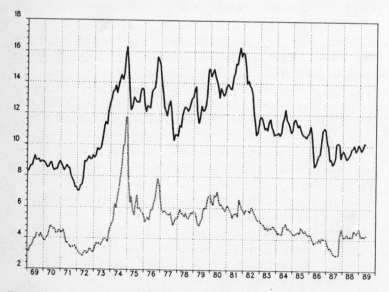

Figure 7.1   Yields on gilt-edged stocks (solid upper line) and on equities (lower line) tend to move the same way. The difference between them is the 'reverse yield gap'. Source: *Datastream International.*

While these forces are always at work, they are not always so easy to spot in the reports of short-term price movements. Investors do not necessarily sit down and work out their assumptions on relative growth rates or returns available elsewhere before buying a share. But prices in the stockmarket reflect a balance of the (often instinctive) views of many thousands of investors. And it is noticeable that the ratings of individual companies do reflect their perceived growth prospects and that, over a long period, there is a remarkable correlation between movements in the yields on equities and those on fixed-interest investments (see chart).

Thus in a period of buoyant economic activity and rising company profits, the equity market as a whole might be expected to show a rising trend (though it will anticipate what is happening in the economy). And when we come down to the particular, any news about a company which adds to expectations of future growth will cause the share price to rise, and events which might depress earnings will cause it to fall, relative to the market as a whole.

Re-rating: up and down

The aim of investment analysts and managers, and of commentators in the financial press, is to find companies which are **undervalued** relative to their growth prospects. The writer who spots that a company is due for an **upward re-rating** before others realize that its earnings prospects are better than expected is (if he is right) offering his reader the chance of a capital profit. It is, of course, equally important to spot companies whose growth prospects are diminishing and whose shares are likely to be **re-rated downwards** — astute investors will want to sell before the share price adjusts downwards. But warnings of this nature are a lot less common in print than the **buy recommendations**. And press commentators along with most other investment advisers are much less adept in forecasting major turning points in the market as a whole than they are at predicting price movements in individual shares. Don't necessarily expect a press warning ahead of a major fall in the stockmarket.

If share prices in the long run depend on a combination of company profits and alternative investment returns, in the short term they can be moved by a variety of other factors. Many of these are purely technical. Investment comment draws a distinction between **fundamental** influences (those relating to company profits or assets) and **technical** influences (mainly those affecting the share price without reflecting on the trading position of the company itself). Here are some of the more important ones:

Company profit announcements

Surprisingly, you will see from market reports that a share price often falls when a company reports good profits. A market report probably talks of **profit-taking**. The reason is as follows. In the weeks ahead of the **profit announcement** the share price rises as investors buy in expectation of the good figures. By the time these figures arrive, there is no reason for the speculators to hang on any longer, so they sell to take their profits. It is another example of the stockmarket **discounting** news well in advance.

Press recommendations

If the press (or a firm of brokers) **tips** a share, the price will usually rise. It will rise furthest if the shares are a **narrow market** — in other words, the recommendation relates to a company which does not have a great number of shares in issue or available on the market. In this case a small amount of buying would push the price up, whereas a recommendation for a large and widely traded company such as ICI might have relatively little impact on the price.

Don't assume, however, that all the price rise that follows a press recommendation is the result of share buying. **Marketmakers** read the press too, and when they see a share recommended they will tend to move up the price they quote in anticipation of likely buying. Thus investors often find they can buy a share only at a price considerably above the one quoted when the recommendation was made.

Marketmakers' manoeuvres

You'll sometimes see reports such as 'marketmakers were short of stock, and prices rose as they balanced their books'. This simply means that marketmakers had sold shares they did not own — they went **short** — and later they had to buy the shares they needed to deliver to clients. This buying moved prices up.

Marketmakers thrive on activity and when there is little activity they may attempt to stimulate it artificially. For example, at a time when there was little news to encourage investors either to buy or sell, they might move their quoted prices down to attract buyers and generate some action. However, there are now many more marketmakers than before and their competitive dealing can also chase share prices a long way up or down when investors' moods change.

Bear operations

It is not only marketmakers that sell shares they do not own. Speculators in the market may also **go short** in expectation of a price fall. They sell shares in the hope they can buy them at a lower price before they have to deliver. Their profit is the difference between the two prices.

It is a dangerous manoeuvre. If they get it wrong and the price rises rather than falling, there is no limit to their potential loss. They might sell shares at 100p and find themselves forced to buy at 120p if some news intervenes to raise the price.

Short sellers have to buy to fulfill their contractual obligations to deliver the shares. If marketmakers sense there has been widescale short selling of a particular share they may deliberately move their quoted prices up, forcing the **bears** (those who had been trading on expectation of a price fall) to buy at an inflated price. This is known as a **bear squeeze**. Quite commonly you will see reports that prices rose on **bear covering**, even when the general trend of prices had been downwards. This simply reflects the forced buying by speculators who had earlier sold short and does not necessarily indicate a reversal of the market's downward trend.

A **bear raid** occurs when speculators descend on a company and deliberately try to force the price down, partly by short selling but possibly also by circulating unfavourable rumours about the company. They hope to buy the shares cheaply once the price has dropped. Bear raiders are, of course, vulnerable to being caught in a bear squeeze.

Technical corrections

Markets seldom continue up or down in an unbroken line. After a period of rising or falling prices you often see references to a

technical correction or to the market **consolidating**. If prices have been rising for a long period, there will often be a break as some investors sell to take their profits and prices temporarily fall. They may well continue on up after the **shakeout** has taken place. A similar process takes place in reverse on the way down. The market tends to move in fits and starts, with investors pausing for breath at various points on the way up or down.

Chartist influences

There is a theory that you can predict from past price movements what a share price (or the market as a whole, as measured by one of the indexes) is likely to do in the future. Whether you believe in this theory or not, you cannot igore the fact that at times it has a strong impact on share prices. Commentators who base their forecasts on these theories are known as **technical analysts** or **chartists** (because they use charts to plot the price movements).

The theory is not as silly as it might sound. Suppose the share price of ABC Holdings had, over the past few months, fluctuated between 100p and 120p. This would suggest that each time the price dropped as low as 100p there were investors who considered it cheap at this price and were prepared to buy. Each time it rose as high as 120p a fair body of investors considered it was becoming expensive and therefore sold. So 100p and 120p became recognized as **resistance levels**.

If subsequently the price dropped significantly below 100p or rose significantly above 120p, this would suggest that something had happened to change investors' perception of the shares. The chartist would not need to know what had happened but simply that the price — reflecting the balance of opinion among buyers and sellers in the market — had broken out from a resistance level and might be expected to continue in the direction it had taken until a new resistance level was reached.

This merely illustrates the principle — in practice the chartist projections may be based on considerably more complex analysis. And nowadays share prices are often plotted with the help of computers rather than on graph paper, and the computer can be programmed to give buy and sell prompts at appropriate points.

Since most **chartists** work on broadly similar theories, their predictions can be self-fulfilling. If all chartists reckoned the

ABC Holdings share price had breached a significant resistance level when it rose through 120p to 125p, all who followed the theory would duly jump in and buy and the price might be carried up to, say, 140p. Chartist techniques are also widely used in other markets such as gold and foreign exchange.

Interest rate and currency movements

We have seen that a rise in interest rates will depress the price of gilt-edged stocks and may also depress equity prices by raising the returns available on other investments. But it will have different impact on different kinds of company. It might depress, say, housebuilders more than the average because higher interest rates mean higher mortgage costs and could deter housebuyers. It would depress highly-geared companies which use a lot of variable-rate borrowed money, because higher interest costs will depress their profits. It might actually help companies which are sitting on large amounts of cash and will therefore earn a higher interest income. But, all else being equal, higher interest rates raise the cost of borrowing for consumers and for industry and may be expected to damp down economic activity, which is bad for company profit prospects. This is quite separate from the purely technical factor that higher interest charges may depress share prices because of the higher returns available elsewhere.

The effect of **currency movements** is also complex. A fall in sterling, bringing the prospect of higher interest rates to defend the pound, will usually hit gilt-edged prices and might be expected to have a knock-on effect on share values. But a lower level of sterling improves British industry's competitive position in home and export markets and thus improves profit prospects. So sometimes a weakening in sterling will depress bond prices but boost ordinary shares.

Weight of money argument

Share prices tend to rise when there are more buyers than sellers. If there is a lot of money available for investment in stockmarkets, prices will tend to rise — hence the **weight of money** factor.

It used to be fairly simple to calculate. **Pension funds** and **insurance companies** have about £21 billion a year to invest. This is spread mainly between gilt-edged stocks, UK ordinary shares,

UK property and overseas investments. Calculate how much will be needed to subscribe for new gilt-edged issues (if the government is a net borrower at the time) and how much will be absorbed by buying new shares issued on the stockmarket. Allow for the proportion invested in property and overseas and what is left is available to buy existing gilt-edged stocks or equities. If it exceeds likely sales from other quarters (private individuals are normally sellers on balance), prices should rise.

Today's sums are more complex, partly because of the freedom to invest overseas without penalty since exchange controls were suspended in 1979. But more important, it is very difficult to estimate likely overseas investment in UK stockmarkets. There are so many options for UK and foreign investors nowadays that weight of money calculations are no guarantee of future equity trends in any one market.

Too many shares

When a company raises capital by issuing new shares or issues shares in a takeover, the price will often fall. This is simply because initially there are not enough buyers around to absorb all the new shares. And if it is known that there are owners of large blocks of shares who want to dispose of them (possibly **underwriters** left with shares they do not want — see Chapter 8) the price may be weak until these have been disposed of. You will see references to large blocks of shares **overhanging the market**.

Politics

As a general rule, particularly in the run-up to an election, evidence that the Conservatives are doing well will boost gilt and equity prices and evidence to the contrary will depress them. This is not always totally logical. The Labour party is associated with high inflation and high interest costs, but in the past ordinary shares have often performed well under a Labour government. Sometimes share prices will rise in anticipation of a Conservative win, but fall on heavy profit-taking when the expectation is fulfilled. Betting on elections can be dangerous.

Sentiment

This is the undefinable factor. On some days investors feel cheerful and decide to buy. It may be good political or economic news, it may simply be that the day is sunny or England has won a game of cricket. But one strong and consistent influence on the London stockmarket is the performance of share prices across the Atlantic on **Wall Street**. A big rise or fall on Wall Street is often reflected in the behaviour of equities in London. Sometimes this is logical. The same political or economic news has an impact on both markets, and a movement in the returns available on Wall Street will affect expectations elsewhere; many of the same shares are in any case traded on Wall Street and other markets. But sometimes the Wall Street rise or fall simply influences **sentiment** in London. Though, for London, the Wall Street link is probably the strongest, the crash of October 1987 (with its knock-on effect on all world markets) demonstrated how quickly market movements now travel across most frontiers.

Takeovers

We have left **takeovers** to last because at times they dominate stockmarket thinking. The assumption is that if Company A bids for Company B it will need to pay above the current market price of Company B shares, though in practice the company B share price often rises as a result of leaks or inspired guesses in the weeks before a bid is announced.

Actual takeovers, and rumours of takeovers, raise the prices of individual shares. Investors' thinking becomes obsessed with takeovers and they look for other possible bid candidates and force up the prices by buying the shares. The equity market as a whole is carried upwards by the takeover fever.

Price rises on takeover talk seem to fly in the face of the idea that a company's earnings prospects determine the value of its shares. This is not so. The bidder is simply paying a price that takes account of the expected earnings growth of the victim company over the next two or three years, or the earnings he expects to be able to squeeze out of his victim (possibly with the help of creative accounting). Thus for any share there are at least two possible values. What it is worth in the market on its own earnings prospects. And the price a bidder might have to pay, which preempts a few years of earnings growth or which is based on the potential for **asset-stripping** (see glossary) or selling off the constituent businesses. Shareholders in the victim company get jam today rather than jam tomorrow.

7b

What moves share prices
In the crash of '87

For investors nurtured on the bull market of the 1980s the roof fell in on Monday 19 October 1987. And it was not only investors who suffered falling roofs. The Friday morning of the previous week, a once-in-a-century freak storm had devastated much of southern England, causing widescale property damage but also disrupting transport and all forms of communication. On that day The Stock Exchange in London had barely functioned. Many securities dealers had not arrived for work. The Stock Exchange's SEAQ price information system was out of commission much of the day and such dealing as took place reverted to old systems of direct contact. No Stock Exchange indexes were calculated in London that day.

America was spared the storm, but nasty things had been happening on Wall Street. On Saturday 17 October the *Financial Times* led with a story headed 'Wall Street ends two worst weeks with record daily fall'. The Dow Jones Industrial Average — the most commonly used index of the American market — had fallen over 17 per cent from its August peak. On Friday 16 October alone it had dropped almost 5 per cent. The *Financial Times*'s market report commented 'It was not simply that the stockmarket fell....It was more: last week the US stockmarket lost its optimism'.

Had London been fully functioning that Friday, and had share price indexes been calculated, some indication of what was to come this side of the Atlantic might have filtered through. As it was, London was worried; but there was little sense of market cataclysm that weekend. Monday's *Financial Times* led with a story 'Bull yields to bear as Wall Street accepts the party's over'.

But it was writing mainly of the United States. In Britain, the biggest ever sale of government-owned shares was about to take place: the £7.2 billion offer of the government's stake in British Petroleum. Monday's paper contained a piece on the BP sale headed: 'A test for the bull market's resolve'. In Britain we were still talking of bull markets.

By Tuesday the worldwide bull market was history. At the close on Monday 19 October the London market was down almost 10 per cent from its close the previous Thursday, as measured by the FTA All Share Index.

But on that Monday the United States had again held centre stage. The Dow Jones Industrials crashed by over 500 points to 1738.42: a one-day fall of over 22 per cent, the worst of which happened after the London market had closed. By Tuesday's close London was a further 11.4 per cent down for a two-day fall of 20 per cent. And, with only modest occasional rallies, it continued down well into November. At its nadir the FTA All-Share Index was down 36.6 per cent from its July 1987 peak. Other markets worldwide had suffered a similar fate. On Monday 19 October and the following day the Tokyo stockmarket lost 17 per cent and the Australian market was down almost 28 per cent. Hong Kong could not be measured at this point. The market had closed.

Once the full extent of the market rout was apparent, the economic gurus were out in force to rationalize the week's events. The instability in the financial system as a result of world trade imbalances, and particularly the budget and trade deficits in the United States, was apparently to blame for the mayhem in the world's financial markets. The economists singularly failed to explain why, since these imbalances had been with us for some considerable time, the crash had not happened before.

There was in fact a far simpler and, at least with the benefit of hindsight, more accurate explanation of the week's events. Most speculative booms in stockmarkets end with a bust: what sparks the fall is almost irrelevant. Professor J K Galbraith summed up the phenomenon in his book on an earlier and ultimately far more serious stockmarket crash in the United States, *The Great Crash 1929*. '... it was simply that a roaring boom was in progress in the stock market and, like all booms, it had to end. ...When prices stopped rising — when the supply of people who were buying for an increase was exhausted ... everyone would want to sell. The market wouldn't level out; it would fall precipitately'. On Monday 19 October 1987, this happened again on Wall Street — and in London and across the world.

The price falls in the 1987 crash were as nothing compared to the bear market of 1973-75, when share prices fell to around a quarter of their previous peak. It was the speed of the fall that created the drama. A decline in share prices that in previous decades might have taken place gradually, over a year or more, was telescoped into a day or a few days. Again, many explanations have been advanced for the suddenness of the fall, and computers (or the men and women who programme them) were singled out for a large share of the blame.

There was much talk of the perils of **programme trading**, though the phrase appeared to mean different things to different commentators. In the United States widescale arbitrage habitually took place between the cash market and the financial futures market, with computers signalling the minor discrepancies in pricing between the two that offered the chance of a profit (see Chapter 17). **Portfolio insurance** was also common in the States. This is a tactic by which major institutional investors may seek to lock into the profits on their portfolios. It can involve operations in the futures or options markets (the value of the futures or options positions rises if the value of shares in the portfolio falls). It can also involve a set programme for turning part of the share portfolio into cash if prices fall more than a certain amount. And on top we have the familiar **chartist** theories (see earlier in this chapter) whereby a price fall can itself signal a larger price fall and stimulate selling which makes the prediction self-fulfilling.

All of these factors and more were probably at work on Wall Street during the crash. The interaction of the stockmarket and the futures market meant that a fall on one stimulated selling on the other, which in turn led to further selling on the first. And the use of semi-automatic programmes made the spiral twist even more rapidly down.

But perhaps this form of computerized trading (which in any case was not widespread in London) was the least significant aspect of computers in the crash. More important was the instant dissemination of information across the world by electronic message and computer screen. The trader knew instantly what was happening in other financial centres and marked down share prices in his own in consequence. As panic spread through the

Figure 7.2   This graph of the FTA All-Share Index shows clearly how speculative fever took share prices to unrealistic heights in 1987. Source: *Datastream International.*

world's financial centres it became clear that instant information had negative as well as positive features.

So much for the techicalities. Why had share prices been poised for a fall? If we take the London market in isolation (and many of its features were mirrored overseas) the charts tell much of the story. Look first at Chart 7.2, plotting the FTA All-Share Index since 1983. Share prices had been climbing steadily through to the end of 1986. In the first half of 1987 the rate of increase accelerated (a typical feature of the late days of a bull market) as more and more investors or speculators climbed on the bandwagon, attracted by the profits made from the market in recent years. By its peak in the middle of July, the index had climbed 48 per cent from its beginning of the year level. Then look at Chart 7.3, showing the average price earnings (PE) ratio on the FTA 500 Share Index (we cannot use the All-Share because it includes financial stocks, on some of which a PE ratio cannot be calculated).

The immediately striking point is that though on balance PE ratios were rising up to the end of 1986 — again, this tends to happen in a bull market — they were not rising anything like as fast as share prices. In other words, company profits and earnings were rising rapidly, providing justification for the increase in share prices. But the rise in share values in the first half of 1987 finally lost contact with the **fundamentals**. Company profits did not rise 48 per cent in half a year, as shares did. Outright speculative fever had taken hold. If we look at Chart 7.4, showing average dividend yields against average redemption yields on gilt-edged stocks, we get another facet of the same picture. Up to the end of 1986, company dividends had been increasing fast enough to prevent a great drop in yields despite booming share prices. In 1987 share prices shot ahead of dividend growth and dividend yields fell sharply to below 3 per cent on average. In the process, as the chart shows clearly, the traditional relationship between gilt-edged returns and dividend yields was sharply distorted.

Thus, in 1987, share prices totally lost contact with the fundamentals — earnings, yield and alternative investment returns — which are the ultimate support for share values. When

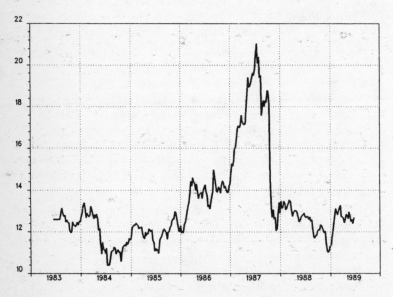

Figure 7.3 Average PE ratios. Because company earnings were rising fast, share prices could show good growth without making PE ratios unrealistic in the earlier years of the bull market. This graph shows how the average PE ratio suddenly shot up above 20 in 1987 when share prices lost contact with the fundamentals of company earnings. Source: *Datastream International.*

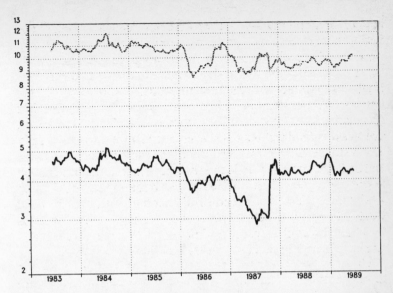

Figure 7.4   Yields on gilt-edged securities (upper dotted line) and on ordinary shares (lower thick line) normally maintain a relationship with each other. But in the final share price boom of 1987, the average yield on ordinary shares dipped below 3 per cent, distorting the relationship with gilt-edged yields and pointing to trouble. The crash in share prices restored the relationship. Source: *Datastream International.*

prices began to fall, there was nothing to stop the rout until a rational relationship with the fundamentals was re-established. In fact, for all the drama, the crash did no more than return share prices to their value of a year earlier, when the final speculative fever had taken hold. The crash is a vindication — not a negation — of the theory that company profits and dividends determine share values in the long run.

What of the aftermath? Company profits and dividends continued to grow after October 1987, though the rate of growth was probably slowing by 1989. The economic collapse, which many felt that the crash foretold or would cause, simply failed to happen over the following eighteen months. Shares again began to look quite attractive on the fundamental criteria.

But the crash had left its scars. Whatever the fundamentals were saying, institutional investors remained highly nervous of a repetition. Into 1989, share dealing volumes were well down on pre-crash days and marketmakers' spreads were up, thus increasing dealing costs again. The **liquidity** of the market had been exposed as an illusion. The events of 1987 showed that shares were easy to buy and sell while prices were rising. But once the fall began, those who hoped to get out fast found they were lucky if they could get through to their broker or to the marketmakers. The trading system introduced in the Big Bang is already being revised. And it is clear that, without a raging bull market, there is not enough income generated in the securities business to support all the securities houses who in 1989 were still fighting for a profitable share.

Could a crash on a similar scale happen again? Unfortunately, the answer is 'yes', though trouble is more likely to start on the other side of the Atlantic than in Britain, where the finances of companies are far more soundly based (the **fundamentals** are better). But a crash is most likely after a period of feverish speculative activity in the markets. Before the crash the British government had encouraged such speculative fever, by hypeing privatization issues and by selling state assets to the public at below their worth. The illusion of the stockmarket as a source of instant profits had been created. It fuelled the boom that preceded the bust.

If such speculative fevers could be prevented in the future, perhaps crashes could be prevented as well. But investors and market professionals have short memories. Once the stockmarket gets a head of steam behind it, nobody wants to miss the fun. Everybody holds on for the last five per cent of profit as the market approaches its peak, and everybody succumbs to the delusion that he or she will be able to spot the warning signs of the downturn ahead of the herd. The 1987 crash showed what happened when investors put this delusion to the test of reality and, in the event, all rushed to sell at the same time.

8

Stockmarket launches

When the stockmarket is buoyant you can expect a spate of new companies **coming to the market** — achieving a **quote** for their shares for the first time — encouraged by the high valuation that will be put on their shares.

The term 'new companies' is perhaps misleading. They are not new businesses, but businesses which are new to the stockmarket. For the first time their shares can be bought and sold on the stockmarket. The larger ones may apply for a **listing** on The Stock Exchange itself (the **main market**). Smaller or younger companies (or companies which wish to **float** only a small amount of their share capital) may apply for a quote on the **Unlisted Securities Market (USM)**. And still smaller or newer companies may chance their arm on the new **Third Market** run under Stock Exchange auspices. Normally a five-year profit record will be required for a company coming to the main market and at least three years for a USM stock.

For many individual investors, applying for shares in **new issues** is their first introduction to Stock Exchange affairs. They **stag** new issues by applying for shares in the hope that these can be sold at a profit as soon as **dealings begin** (we will see later why this is often a good bet). First, the mechanics of a new issue.

Type of launch

There are three main ways a company may float its shares on the market (flotations attract nautical metaphors just as takeovers attract marital ones, and a new issue may also be described as a **launch**):

- The **offer for sale**. Shares are offered for sale to the public, partly via the medium of the newspapers which carry a **prospectus** with details of the company (a prospectus is a legal requirement when shares are marketed) plus an **application form** for the shares. This is the method of most interest to the general public and we will look at it in detail later.
- The **placing**. In this case the company achieves an initial spread of shareholders by arranging privately to sell shares to a range of investors: usually several hundred of them. The placing is usually arranged by the company's broker and most of the shares will probably be placed with his clients. The general public who are not clients probably do not get a look-in at this stage. After the placing, permission is given for the shares to be traded on the stockmarket, and anybody can buy in the normal way. Many USM issues — where the quantities of shares sold may be fairly small — are made via a placing.
- The **introduction**. This is less common. It happens when a company already has a large spread of shareholders and simply wants permission for the shares to be dealt in on the stockmarket. An introduction does not involve the raising of capital, and it is the cheapest way of coming to market. If a company moves up from the USM to the main market it will probably be by way of an introduction.

Who is raising money?

In any report of an offer for sale or a placing, one of the first points to focus on is: who gets the money from the sale of the shares? The shares may come from one of two sources:

- Shares being sold by the existing shareholders — perhaps the founders of the company who built it up from its inception. In this case the cash raised goes to these original shareholders, not to the company.
- New shares created by the company. In this case the cash from the sale of the shares goes into the company's own coffers, not to its original owners.

In practice, the shares made available may be a mix. Some are existing shares sold by the owners and some are new shares sold to raise cash for the company.

Pricing an offer for sale

Offers for sale to the public are of two main types: **fixed-price offers** and **tender offers**. The fixed price offer is the more common. How is the price fixed?

Every issue requires **sponsors**. The issue may be sponsored simply by a broker or both a merchant bank and broker may be involved. Normally — though not always — a company coming to market makes in its prospectus a forecast of profits and dividend for the current year, as well as giving details of its historical profits. Working with these figures, the sponsors will look for existing quoted companies in a similar line of business. By reference to the **ratings (PE ratio** and **yield)** these companies enjoy — and adjusting for the superior or inferior **growth prospects** of the newcomer — it should be possible to fix the appropriate rating, and therefore the price, for the shares of the newcomer.

Two points should be born in mind. The sponsors want to make sure the new issue gets off to a good start: in other words, when trading begins in the shares the price in this **aftermarket** should not be below the offer for sale price and preferably should rise some way above. So they will try to pitch the shares at a price a little below what they are likely to be worth. Too far below and they will be accused of failing to get a sufficiently good price for their client.

Secondly, the company itself almost certainly errs on the side of caution in arriving at its profits forecast. There is nothing worse for a market newcomer than to fail to meet its **prospectus forecast**. So the forecast will be pitched some way below what the directors expect profits to be.

The first point means that — unless the sponsors have got their calculations badly wrong or the stockmarket drops sharply between the price being fixed and the start of dealings — the shares are being sold at less than their likely value and there is therefore a very good chance of a quick profit for **stags** who manage to secure an allocation of shares. The second means that you should not take too seriously the reports which appear later when the company publishes its first profit figures after going public. They are often headed 'XYZ Holdings exceeds forecast' as if this implied unexpectedly good performance. The truth in most cases is that investors should have been worried if the company did not exceeed its forecast. It had planned to do so.

The tender offer

Some companies are almost impossible to value — for example there may be no comparable quoted company — and in these circumstances a **tender offer** can make sense. Investors are invited to apply for the number of shares they want and asked to state what price they are prepared to pay above a stipulated minimum. Assuming the issue is **fully subscribed** — applications are received for at least the total number of shares on offer — the sponsors will calculate at what price all the shares available can be sold. This becomes the **striking price** and anybody who applied for shares at this price or above has a chance of getting some. The shares are allocated at the striking price, even to those who bid at a higher price. Those who bid below the striking price get none.

The striking price will not always be the highest possible price at which all the available shares can be sold. As this becomes a bit complicated, an example helps. Suppose XYZ Holdings offers 10m shares to the public and invites tenders at a price of 120p or above. Applications were received as follows:

No of shares applied for at each price	Price	Cumulative total of shares that could be sold at each price
2,000,000	140p	2,000,000
3,000,000	135p	5,000,000
5,000,000	130p	10,000,000
2,000,000	125p	12,000,000
4,000,000	120p	16,000,000

The right-hand column shows that, at a price of 130p, all of the 10m shares available could be sold, since there were applications for 5m at 130p, 3m at 135p and 2m at 140p. So 130p would be the highest possible striking price. But the sponsors may decide they would rather sell at a slightly lower price to ensure the shares get off to a good start when dealings begin. So they fix on 125p as the striking price. Since there were applications for 12m shares at this price or above, not all the applicants will get all the shares they asked for.

Oversubscription and allotments

Sponsors pitch their price at a level that they expect will attract applications for more shares than are on offer. Or, with a tender offer, they may settle for a striking price below the highest possible. If they are right and there are applications for more shares than are on offer, the offer is **oversubscribed**. Press reports normally give the extent of the oversubscription.

Then comes the problem of deciding who gets shares, and how many: the **allocation** or **allotment**. This depends on policy and on the extent of oversubscription. It may be decided to hold a **ballot** of all applicants, with the successful ones receiving a standard allocation, whatever they applied for. Or those applying for large numbers (over 100,000, say) may have their applications **scaled down** to, perhaps, 10 per cent of what they asked for. Those applying for fewer than 100,000 might each get 100 shares, or might be put in a ballot with the successful ones getting 300 shares each and the remainder nothing. It depends on the spread of shareholding the company and its sponsors want (in the British Telecom and British Gas offers the issues were structured to favour small investors).

Underwriting an issue

Most new issues are **underwritten**. This means that big investors — particularly institutions — agree for a fee to buy any shares which are not bought by the public if the offer is **undersubscribed**. The vendors — the company or its original shareholders — are thus sure of getting their money. The merchant bank sponsoring the issue takes a fee (a percentage of the value of the shares on offer) and pays part to **subunderwriters** — investors who agree to take a certain maximum number of shares if required to do so. **Underwriting fees** are a useful source of income for merchant banks and investing institutions and the City does not like tender offers which are not invariably underwritten.

It is unusual for the underwriter or subunderwriters to be called on to take up shares. But if an offer for sale is undersubscribed and **left with the underwriters** you may see references in the press to shares **overhanging the market**. This may mean that underwriters, who were forced to take up more shares than they wanted, will want to sell them (**lighten their holdings**). The share price is unlikely to rise far until these shares overhanging the market have been sold and end up in **firm hands**: with investors who want to keep them.

The most dramatic case of a **new issue flop** was the sale of the government's £7.2 billion stake in British Petroleum in October 1987. It coincided with — and probably helped to cause — the stockmarket crash of that month. Most of the shares were left with the underwriters and subunderwriters, who suffered massive losses. They would have suffered still worse losses if the Bank of England had not effectively re-underwritten the part-paid shares by offering to buy them at 70p — a startling case of government subsidy for the private sector securities houses of Britain and North America.

The offer for sale timetable

The sponsors of an issue want as little time as possible to elapse between fixing the price of an issue and the receipt of applications. They are vulnerable if the market falls in the interim — as with the BP issue — and the shares on offer consequently look overpriced.

Normally a **pathfinder prospectus** is made available to major investors and the press some days ahead of the issue. This contains the details of the company and the offer, so that investors can assess them, but leaves blank the vital information on price and prospective yield and PE ratio. This is then filled in just before the prospectus is published. Applications then have to

LONDON RECENT ISSUES

EQUITIES

Issue Price	Amount Paid up	Latest Renunc. date	1989		Stock	Closing Price	+ or -	Net Div.	Times Cov'd	Gross Yield	P.E. Ratio
			High	Low							
§140	F.P.	-	178	140	✠Alan Paul 5p	171	-1	L2.5	2.6	1.9	20.6
§110	F.P.	-	116	111	✠Allen	112	+1	L4.2	2.8	5.0	8.7
165	F.P.	-	213	198	✠Ball (A.H.) 5p	213		L6.0	1.9	3.8	17.0
§100	F.P.	-	126	108	✠Boxmore Intl. 10p	118		u5.2	1.9	5.9	11.4
175	F.P.	-	201	185	Butler Cox 5p	198	+1	L4.0	2.5	2.7	18.5
180	F.P	23/6	218	180	Community Hospital £1	218	+1	R4.5	1.4	2.8	19.9
Fl.47	F.P.	-	£17$\frac{1}{4}$	£16$\frac{1}{16}$	DAF N.V. Fl.5	£16$\frac{5}{8}$	-$\frac{1}{4}$	HQ2.5	1.8	4.2	13.1
85	F.P.	-	96	84	✠Diamond Group Hldgs 5p	93		L1.13	4.7	1.6	17.7
50	F.P.	-	65	56	Donelon Tyson 10p	60	+1	u0.75	1.6	1.7	50.2
130	F.P.	-	141	130	✠Faupel Trading 5p	133		L4.88	2.4	4.9	10.2
§160	F.P.	-	183	179	Gowrings 10p	181		6.66	1.5	4.9	18.3
160	F.P.	-	185	160	✠Hadleigh Inds. 50p	183	+3	4.5	3.1	3.3	10.8
†	F.P.	-	140	125	Hardy Oil & Gas 50p	135	-1	-	-	-	-
Ir76	F.P.	-	77	65	✠Kingspan Gp Ir20p	76		L1.71	3.6	3.0	10.0
§58	F.P.	-	66	56	✠Miskin Group 20p	60	+2	Wd1.38	4.5	3.1	8.0
†	F.P.	-	£11$\frac{7}{8}$	£11$\frac{1}{2}$	Mitsubishi Tst & Bank Y50	£11$\frac{5}{8}$	-$\frac{1}{4}$	Q16%	8.2	3.0	39.9
§55	F.P.	-	60	55	✠Molyneux Estates	58	-1	-	-	-	79.1
†	F.P.	-	55$\frac{1}{2}$	45$\frac{1}{2}$	✠Oliver Resources Ir5p	50	+$\frac{1}{2}$	-	-	-	-
90	F.P.	-	108	90	✠Plastiseal 5p	101		L3.78	2.3	5.0	11.8
§125	F.P.	-	152	135	Sheffield Insulations 10p	150	+2	L4.25	2.2	3.8	15.8

Table 8.1 New issue information. Source: *Financial Times*.

be in, usually within a week, and the basis of allocation is announced a few days later.

Allotment letters go out to successful applicants as soon as possible after the basis of allocation is decided, and unsuccessful applicants get their money back. The Stock Exchange fixes a date on which official dealings in the shares will start. In the *Financial Times* the prices of shares in newly-floated companies are listed for a time in a special table towards the end of the companies and markets section of the paper and ahead of the main prices pages under the heading **London recent issues**.

The major **denationalization** or **privatization issues** — British Telecom, British Gas and the like — worked to a longer timetable because of the size of the issues and the number of unsophisticated investors they were expected to attract. And when there are a lot of companies coming to market, the timetable may in any case vary a little.

Grey markets

In practice, shares may be traded in a **grey market** before shareholders get their allotment letters or even before the basis of allotment is known. The Stock Exchange was disparaging of unofficial grey markets which used to be run by licensed dealers rather than Stock Exchange members. Dealings are risky, because applicants do not yet have shares, so there is no guarantee that they can or will deliver. But in the case of the TSB Group (Trustee Savings Bank) launch, the Stock Exchange's own **official market** got under way before many applicants knew whether or not they had been allocated shares, to the considerable annoyance of many of them. And with British Gas the start of official dealings was deliberately set a week before allotment letters could be received. One reason was supposedly the risk of the Exchange's new computerized systems collapsing under the strain unless the start of dealings was staggered.

Part-paid shares

Most shares are **fully paid**. In other words, suppose we are talking of 20p shares being sold at 100p, the buyer or subscriber pays the whole 100p at one go. But sometimes — mainly with the privatization issues and in the case of some gilt-edged stocks (see

Chapter 13) — the price is paid in two or more instalments. This means the vendor gets his money spread out over a period rather than in a single lump.

Thus when XYZ Holdings launches, it might decide to sell its shares at 100p but ask for 30p immediately, a further 30p in six months and the remaining 40p in a year. When only 30p has been paid, the shares will be **part paid**. The *Financial Times's* **London recent issues** table shows the amount paid for each share in a column headed **Amount paid up** (in pence). Usually the entry is 'FP' for fully paid, but not in every case.

Part-paid shares are speculative because they are **highly geared**. Suppose investors think the right price for XYZ shares is 130p: a 30p premium on the issue price of 100p. In their 30p-paid form, the shares might also be expected to stand at a premium of 30p, so the market price is 60p. This means that anyone who was allotted the part-paid shares at 30p has a 100 per cent profit on his outlay to date, though the shares are only thought to be worth 30 per cent more than their issue price. But it works the other way round, too. If the shares are thought to be worth only 90p against an issue price of 100p, in their 30p-paid form they might be expected to stand at 20p. At that point a subscriber has lost a third of his outlay to date. The problems of the BP issue were exacerbated by the fact that only 120p of the 330p sale price was payable immediately, and the value of the part-paid shares roughly halved at one point.

New issue fraud

Multiple applications for shares in an offer for sale are, at best, discouraged and in the case of the privatization issues those making multiple applications were threatened with prosecution. A multiple application is when one person fills in a number of different application forms, perhaps with different names and addresses, hoping to get more shares or increase his chances of getting some shares. It is most likely to happen with a popular issue that is expected to be **heavily-stagged** and where there is an almost certain profit when the shares begin trading.

The issuing bank's normal way of discouraging multiple applications is to threaten that all cheques sent in will be cashed. If the multiple applicant has borrowed heavily to stag the issue, he is paying large interest charges until he gets the money back in

respect of his unsuccessful applications. The government —
perhaps because it was selling state assets at less than their true
worth to attract the public into its version of popular capitalism
— decided that one handout per person should be the limit and
adopted the prosecution route for anyone who attempted to grab
more.

9

Rights, placings and scrip issues

There is an old principle, enshrined in British company law, that when a company issues new shares to raise cash, those shares should be offered first to the existing shareholders: the owners of the business. This principle of **pre-emption rights** is under attack as part of the 'all change' atmosphere that accompanied and followed the Big Bang. And the government has fuelled the controversy by hinting that the pre-emption rights provisions might be removed from a future Companies Act. Pre-emption rights count for little in the United States, and Britain showed signs after the Big Bang of moving towards a US pattern where a company may issue new shares *en block* to a securities house which subsequently sells them through its marketing network, or where new shares are placed direct with investors who may not be existing shareholders. It is faster and cheaper for the company, the big company men claim. This poses a paradox. How can a procedure be good for a company if it is not good for the shareholders who own the company? You are likely to see frequent echos of this debate in the financial columns of the press.

Anything we say about traditional methods of issuing new shares for cash must therefore be read with a note of caution. In many big companies the old order of **rights** issues has been challenged by the new regime of **placings**, **vendor placings** and **bought deals**, though there were indications by 1989 that traditional methods might be regaining ground. It is the rights issue we need to look at first.

Mechanics of the rights issue

The **rights issue** procedure — 'rights' because existing shareholders have the first right to put up the new money — goes like this.

The company announces it intends to raise a particular amount by creating and selling new shares. The new shares will be offered to the shareholders in proportion to their existing holdings. And they will virtually always be offered at a price below that of the existing shares in the market, to give shareholders an incentive to put up money for the new shares. If they are offered at a price way below the existing price — say, at half the market value — the issue would be described as a **deep discounted** rights issue or as having a very large **scrip** element. But this is the exception rather than the rule. Discounts of 20 per cent or so are more common. This is a point that often causes confusion. You will come across phrases in the press like: 'XYZ Holdings is offering shareholders one new share for every five held at the very favourable price of 200p against a market price of 400p' or 'XYZ Holdings is making a rights issue on very attractive terms to investors'.

This is usually sheer nonsense. The shareholders already own the company. The company cannot offer them anything that is not theirs already. The price at which the new shares are offered is a technicality, provided they are offered to existing holders. Investors are not getting anything on the cheap. An example illustrates the point.

Adjusting the price

Suppose XYZ Holdings, whose shares are quoted in the stockmarket at 260p, decides to raise £40m by creating and selling 20m new shares at 200p each. The shares are offered to shareholders in the ratio of two new shares for every five existing shares they hold (a 'two-for-five' rights issue). For an investor who decides to take up his rights, this is how the sums go. For every five shares worth 260p each that he holds, he buys two new shares at 200p each. The average value of his shares after the issue would be 242.9p:

5 existing shares at a market price of 260p	=	1300p
2 new shares for cash at 200p	=	400p
Total for 7 shares	=	1700p
Value of 1 share (1700p/7)	=	242.9p

If all else were equal, 242.9p (call it 243p for simplicity) would be the price at which the XYZ shares would stand in the market after the rights issue. In other words, the market price would adjust down from 260p to 243p to reflect the fact that new shares had been offered below the previous market price. In practice, the general level of the stockmarket and the prices of individual companies are constantly moving up or down, so the sums may not be quite so clear cut. But the principle holds good.

It follows from this that the right to buy new shares at below market price has a value in itself, which is why it needs to be offered first to existing shareholders. A shareholder who simply ignored the rights issue would start with 5 shares at 260p worth 1300p in total and end with 5 shares at 243p after the price adjustment, worth only 1215p. In practice, when the shareholder does nothing the company will normally sell his entitlement to the new shares on his behalf and send the proceeds to him.

Cum-rights and ex-rights

When a company announces a rights issue, it says that the new shares will be offered to all shareholders on the company's **register of shareholders** at such-and-such a date. But since it can take time for purchases and sales to be reflected on the register, The Stock Exchange adopts its own different cut-off date. Anybody buying existing shares in the market before this date buys them with the right to subscribe for the new shares (**cum-rights**). Anyone buying on or after this date does not have the right to the new shares — this remains with the seller. The date is the day on which the shares go **ex-rights** for Stock Exchange dealing purposes, and it is therefore the day on which the market price will adjust downwards — from 260p to 243p in the example. After this date the share price in the Stock Exchange Official List and in newspapers will be marked for a time with an **xr** to tell buyers that they are not acquiring the right to subscribe for the new shares.

Dealing in rights

The rights to subscribe for new shares can be bought and sold in the market in much the same way as shares, and the value of the rights will be roughly equivalent to the **ex-rights price** (the price which has been adjusted downwards to take account of the issue) less the subscription price for the new shares. In the example, the right to buy for 200p a new share which will be quoted in the market at 243p ex-rights will be worth about 43p (243p minus 200p), though technical considerations can affect this a little. Shareholders who do not want to put up money for new shares will sell their rights and thus end up with some cash plus a smaller proportionate stake in the company.

Shareholder has 5 shares at 260p	=	1300p
Sells rights to two new shares at 43p	=	86p
Retains 5 shares at adjusted price of 243p	=	1215p
Has cash and shares of		1300p
(adjusting for rounding-up errors)		

The rights themselves are a short-life high-geared investment rather like an **option** or **warrant** (see Chapter 17), and often appeal to gamblers. Suppose XYZ's ex-rights share price rose 10p from 243p to 253p: an increase of 4 per cent. The value of the **nil paid** rights (the subscription price for the shares has not been paid) might be expected to rise from around 43p to around 53p: an increase of 23 per cent. Like all gearing, it works in reverse and the value of the rights can disappear entirely if the XYZ share price suffers a sharp fall.

The *Financial Times* carries in its 'Companies and Markets' section a table of **rights offers** showing the prices (technically the **premiums**) quoted for rights to buy new shares. It gives the price at which the new shares are being issued (which would be 200p for XYZ), the proportion of this price which has already been paid (if any — see Chapter 8) and the highest and lowest price at which the rights have traded. You can see that the percentage swings can be very large. The **pm** after the price simply means that the price is actually a premium which the buyer pays for the right to subscribe to a new share.

The price for the new shares in a rights issue is normally pitched sufficiently far below the market price to allow a bit of leeway in case the share price falls in the interim — investors will not put up money for the new shares if they can buy existing shares more cheaply in the market. Nevertheless, to make sure the company gets its money, the issue will normally be **underwritten** — institutions agree for a fee to put up the money for any shares the company cannot sell (see Chapter 8).

To XYZ Holdings it makes little difference if it issues 20m new shares at 200p each or 40m at 100p each. It still raises the £40m it

RIGHTS OFFERS

Issue Price p	Amount Paid up	Latest Renunc Date	1989 High	1989 Low	Stock	Closing Price p	+ or -
9	6	8/9	10¾pm	7½pm	Bear Brand	10½pm	
62	Nil	-	8pm	3pm	‡Eadie Hldgs.	3pm	
61	Nil	-	12pm	7½pm	Fife Indmar	12pm	
10	Nil	-	28pm	13pm	‡Global Group 10p	15pm	
78	Nil	-	21pm	9pm	‡Midland & Scottish Resources	19pm	
220	Nil	-	20pm	13pm	Plaxton Group	18pm	-2
435	Nil	4/8	74pm	50pm	RTZ 10p	62pm	-2
60	F.P.	27/7	71	68	Richardsons Westgarth 10p	68	
8	Nil	-	½pm	¼pm	‡Southwest Res. A 2p	¼pm	

Table 9.1 Stockmarket prices for 'rights'. Source: *Financial Times*.

needs. And if it pitches the **subscription price** at 100p against a market price of 260p for the existing shares, there is very little risk that the market price might fall below the subscription price and prevent the new shares from being taken up. A **deep-discounted rights issue** such as this would therefore not need to be underwritten — a considerable cost saving. In practice, very few companies follow the deep-discounted route. The reason usually given is that there is a slight tax disadvantage for some shareholders in the deep discount process. The City, for which **underwriting fees** are a useful and normally an easily-earned perk, does not encourage deep-discounters.

> 'Prudential Corporation, Britain's largest life assurance company, yesterday surprised the stockmarket by seeking £357m from its shareholders through a rights issue.
>
> 'The market was even more surprised when the Pru revealed that the issue would not be underwritten. A rights issue not underwritten is rare and the Pru's current issue is by far the largest of its kind to date. Its terms are one new share at 600p for every five held and it will involve the issue of 60,257,503 new shares.' (*Financial Times*, 2 May 1986)

When XYZ's market price is 260p the company is being no more and no less 'generous' if it offers new shares at 100p than at 200p. Remember the principle. The company belongs to the shareholders and there is nothing they can be given that they do not already own. The only benefit they may derive is if the **dividend per share** is maintained on the increased capital, which has the same effect as a dividend increase. This is a totally different decision, but it is often confused with the rights issue itself. If XYZ was paying a

10p per share gross dividend before the issue, the yield on the shares at 260p would have been 3.8 per cent. If it paid the same dividend per share after a two-for-five rights issue at 200p, the yield at the **ex-rights price** of 243p would rise to 4.1 per cent.

New developments in capital raising

The rights issue is far from dead, but the other arrangements for issuing new shares for cash which have sometimes supplanted it include:

- The **vendor placing**. This technique replaces a rights issue used to raise cash for an acquisition. Company A agrees to buy a business from Company B. It issues its own shares to Company B to pay for the acquisition, but arranges in advance for all of these shares to be **placed with** (sold to) investors — mainly the institutions. Thus Company B ends up with cash for the business it sold.

- The **placing** is much like a vendor placing, except that no acquisition is involved. The company creates new shares and its financial advisor places them with a range of investors. Sometimes a tranche of new shares is offered on an overseas stockmarket without being available to investors in London.

- The **bought deal**. Instead of placing shares with a number of investors, a company can invite bids for all the shares from the **securities houses**. The securities house offering the highest price gets the business and pays cash for the shares, hoping to make a profit by selling them via its distribution network to a range of investors. The bought deal is not limited to new shares a company creates. A company which held a large investment portfolio of other companies' shares that it wanted to dispose of could invite offers for the lot. This type of business can be very profitable for the securities houses, though is also very high risk — they could lose heavily if the share price dropped between their buying the shares *en bloc* and selling them to the final purchasers. It requires large amounts of capital — one of the reasons why British securities houses need big financial backing to be able to compete with their American counterparts. Equally important, it demands a large efficient marketing department with a wide spread of investor contacts.

'Granada is to finance the purchase of Laskys by issuing 10.8m new shares. The entire issue has been taken up by Salomon Brothers, the US investment bank, in a bought deal, a common US stockmarket tactic which is increasingly being imported to the UK.

'Salomon has paid 282p a share, just 2p less that Granada's 284p closing price on Wednesday. This was a smaller discount than would have been necessary in a conventional vendor placing, Granada said.' (*Financial Times* 17 October 1986)

● Various other arrangements are evolving for issuing shares in the international markets. In a **euroequity** issue a company bypasses the domestic stockmarket and, via a securities house, sells shares direct to investors in a number of overseas countries. Or it may issue a **convertible loan stock** rather than shares and sell it through the **eurobond market** mechanism.

Pre-emption rights controversy

In the case of a placing, a vendor placing or, particularly, a bought deal, the price for the new XYZ shares would probably be far closer to the market price than in the case of a conventional rights issue. But it will still normally be at some discount to the ruling market price. And this is where the controversy arises. It makes no odds, as we've seen, whether XYZ choses to offer its new shares at 200p or 100p as long as they are offered first to existing shareholders. But if they are offered below market price to investors who are not already shareholders in XYZ, there is a transfer of value from existing shareholders to the new buyers, which is a totally different matter.

The pension funds and insurance companies are the major existing shareholders in most larger companies, and they have not taken kindly to seeing their birthright eroded. They have therefore argued that most or all of the new shares sold via these new techniques should be offered to existing shareholders as a **clawback**. The process then is as follows. XYZ arranges with its financial adviser to sell the new shares it creates, so it is sure of its money. But at the same time the financial adviser makes an **open offer** of the new shares to the XYZ shareholders, pro rata with their existing holdings. Those who want to can take up the new shares. Shares which are not taken up remain with the (mainly institutional) investors to whom they were provisionally sold.

Note this does not produce the same result as a conventional rights issue for all shareholders. A holder who does not take up his entitlement under the clawback has no **rights** to sell for cash. The benefit of new shares at below market price goes to somebody else.

> 'The purchase of Celebrated, owner of four English hotels, is to be satisfied by the issue of 61.2m new ordinary shares in Norfolk which will represent 21 per cent of the enlarged equity.
>
> 'Morgan Grenfell is placing the shares conditionally with investment clients but existing shareholders are to be offered them for 25p each. Norfolk's shares closed yesterday at 29p, down 1½p'
> (*Financial Times*, 27 January 1987)

The investing institutions have used their collective muscle to impose tight restrictions on the amount of new share capital companies may issue without offering the shares to existing holders.

The scrip issue

From the new, back to the old. There is one further type of share issue any reader of the financial press has to understand: the **scrip issue** or **capitalization issue**. It arises almost by historical accident, but poses a pitfall for the unwary. It is sometimes referred to in the press (and, even less excusably, by companies themselves) as a **free issue** or a **bonus issue**, again conjuring the vision of shareholders receiving something for nothing. In the case of the traditional scrip issue, this is misleading nonsense.

The historical accident is the fact that the nominal value of the share capital of British companies is distinguished from other funds belonging to shareholders and that the shares themselves therefore have a **par** value: 5p, 10p, 20p, 25p, 50p, £1 or whatever. The equivalent unit of **common stock** in American companies may not need to have a par value.

A scrip or capitalization issue in the UK is the process whereby a company turns part of its accumulated **reserves** into new shares. Suppose ABC Company's shares stand in the market at 800p and its **shareholders' funds** look like this:

	£m
ORDINARY SHARE CAPITAL (in 20p shares)	100
REVENUE RESERVES	600
CAPITAL RESERVES	300
SHAREHOLDERS' FUNDS	1,000

Because the company has accumulated considerable **revenue reserves** by ploughing back profits over the years, the £100m of share capital gives little indication of the total size of the shareholders' interest in the company. Also, as profits have risen so the share price has risen, to the point where — at 800p — it is **heavy** by British standards. In many other countries, shares which each cost the equivalent of tens or hundreds of pounds are common. Britain has the tradition of units with a smaller value and shares are considered to become less easily **marketable** (less easy to buy and sell in the stockmarket) when the price pushes up towards £10 or so.

So ABC might decide to convert part of its reserves into new shares. Suppose it decides to use £100m of its revenue reserves for this purpose. It creates £100m nominal of new shares (500m shares, since they are 20p units) and uses £100m of the revenue reserves to make them **fully paid**. The new shares are distributed to existing shareholders (in this case in a one-for-one ratio) and the shareholders' funds after the operation look like this:

	£m
ORDINARY SHARE CAPITAL (in 20p shares)	200
REVENUE RESERVES	500
CAPITAL RESERVES	300
SHAREHOLDERS' FUNDS	1,000

All that has happened is that £100m has been deducted from one heading (revenue reserves) and added to another (ordinary share capital). It is a **book-keeping transaction**, pure and simple, and in no way affects the value of the shareholders' interest in the company nor does it raise money for the company. Shareholders' funds remain unchanged at £1,000m.

Adjusting the price for a scrip issue

In our example the shareholder now has two shares where he had one before. But since the value of the company has not changed, the market price will simply adjust to reflect the issue. Previously the shareholder had one share worth 800p. After the issue he has two shares worth 400p each. The greater number of shares in issue and the less heavy price may make them slightly more marketable.

A scrip issue need not be in the ratio of one-for-one (also

referred to as a 100 per cent capitalization issue). It could be one-for-ten (a 10 per cent issue), two-for-five, two-for-one and so on. The complication in each case is that the market price has to be adjusted for the issue. If the issue were one-for-ten, the market price would come back from 800p to 727.3p. The investor starts with 10 shares at 800p, worth 8,000p in total and he ends with 11 shares. Dividing the 8,000p by 11 shares gives a price of 727.3.

As with a rights issue, The Stock Exchange sets a date after which a buyer of ABC's shares in the market will not acquire the entitlement to the new shares resulting from the scrip issue, and that is the day the price adjusts downwards. After the adjustment the letters **xc** will appear after the price, meaning **ex-capitalization**.

If a scrip issue by itself is significant only in a technical sense it can, like a rights issue, have implications for the shareholder's income. If ABC makes a one-for-one scrip issue and wants to pay out the same amount of money by way of dividend after the issue, it will have to halve the rate of dividend per share. The shareholder who received 10p on one share gets the same income from 5p on two shares after the issue. If ABC holds its dividend at 10p per share, it is effectively doubling the payment. Occasionally, companies increase their dividends by paying a constant amount per share, but making regular small scrip issues such as one-for-ten.

How scrip issues complicate comparisons

With a one-for-one scrip issue, when the market price halves, it is not easy to miss what is happening, though brokers still get calls from clients asking why their shares have performed so badly. A one-for-ten issue, with a comparatively minor downwards adjustment in the price, is far easier to miss. When tracking the performance of a share price over the years, the investment analyst or journalist has to **adjust** for every scrip issue. Not only must the price be adjusted. Previous years' earnings and dividends per share will also need adjustment. Suppose ABC earned 25p per share and paid a 10p gross dividend for the year before it made its one-for-one scrip issue. In the year after the scrip issue the earnings per share were 15p, the dividend was 6p and the share price has touched 550p. What has really happened? All of the earlier year's figures have to be adjusted for the issue:

One share at 800p	=	two shares at 400p
25p earnings on one share	=	12.5p divided between two shares
10p dividend on one share	=	5p dividend on two shares

Therefore, in comparing the previous year's performance with the latest one, we are comparing **effective** or **adjusted** earnings per share of 12.5p with the latest year's 15p, and an effective or adjusted previous year's dividend of 5p with a current one of 6p. The share price has risen from the **equivalent of** 400p to the current 550p. Net asset values must be adjusted in a similar way.

Discussions of company performance in the financial press are thus studded with words like 'effective', 'adjusted' and 'equivalent', and reflect this particularly irritating technicality of British company practice. In theory, all figures should also be adjusted for a rights issue at below market price, though practice varies. Certainly, a deep-discounted rights issue (which really contains strong elements of a scrip issue as well as a money-raising issue) requires adjustment.

Less common forms of scrip issue

Two other quirks of the scrip issue process crop up from time to time. Occasionally, companies give shareholders the option of taking new shares (created by capitalization of reserves) in place of dividend. The practice was more widespread in the past when it sometimes carried tax advantages. And in some of the government **privatization issues**, shareholders who retain their shares for a specified period are promised a **loyalty bonus** in the form of a scrip issue. In this case the issue does have a value since it does not go to all shareholders alike. Those who receive the extra 'loyalty' shares are increasing their proportionate stake in the company at the expense of the other shareholders who do not qualify.

10

Bidders, victims and lawmakers

Takeovers are the jam on the bread and butter of normal investment business. When Company A bids for Company B, it will almost always be at a price above that which Company B commands in the market on its own merits. Therefore there are instant profits for shareholders of Company B. Moreover, the **market professionals** have a strong vested interest in takeovers. They generate high share dealing **volumes**, and activity is the lifeblood of brokers and marketmakers. They generate big fees for the **merchant banks** who advise the companies involved in the takeover. And there are spin-off benefits for the accountants, solicitors and other professionals drawn into the affair. The City has a strong vested interest in a high level of takeover activity and there will be fierce resistance to efforts to curb it.

In the press, takeover activity is covered at several levels. There are the takeover tips: 'buy shares in XYZ Holdings; a predator is sniffing round'. There are the blow-by-blow accounts of disputed takeovers which can occupy many column-inches week after week. And there is an increasing number of more thoughtful pieces questioning whether frenetic takeover activity harms Britain's economy and dissecting some of the less desirable tactics employed. Much of this is self-explanatory, but a little background is needed.

Take the last point first. Takeover activity tends to go in waves and often reaches its peak when share prices are close to their peak after a prolonged bull market. At these times takeover considerations can almost totally dominate stockmarket thinking as a form of collective fever takes hold. Everybody is looking for the next takeover victim, buying its shares and forcing prices up. The process becomes self-fuelling. Financial journalists catch the fever like everybody else. Remember this when reading the financial pages: some of the comment on share prices loses all contact with fundamental values. **Takeover activity** reached a peak in the early 1970s and again in the mid-1980s.

The justification put forward for takeovers is that they increase **industrial efficiency**. Sleepy companies are gobbled up by more actively managed **predators** which can get better returns from the victim company's assets. In some cases this may be true. But there is little if any consistent evidence that takeovers improve industrial and commercial performance in the long term. Contested takeovers are almost unknown in West Germany and Japan, two of the strongest industrial performers. Takeovers may, however, suit the biggest owners of British companies: the insurance companies and pension funds. Finding it difficult to exert positive influence to improve management in the companies they invest in, they may welcome a takeover approach from an actively managed company that will do the job for them.

The increasingly strong opposition to excessive takeover activity that finds its echo in the financial pages homes in on other arguments. The threat of takeover induces short-sighted attitudes in company managements. They will not undertake long-term investment if the cost threatens to depress profits before the benefits appear. Depressed profits depress the share price and make the company vulnerable to takeover. Institutional investment managers, too, are being forced to take a short-term view of their performance: **short-termism**. If they are judged over a three-month period on the performance of the investments they manage, they will be inclined to back a takeover which shows them short-term profits.

Finally, there are criticisms of **merger accounting**. This is one of the ways the accounts of the combined group may be shown in some cases after a takeover, and it can result in an artificially bright picture of the profits in following years. Note that except in this context the word **merger** does not normally have a precise technical meaning (see below).

Takeover mechanics

Takeovers in Britain are fought within the framework of formal rules, rather like the moves of medieval combat. As with most rules, frequent revisions of the detail are needed as new techniques emerge. We will come to the more important ones later, but the point to grasp at the outset when reading of any takeover is that a form of corporate democracy prevails. Company A gains **control** of Company B by persuading the holders of at least 50.01 per cent of the Company B **votes** to sell to it or accept its offer. If it already owns some shares in Company B it may require fewer votes to take it to the magic control point. Most companies have a one-vote-per-ordinary-share **capital structure**, so in practice Company A usually has to secure over 50 per cent of the Company B shares.

Within this general rule there are numerous permutations. The first thing to look for in the press report is whether the bid is agreed, defended or contested:

- The directors of Companies A and B may have met and decided that a merger is in the interest of both parties. In this case the bid for Company B will be **agreed**, though this is not a guarantee that it will succeed. The shareholders, not the directors, have the ultimate word. An agreed bid between two companies is often referred to as a **merger**.
- Company A may announce that it is bidding for Company B and the Company B directors may decide to try to fight off the bid. In this case it is **defended** or **contested**. It is certainly **hostile**.
- Two or more companies may bid at about the same time for Company B, which perhaps does not want to be taken over by either of them, or might back the bid from Company C against that from Company A. This will be a **contested** bid. A company at the receiving end of an unwelcome bid often searches for a **white knight**: an alternative bidder that would be acceptable to it and might keep it out of Company A's clutches.

Form of the offer

When Company A bids for Company B, it has several options. It can make a:

- **Cash offer**. In this case it simply offers a certain amount in cash for each Company B share. Shareholders in Company B who decide to accept have no further interest in the combined group. But acceptance counts in much the same way as if they had sold their shares for cash in the stockmarket, and they may be liable to **Capital Gains Tax** on profits.

- **Paper offer**. Company A offers to swap its own shares in a certain proportion for those of Company B. This will also be referred to as a **share exchange offer**. Company A might offer three of its own shares for every five of Company B. If the Company A shares stand at 360p in the stockmarket, this puts a value of 216p on each Company B share. Sometimes a bid will provide a mix of cash and paper.

In a paper offer, instead of offering its own shares Company A might offer to swap some other form of security for the Company B shares. It might offer 216p nominal of Company A 6 per cent convertible loan stock for each Company B share, again valuing them at 216p if the convertible is worth its nominal value (there can be heated arguments on this point). Or it might offer a mix of convertible and shares, or a choice between the two. When the bid terms become very complex, involving rare and wonderful forms of security, these securities are sometimes referred to as **funny money** (see glossary). When a company issues massive quantities of its shares in a succession of takeovers, the press sometimes talks in terms of a **paperchase** or makes references to **wallpaper**.

Note that with any paper offer, the value of Company A's shares in the stockmarket determines the value of the offer for each share in Company B, and therefore the chances of the bid succeeding. Company A thus has every incentive to keep its own share price up, and its friends and associates may help its chances by buying its shares to **support** the price (see below).

In a paper offer, the bidder will often establish a floor value for its bid by arranging **underwriting** for the shares it offers. Take the share exchange offer we looked at earlier. Company A offers three of its own shares for every five in Company B. With Company A at 360p Company B shares are valued by the offer at 216p. But Company A arranges with institutions that they will agree to buy any new shares it offers at, say, 340p cash or perhaps it offers a 340p cash alternative from its own resources. So a shareholder in Company B who accepts the Company A offer knows he can take 340p in cash, which gives an **underwritten cash value** for the bid of 204p per Company B share. Of course, if the Company A share price stays high after the bid, he would do

better if he wants cash by taking the new Company A shares and
selling them in the stockmarket.

Market purchases

So far we have assumed that a takeover simply involves an
approach by Company A to the shareholders of Company B
outside the stockmarket. But in many cases Company A will use
the stockmarket as well. It will perhaps build up a stake in
Company B by buying shares in the stockmarket before it makes
a formal offer. Or, once an offer has been made, it will increase its
chances of success by buying the shares of Company B in the
market — the shares it acquires via **market purchases** can then be
lumped together with acceptances by Company B shareholders to
reach the magic control figure.

But there are rules governing market purchases in the course of
a bid (see below), and Company A has to be careful. By market
purchases it may force up the Company B share price, which can
make it more difficult or more expensive to gain control.

Rules of the game

Takeovers are policed by the **Panel on Takeovers and Mergers**
(the **Takeover Panel**) which applies the **City Code on Takeovers
and Mergers** (the **Takeover Code**). The Takeover Panel has
always been a non-statutory body with the main City institutions
represented on its board, though it now has the backing of the
Securities and Investments Board's range of sanctions, and it has
generally been one of the better examples of **self-regulation** at
work. With a full-time executive, it can give quick judgements on
contentious points arising in a takeover, and these are generally
respected by the parties involved. In the more legalistic atmosphere following the Big Bang there is perhaps a greater tendency
for the contestants to bring their lawyers with them to discussions
with the Panel, but there have been very few legal challenges to
Takeover Panel decisions. Certain aspects of takeovers are also
governed directly or indirectly by the **Companies Acts**.

The Takeover Code has been expanded over the years to
incorporate points raised by specific cases which have a general
application. You do not have to understand all its ramifications
to follow a press report of a takeover. But the rules can play an
important part in some of the big contested bids and a general

understanding of the principles, which are relatively simple, is useful.

Underlying the Takeover Panel's approach is the principle that all shareholders should be treated equally when one company tries to gain control of another. This is a counsel of perfection, but at least some of the worst abuses have been eliminated. In the bad old days of the jungle, before the Panel existed, one company might pay a high price for a controlling interest in another company, but make no offer to the remaining **minority shareholders**, who were left out in the cold. Those closest to the market would have the best chance of knowing what was going on and selling at the higher price. So much of the rulebook is concerned with preventing control from changing hands until all shareholders can see what is happening.

The trigger points

When a company acquires shares in another, it may come up against **trigger points** which affect its subsequent actions.

A company which builds up a stake of **30 per cent** in another is obliged to make a bid for all the shares in the target company unless specifically exempted by the Panel. This is because 30 per cent is pushing close to **effective control**: it is difficult for anyone else to bid successfully when one party has a stake of this size. So a **mandatory bid** follows acquisition of a 30 per cent stake. You will often see in the press that one company has built up a stake of 29.9 per cent in another: just below the level that triggers a bid.

When Company A builds up a stake of 30 per cent in Company B, the price it offers the remaining shareholders must usually be at least as high as the highest price it paid over the previous year. If in the course of the bid it buys Company B shares at a price above the bid value, it will have to increase the bid.

There are also provisions designed to limit the speed with which Company A can acquire shares in the market once it has taken its stake over 15 per cent via market purchases. These give the directors of Company B a breathing space in which to advise their shareholders on whether or not to sell (and if not, why not), and allow smaller shareholders as well as professional investors who are close to the market to decide whether to take advantage of the price the predator is paying. A **dawn raid** is when a company swoops on the stockmarket to buy a stake of up to 15 per cent in another company in double-quick time. An alternative (though it is less common) is to invite shareholders to tender shares for sale, up to the maximum required.

Takeover bids are **conditional** upon a number of factors. In other words, the bid may lapse unless the conditions are met. The most important conditions are those regarding **acceptances**. Normally the offer will lapse unless the bidder gets over 50 per cent of the victim. Between 50 and 90 per cent it has the option of letting the bid lapse or declaring it **unconditional** — except in a mandatory bid, where the offer must go unconditional at 50 per cent. Above **90 per cent** the bid has to become unconditional. The **Companies Acts** allow the bidder to acquire any remaining shares **compulsorily** when it already has over 90 per cent of the shares it bid for.

The other common condition built into a takeover is that the bidder must withdraw if the bid is referred to the **Monopolies Commission,** If called on to do so, the Monopolies and Mergers Commission — to give it its full title — will investigate a proposed takeover and can veto it, usually on the grounds that it would seriously diminish competition. Whatever its finding, its researches normally hold up a takeover for more than six months, and few potential predators are prepared to wait. The **Office of Fair Trading** recommends whether a particular bid should be referred to the Monopolies Commission, though the Industry Secretary has the last say. Policy in this area is not always wholly clear.

There are also important trigger points for **disclosure of shareholdings** in another company (most of these apply outside takeovers as well). Any person or company acquiring **5 per cent** or more of another company (this trigger point is to be reduced to **3 per cent**) must declare the holding to the company. You will often see references in the press to the fact that one company has acquired over 5 per cent of another, perhaps presented by the writer as a prelude to a possible bid. Following the Guinness affair (see below), the Takeover Panel tightened its rules to require disclosure of transactions which resulted in a stake as small as **one per cent** in the parties to a bid or which resulted in changes to stakes of over one per cent, once the bid had been announced.

Sometimes in the past, when Company A wanted to prepare the ground for a bid for Company B, it would persuade its friends, Companies C and D, to buy Company B shares, effectively **warehousing** them on its behalf. Nowadays, Companies A, C and D would be held to be **acting in concert** (or would constitute a **concert party**) and their shareholdings would be lumped together for the purposes of the various disclosure and trigger points. In practice it may be difficult to prove that parties are acting in concert, particularly when the beneficial owners of shareholdings are obscured behind overseas **nominee names**.

Share price support

We have seen why it is vital for the bidder to maintain its own share price if it is offering shares. But there are limits — in theory at least — on what can be done by way of support.

First, all **associates** of the bidder must declare their dealings in the shares of either party. The most common forms of associate are the merchant bank advisers and funds under their control.

Secondly, any buyer — even if he is not an associate — will have to declare his holdings if they pass one of the trigger points for disclosure.

Thirdly, the company itself must not support its own share price with company money. This revolves on a **Companies Act** provision that companies may not, except with the permission of their shareholders and in very closely defined circumstances, give **financial support for the purchase of their own shares**. It was the main point at issue in the Guinness scandal (see below).

Again, the practice diverges some way from the theory. In the course of a bid, **friends** of Company A may try to help by buying shares in Company A to boost its price and selling those in Company B to depress it. The friends could include friendly institutions and are often referred to as a **fan club**. Whether or not the help is given in the expectation of future favours (in which case the company might be deemed to be giving financial assistance for the purchase of its own shares) is often difficult to establish. In the United States **arbitrageurs** or **arbs** — of whom **Ivan Boesky**, the disgraced **insider trader**, was the best known example — make a business of acquiring large share stakes in takeover situations. Sometimes they simply gain by buying shares in the victim and selling at a profit. Less legitimately, it is suspected that some offer their services to support or depress a particular share price to aid or frustrate takeover ambitions. Though less active in Britain, they crop up frequently in accounts of the Guinness affair (see below).

The bid timetable

To prevent bids from dragging on interminably, there is an established **bid timetable**. The Take-over Panel sets a time limit of 60 days for an offer or series of offers from the same party to remain on the table, starting from the day the **formal documents** go out. If the bidder cannot gain control within this time, he has to wait a year before making another attempt. However, if a second or subsequent competitive bidder emerges, it in turn has 60 days and its deadline also becomes the deadline for the first bidder.

A takeover often starts with a sustained rise in the price of the victim company's shares (yes, for all the insider dealing penalties, it is the exception rather than the rule for a bid to remain unheralded until it is declared, though legitimate buying by the prospective bidder could account for the movement, while some forthcoming bids are not too difficult for the market to spot in advance).

Then Company A announces to the Stock Exchange and press that it is bidding for Company B, usually giving the terms. Company B, if it resists, will usually rush out a statement describing the bid as inadequate and wholly unacceptable, and telling its shareholders to stay firm.

Some time later Company A posts its formal **offer document** to Company B shareholders, giving details of itself and of the offer and — with a paper offer — stressing its own management strengths, the (possibly dubious) **industrial logic** of the offer and the advantages of acceptance. Company B studies the offer and comes out with a formal **defence document**, knocking down the Company A arguments and extolling its own virtues, usually with the help of profit and dividend forecasts and, possibly, asset revaluations.

Salvoes of this kind may be fired by both parties several times during the course of the affair. The more important ones are reported in the press. By the **first closing date** of the offer, Company A must decide — if it does not already have control — whether simply to keep the offer open in the hope of further **acceptances**, raise the bid if it clearly needs to offer more or let it **lapse** if it does not fancy its chances of winning. If it lapses, any acceptances that have been received become void. Offers may be raised several times during the affair. Alternative bidders may appear at any point to complicate the decisions. Throughout, Company A and any competitive bidders may be buying

Company B shares in the market and friends or associates of all the parties may be supporting the price of their respective proteges. But by the **final closing date** the bidder must announce that the offer is **unconditional** as to acceptances — the bid goes through if the other conditions are met — or allow it to lapse.

Throughout the **offer period** the price of Company B's shares in the stockmarket will give some indication of the expected outcome. If it lags just a little behind the value of the latest bid it can mean that the bid is expected to succeed. If it jumps ahead, the market is probably expecting a higher offer, though it could just possibly be that Company B has justified a higher price for its shares on their own merits.

The United States scene

The takeover scene is considerably rougher — as to the tactics permitted and employed — in the **United States** than in Britain. The Takeover Panel has been effective in preventing widespread use in the UK of some of the more questionable American techniques. **Greenmail** — a form of corporate blackmail — is a prime example. A company builds up a large stake in a potential takeover candidate. It threatens to bid or sell the stake to another prospective bidder unless the target company buys the stake from it at an inflated price — possible, because of the greater freedom to buy their own shares enjoyed by American companies.

The **poison pill** bid defence is another American tactic which has also cropped up only in its milder forms in the UK. The target company builds in a tripwire to make itself less attractive to a bidder. It might, say, create a new class of stock which becomes automatically redeemable at a high price in the event of a successful takeover.

Geared or **leveraged** takeovers have also been less common in the UK, though the idea is beginning to catch on. A bid is made using a high proportion of borrowed money. The resultant company is very highly-geared and forced to concentrate on short-term profitability to meet the interest charges (see Chapter 11). Sometimes these bids involve borrowing money by the issue of **junk bonds** — bonds which offer a high rate of interest but which would not normally count as being of investment quality because they are issued in large quantity by relatively insubstantial companies. The US authorities have become worried by the level of gearing introduced into American companies.

We have already seen how the **arbs** take positions in takeover stocks. Recent revelations suggest their success was based more on **insider dealing** — acting on confidential information, often unlawfully purchased — than on successful prediction, and they are likely to be less active in future. But often in the US they have built up stakes of sufficient size in a takeover candidate to sway the outcome of the bid.

Leverage and level playing fields

Cross-frontier takeovers are usually for cash; shares are rarely a widely accepted currency outside their country of origin. Thus British companies have made major acquisitions for cash in the United States in recent years, and most large overseas bids for British companies are for cash. British companies at the receiving end of hostile takeovers from overseas have frequently complained about lack of **reciprocity** and the lack of a **level playing field**: the predator companies may be protected from hostile takeovers in their country of origin, though perhaps more by patterns of shareholdings and by local custom and practice than by specific legislation.

Overseas bids for British companies are frequently highly **leveraged** and a trend towards bids made with borrowed money has been reinforced domestically by the growth in **management buy-outs** and **management buy-ins** (see Chapter 11), some of which are aimed at stockmarket-listed companies. There has been no shortage of cash from the banks to back management teams dissatisfied with the share price performance of their company, who reckon they could do better by buying it and taking it private. If the company is listed, this involves making a takeover offer to its existing shareholders.

The Guinness affair

No review of takeovers is complete without a glance at the *cause celebre* that has filled so many column-inches of the financial press since late 1986: the £2.6 billion Guinness bid for whisky giant Distillers in 1986.

Drinks group Guinness was competing with the Argyll supermarket business to take over Distillers, which backed the Guinness offer. The Guinness offer was mainly in shares and its value — and therefore Guinness's chances of beating Argyll — depended heavily on the Guinness share price. Having been below 300p in January 1986, the Guinness share price staged a remarkable rise to over 350p at one point. The value of the Guinness offer surpassed that of Argyll's offer and Guinness won the day.

The revelations which followed the appointment of Department of Trade inspectors to investigate Guinness's affairs at the begining of December 1986 made it clear that there had been a massive support operation to boost the Guinness share price. More serious were the allegations that Guinness had used its own money in one way or another to recompense those who bought its shares on a large scale and boosted the price: by paying them fees, by making large cash deposits with them or by guaranteeing to cover any losses they might suffer on the shares. Resignations and sackings — at Guinness itself and at its then merchant bank advisers, Morgan Grenfell — preceded the DTI inspectors' findings. Criminal charges against some of the main players followed later.

It provided a field day for the financial press and — taken with allegations of insider trading elsewhere in the City — considerable embarrassment for a government which had been selling the benefits of stockmarket investment to the public. The government probably worried unduly. To a cynical public, evidence of share rigging and insider dealing in the City scarcely ranked as a revelation.

11

Venture capital and leveraged buy-outs

'Small is beautiful' has been the cry in British business for much of the past ten years, and various initiatives have emerged to provide finance for smaller companies and start-up enterprises. Several of the more serious national daily papers now include a weekly small business feature.

Bank loans and overdrafts traditionally provide the finance for businesses in their very early years and the stockmarket allows more mature companies to raise debt or equity capital. But between the two, it is argued, lies a **financing gap**. Businesses which are too large or too fast-growing to subsist on bank finance, yet too small to launch on the stockmarket, may be held back by lack of funds. In particular, smaller businesses find it very difficult to raise equity finance as opposed to loans.

Management buy-outs

We have seen, too, the phenomenon of the **management buy-out**. A group of managers within a large industrial company decide they would like to own the particular part of the business they run and to operate it as an independent entity. It may suit the large company to sell it to them if the division in question is peripheral to its main business. Alternatively, managers of listed companies may decide they would like to run and part-own the whole of the enterprise they currently manage on behalf of the shareholders (see below). Occasionally a company is acquired with a view to putting in a new management team not previously associated with it (a **management buy-in**). But in all cases the managers themselves rarely have the money to acquire an established

145

business and they require help in the form of outside equity and loan finance.

Venture capital and development capital funds

To satisfy these different financing needs, there has been rapid growth in **venture capital funds**: organizations which provide finance — often a mixture of equity and loans, but sometimes just one or the other — for unquoted companies. Most of the venture capital funds are offshoots of existing financial institutions: clearing or merchant banks, insurance companies or pension funds. At the end of 1988 there were 107 full and 50 associate members of the **British Venture Capital Association**, the umbrella body for these funds.

The biggest venture capital organization in the UK, however, has a longer history. It is **Investors in Industry** or the **3i** group, whose original venture capital arm was known as Industrial and Commercial Finance Corporation (ICFC) and was founded shortly after the last war. Owned by the clearing banks and the Bank of England, it now provides most forms of banking and finance service, other than overdrafts, and has gross assets of over £2 billion. It has financed almost 10,000 businesses, and will consider requests for quite small amounts of money as well as very large sums.

The typical **venture capitalist** puts up money for a growing business or to finance a management buy-out in return for a proportion of the share capital. Individual funds rarely want control of the companies they back, but where the funds required are very large the financing may be **syndicated** among a number of venture capitalists. Each puts up part of the money and collectively they may control the enterprise they finance.

The original entrepreneurs, or the managers in the case of a buy-out, thus concede a large part of their ownership of the business in return for the finance they need if it is to grow. Often their eventual stake in the business is geared to how well it performs (a **ratchet** arrangement). The venture capitalists usually want to cash in on their stake in successful businesses after five years or so and at this point will want an opportunity of selling the shares — a **take-out** — possibly via a **stockmarket launch** of the company.

Most of the major venture capital funds do not consider it worth investigating a **financing proposal** unless the sums involved are quite large — £250,000 or more is not unusual as a minimum — and they are generally wary of business **start-ups** (entirely new businesses) where the risk is highest. They prefer to put up **development finance** for companies which are already past the initial stage and need more equity if they are to advance to a bigger league. The same is generally true of another type of fund providing capital for unquoted companies — the **Business Expansion Scheme fund** — although these funds will sometimes provide finance in smaller quantities.

Leveraged buy-outs and takeovers

Leveraged buy-outs and **leveraged takeovers** have been popular for some time in the United States and the principle has now spread to Britain just as America is beginning to worry about some of the consequences. 'Leveraged' simply means 'geared up' in British terminology.

The principle is that most of the money to buy a company — often a major listed company — is put up in the form of debt by banks and others, with only a small proportion of the finance taking the form of share capital. Typically the debt will be in several layers: **senior debt** which is reasonably well secured, some intermediate layers and perhaps an issue of high-yielding high-risk **junk bonds** (see Chapter 10). You will also see references to **mezzanine debt** which is a form of halfway house between debt and equity: debt offering a high return which may also include some rights to share in equity values. Funds are springing up to provide mezzanine finance and various forms of venture capital fund may provide the relatively small amounts of equity finance involved in the leveraged operation.

A company acquired by way of a leveraged bid (80 per cent and sometimes a lot more of the finance may be in the form of debt) finds that interest charges absorb most of its profits and it is probably under pressure to dispose of parts of its business to raise cash to reduce its borrowings as rapidly as possible. Leveraged buy-outs are a very high risk game whose dangers become more apparent when economic activity turns down. The biggest so far (as of summer 1989) was the $25m buy-out of food and tobacco group RJR Nabisco in the United States.

147

Business Expansion Scheme

The **Business Expansion Scheme (BES)** was started by the government (originally as the Business Start-up Scheme) in 1981 to persuade higher earning individuals to invest direct in smaller companies by subscribing for their shares. Individuals can invest up to £40,000 a year in new shares of qualifying companies, and receive full relief from income tax on the £40,000. The real cost of such an investment for somebody paying 40 per cent tax on at least £40,000 of his income was thus £24,000 in 1989.

To qualify for BES investment, companies must conform to criteria that have been progressively tightened since the scheme was introduced. Investment companies and those which merely sit on appreciating assets — property investment companies, other than a specific type of residential property concern (see below) are excluded. The company's shares must not be quoted on a **recognized stock exchange** for three years after the BES investment is made, and the individual who puts up money under the BES cannot sell the shares for five years if he wants to retain tax relief. But BES company shares may be traded on The Stock Exchange's **Third market** without the company's losing its BES status. The 1988 Budget restricted the amount that could be raised by a BES company to £0.5m, except for those investing in residential property let on new-style assured tenancy terms, where the limit is £5m. This has led to an explosion in BES residential property schemes.

Companies wishing to attract BES money may make **offers for sale** directly to the public (though this may not be worthwhile for a company limited to raising £0.5m), or arrange a placing for their shares. Some investors channel their money via a **BES fund**, where it is pooled with that of other investors and invested in a range of qualifying companies by professional managers. This indirect route provides the same tax relief. BES funds invite subscriptions from investors each year — normally keeping the subscription lists open for some weeks — then endeavour to invest the money in qualifying private company shares in time to reap the tax benefits.

Loan Guarantee Scheme

Another government initiative was aimed at helping small companies which had found it difficult to borrow money from normal banking sources, often because neither the company nor its founders could provide the **security** considered necessary for a loan. Most owners of small companies which want to borrow money are required to offer their houses and other assets as security for the debts of the business.

The scheme — the government **Loan Guarantee Scheme** or **LGS** — does not itself provide money for businesses but it removes part of the risk for traditional lenders. A bank can advance a loan of up to £100,000 to a business, secured on the assets of the business but without personal guarantees from the owners. The bank charges its normal interest rate plus a **premium** of two-and-a-half percentage points on the guaranteed portion of the loan, which goes to the government to provide the guarantee element. In return, 70 per cent (or 85 per cent in 16 Inner City Task Force Areas) of the value of the loan is covered by the **government guarantee**. If the business goes to the wall and the whole of the loan is lost, the government reimburses the lending bank 70 per cent of its advance.

The scheme has undoubtedly helped some businesses that would not otherwise have got off the ground. Its main disadvantage is that it supplies loan finance in circumstances where equity is often what is needed, with the result that the business becomes excessively high geared, which may hasten its demise. Failures among companies taking advantage of the scheme were high in the early years.

12

The gilt-edged market

The government needs an efficient market in its own longer-term debt: this is the part of the stockmarket known as the **gilt-edged market** which we touched on briefly in Chapter 1. The government's agent in this market is the Bank of England, which advises on debt issues and organizes the selling, servicing, purchase and redemption of government stocks; these stocks are created in the first instance by the Treasury. In 1988 the total **turnover of gilt-edged stocks** was £1,129 billion (over half representing trades between marketmakers) and the total value of all stocks listed was £140 billion.

New issues during the year totalled £7.25 billion, as new stocks were created to replace some of those that **matured**. However, thanks to the fact that the government's income exceeded its expenditure, in 1988 it found itself a net repayer of debt rather than a net borrower — a position that persisted in 1989. Therefore in 1988 the volume of gilt-edged stocks redeemed and bought in by the Bank, at £12.2 billion, exceeded the volume of new issues. During 1988 the Bank of England changed from being a net seller to a net buyer of gilts. Thus, during the year the size of the market reduced. The prospect of continuing government surpluses created the impression of a shortage of stocks for some long-term investors such as insurance companies.

The high turnover in the gilt-edged market relative to the value of the stocks listed partly reflects massive and frequent **switching** from one stock to another, when a particular stock appears to offer a small interest rate or tax advantage to a particular class of holder.

Press coverage of the gilt-edged market is far more restricted than equity market comment. Except for comment of a highly technical nature, there is far less to say. There are no takeover battles. There are no profit announcements affecting individual stocks. The news that moves the gilt-edged market is news of Britain's economic and financial outlook, boiled down to a view of likely movements in interest rates and inflation. Individual news items may affect one sector of the gilt-edged market more than another (see below) but comment on price movements in individual stocks is comparatively rare.

The press comment thus falls into three main categories. There are occasional pieces on the outlook for the fixed-interest market as a whole, usually sparked off by events that could mark a turning point. There are pieces on the Bank of England's intentions and techniques in its handling of the market. And there are the regular but brief daily reports of price movements of government stocks and the reasons for them, amplified where appropriate by news of new issues or the use of new techniques such as the reverse auction (see below).

News that moves prices

If you remember the basic mechanism described in Chapter 1 — interest rates go up, prices of fixed-interest stocks come down — and if you remember that higher interest rates are one way of supporting a weak currency, much of this comment falls into place. Weakness in sterling generally rattles the gilt-edged market because it is feared that interest rates may have to rise or stay high to defend the pound. Domestically, fears of higher **inflation**, caused by overheating in the economy, or excessive **earnings growth** bring fears of higher interest rates.

Remember that it is vital for investors to spot evidence of a change in expectations of inflation or interest rates. The **overall returns** can be very high for those who buy gilt-edged stocks just ahead of a major turning point when interest rates are about to move sharply down. When this happened in 1982, overall returns (income plus capital gains) for the year were over 50 per cent.

Technical influences on the market

The market is also affected by more **technical** factors. If a large amount of new stock is being brought to the market it may depress prices, because for a time the supply of stock will outpace investors' readiness to buy, though the Bank's methods of selling stock are intended to minimize the effect. More recently, the heavy flow of non-gilt sterling bond issues by companies and others have been a factor influencing market sentiment. One other technical aspect of the market is now frequently remarked: investors have the opportunity to take a bet on movements in gilt-edged prices by buying or selling **financial futures contracts** in gilt-edged securities (see Chapter 17). Price movements in the very sensitive **financial futures market** can thus herald trends in the gilt-edged market itself, often referred to as the **cash market** when contrasted with the **futures market**.

Types of security

To understand the more detailed comment, we need to look a little closer at the structure of the market.

While the terms **gilt-edged market** and **fixed-interest market** are sometimes used almost interchangeably, they are not always quite the same thing. Not all government stocks carry a fixed rate of interest, though the vast majority of them do. And not all fixed interest stocks are government stocks. There are loans issued by industrial and financial companies (**industrial loans, corporate loans** or **debentures**), loans issued by local government bodies (**corporation loans**) and loans issued in sterling by foreigners on the UK market (**bulldog bonds**). There are also the **convertible stocks** issued by companies, which were discussed in Chapter 5. Measured by the amount in issue, British government stocks predominate, but since 1988 the flow of new issues has been largely in the form of corporate bonds.

Most gilt-edged securities are **redeemable**: the government will repay the stock at some point, but there are a few that have no fixed date for repayment. The notorious **War Loan** is probably the most familiar of these **undated** or **irredeemable** stocks.

The life of a stock

The **dated** fixed-interest stocks are subdivided according to their **life** or **maturity**: how long they have to run until they are repaid. Those with a life of less than seven years (opinions vary — the *Financial Times* chooses five years) are classified as **shorts**, those with lives of seven to 15 years as **medium-dated** and stocks with more than 15 years to run as **longs**. These classifications reflect the current life of the stock, not its life when issued. A 25-year stock issued in 1976 would initially have been in the 'long' category, but by 1989 would have a remaining life of under 15 years and would be classified as a 'medium'. You will see how stocks are classified according to **redemption date** under the heading of 'British Funds' in the prices pages at the back of the *Financial Times*.

How prices are quoted

You will also see that prices quoted are mainly in a range between 40 and 120. Though the pound signs are omitted, these are the prices in pounds and fractions of pounds (usually 32nds) for a

BRITISH FUNDS

1989 High	Low	Stock	Price £	+ or –	Yield Int.	Red.
		"Shorts" (Lives up to Five Years)				
99$\frac{23}{32}$	98$\frac{11}{32}$	Exch.10pc 1989	99$\frac{23}{32}$xd	–	–	–
99$\frac{13}{16}$	98$\frac{3}{4}$	Exch 11pc 1989	99$\frac{11}{16}$	–$\frac{1}{32}$	11.07	13.34
98$\frac{1}{4}$	95$\frac{5}{8}$	Treas 5pc 1986–89	98$\frac{1}{4}$		5.10	11.91
99$\frac{1}{2}$	98$\frac{5}{8}$	Exch 10$\frac{1}{4}$pcCv '89	99		10.35	12.86
101$\frac{15}{16}$	99$\frac{11}{16}$	Treas 13pc 1990‡‡	100$\frac{9}{32}$xd	–$\frac{1}{32}$	12.96	12.36
130$\frac{1}{4}$	124	Treas 2pc IL '90(84.6)	130$\frac{1}{4}$xd	+$\frac{1}{16}$	2.09	9.98
99$\frac{31}{32}$	98$\frac{13}{16}$	Exch 11pc 1990‡‡	99$\frac{1}{16}$xd		11.09	12.57
101$\frac{7}{16}$	99$\frac{7}{8}$	Exch. 12$\frac{1}{4}$pc 1990	99$\frac{23}{32}$		12.52	12.71
94$\frac{1}{4}$	91$\frac{3}{8}$	Treas. 3pc 1990	94$\frac{1}{4}$		3.19	10.56
96$\frac{7}{8}$	95$\frac{3}{8}$	Treas 8$\frac{1}{4}$pc 1987–90‡‡	96$\frac{5}{16}$		8.57	12.59
98$\frac{13}{32}$	95$\frac{1}{4}$	Treas. 8pc Cv 1990 ‡‡	96$\frac{3}{4}$xd	–$\frac{1}{16}$	8.31	12.04
98$\frac{11}{16}$	96$\frac{3}{8}$	Treas. 10pcCv 1990	97$\frac{1}{16}$	–$\frac{1}{16}$	10.30	12.45
91$\frac{3}{8}$	87$\frac{13}{16}$	Exch 2$\frac{1}{2}$pc 1990	91$\frac{3}{16}$	+$\frac{1}{16}$	2.75	9.56
101$\frac{13}{32}$	98$\frac{11}{16}$	Treas 11$\frac{1}{4}$pc 1991	99$\frac{23}{32}$xd		11.82	12.16
92$\frac{3}{32}$	89$\frac{7}{8}$	Funding 5$\frac{3}{4}$pc '87–91‡‡	91$\frac{13}{16}$	+$\frac{1}{16}$	6.25	10.89
89$\frac{11}{16}$	86$\frac{1}{2}$	Treas. 3pc 1991	89$\frac{1}{16}$	+$\frac{1}{2}$	3.37	9.67
100$\frac{5}{16}$	95$\frac{13}{16}$	Treas 10pc Cv '91 ‡‡	96$\frac{5}{16}$xd	+$\frac{1}{16}$	10.37	12.04
101$\frac{7}{16}$	97$\frac{13}{16}$	Exch. 11pc 1991	98$\frac{1}{2}$	+$\frac{1}{32}$	11.18	11.79
94$\frac{1}{2}$	91$\frac{1}{16}$	Treas. 8pc 1991	92$\frac{5}{8}$	–$\frac{1}{32}$	8.67	11.73
106$\frac{7}{16}$	102$\frac{5}{16}$	Treas 12$\frac{3}{4}$pc 1992‡‡	103$\frac{3}{16}$xd	+$\frac{1}{4}$	12.38	11.36
99$\frac{1}{2}$	95$\frac{15}{32}$	Treas 10pc 1992	96$\frac{13}{16}$		10.33	11.42
94$\frac{3}{32}$	91	Treas. 8pc 1992 ‡‡	92$\frac{1}{8}$	+$\frac{1}{32}$	8.69	11.41
100$\frac{3}{4}$	96$\frac{23}{32}$	Treas 10$\frac{1}{2}$pc Cv 1992‡‡	98$\frac{1}{16}$	+$\frac{1}{32}$	10.72	11.35
85$\frac{3}{16}$	82$\frac{1}{4}$	Treas. 3pc 1992	83$\frac{9}{16}$	+$\frac{1}{16}$	3.59	9.56
105$\frac{13}{32}$	101$\frac{1}{4}$	Exch. 12$\frac{1}{4}$pc '92	102$\frac{13}{16}$	–$\frac{1}{16}$	11.96	11.29
109$\frac{3}{4}$	104$\frac{23}{32}$	Exch 13$\frac{1}{2}$pc 1992	106		12.74	11.20
94$\frac{9}{32}$	90$\frac{1}{2}$	Treas 8$\frac{1}{4}$pc 1993	91$\frac{11}{16}$	–$\frac{1}{32}$	9.01	11.12
100$\frac{7}{16}$	95$\frac{7}{8}$	Treas 10pc 1993‡‡	97$\frac{3}{32}$	–$\frac{1}{32}$	10.29	10.91
108$\frac{3}{4}$	103$\frac{11}{16}$	Treas 12$\frac{1}{2}$pc 1993‡‡	104$\frac{13}{16}$xd	–$\frac{1}{32}$	11.93	10.98
87$\frac{3}{4}$	84$\frac{1}{4}$	Funding 6pc 1993‡‡	85$\frac{1}{2}$	–$\frac{1}{16}$	7.01	10.29
113$\frac{1}{4}$	108$\frac{1}{4}$	Treas 13$\frac{3}{4}$pc 1993‡‡	109$\frac{11}{16}$		12.55	10.92
94$\frac{3}{8}$	89$\frac{3}{4}$	Treas. 8$\frac{1}{2}$pc 1994	91$\frac{23}{32}$xd	+$\frac{1}{32}$	9.28	10.87
117$\frac{23}{32}$	112$\frac{1}{16}$	Treas 14$\frac{1}{2}$pc 1994‡‡	113$\frac{13}{16}$	+$\frac{1}{32}$	12.77	10.89
113$\frac{11}{16}$	107$\frac{11}{16}$	Exch 13$\frac{1}{2}$pc 1994	109$\frac{7}{16}$		12.36	10.95
100$\frac{5}{8}$	95$\frac{15}{32}$	Treas. 10pc Ln. 1994‡‡	97$\frac{1}{8}$	+$\frac{1}{16}$	10.29	10.73
		Five to Fifteen Years				
110$\frac{1}{4}$	104$\frac{7}{16}$	Exch. 12$\frac{1}{2}$pc 1994	106$\frac{1}{4}$	+$\frac{1}{32}$	11.79	10.94
96$\frac{13}{16}$	91$\frac{3}{8}$	Treas 9pc 1994‡‡	93$\frac{5}{32}$	–$\frac{1}{32}$	9.67	10.71
108$\frac{11}{16}$	102$\frac{11}{16}$	Treas 12pc 1995	104$\frac{21}{32}$xd	+$\frac{1}{32}$	11.48	10.89
79$\frac{7}{8}$	74$\frac{1}{2}$	Exch 3pc Gas 90–95	76	+$\frac{1}{2}$	3.97	8.40

Table 12.1   Gilt-edged price information. Source: *Financial Times*.

nominal £100 of the stock. In practice they are **middle prices**, between the buying and selling prices that marketmakers normally quote. Prices and interest rates are, as we saw earlier, expressed in terms of this nominal £100 unit of stock, though it does not mean that buyers or sellers have to deal in round amounts of £100 nominal. But an 11 per cent stock pays £11 of interest on every £100 of nominal value and the stock is normally repaid at this £100 **nominal** or **par value** at redemption.

The range of coupons

The wide range of interest rates or **coupons** on the different stocks — ranging from under 3 per cent to over 15 per cent — gives some indication of the interest rate the government had to pay when they were first issued and hence the very large movements in interest rates over the years. It is not a perfect guide, since most stocks are issued slightly below their £100 **par value (at a discount)** and some used to be issued at a larger discount (see below) so that the yield to a buyer even at the outset was significantly different from the coupon rate.

The name is not important

You will also see from the *Financial Times* that stocks have somewhat curious names such as **Treasury**, **Exchequer** and **Funding**. Nowadays, 'Treasury' or 'Exchequer' is chosen as circumstances dictate to help identification if there are stocks of similar coupon maturing in the same year — 'Exchequer' is chosen if there is already a similar 'Treasury' stock. The word 'loan' in the title indicates that the stock can be held in bearer form. Regardless of the name, all the money raised goes into a central pool. What is important is the interest rate and the redemption date, which follow the name of the stock. Where two redemption dates are shown, the stock will not be redeemed before the first date and must be redeemed by the second. Thus, Exchequer 12 per cent '99-02 pays £12 a year on every £100 nominal of stock (carries a 12 per cent coupon) and is due to be repaid (at the government's option) at the earliest in 1999 and the latest in 2002. Treasury 9 per cent 1994 carries a 9 per cent coupon and will be repaid in 1994.

Calculating the interest yield

9 per cent is not the yield an investor in Treasury 9 per cent 1994 would have received if he had bought the stock early in 1989. The price of Treasury 9 per cent in mid-April 1989 was $93\frac{7}{8}$. Since the investor is only paying £$93\frac{7}{8}$ (or slightly above since the quoted price is a middle price) for this £100 of nominal value, he is getting £9 per year for an outlay of £$93\frac{7}{8}$ and the yield on his outlay is around 9.6 per cent. This is known as the **interest yield**, **income yield**, **flat yield** or the **running yield**. The sum to calculate a yield is simply:

$$\frac{\text{Interest rate (9)}}{\text{Market price } (93\frac{7}{8})} \times 100$$

What a redemption yield means

If Treasury 9 per cent were an **undated** stock, this would be the end of the matter. But it is to be repaid at its nominal £100 value in 1994. Thus a buyer in early 1989 could say to himself 'I'm paying just under £94 for a stock that will be repaid to me at £100 if I hang on to it till 1994. In other words, I'll see a £6 capital profit in 1994, in addition to the income I've been getting. This £6 is really part of the total return I'll get on the stock if I hold on to it. If I apportion the £6 over the five years the stock has to run, it works out at £1.20 a year. So notionally I'm getting an extra £1.20 per year for my outlay of £$93\frac{7}{8}$, which is about 1.3 per cent. This is my **gain to redemption**. If I add it to the 9.6 per cent yield I'm getting from the income, I have a notional combined yield of 10.9 per cent.'

In practice, an investor who did his sums this way would have grasped the general principle, but would be slightly wrong on the detail. To calculate the total return requires a compound interest sum and is best done with a computer programme. But he is right inasmuch as the *Financial Times* quotes two yields for each dated gilt-edged stock. First the **income yield**, then the **redemption yield**, which combines the interest yield with the notional **gain to redemption**. When Treasury 9 per cent 1994 at $93\frac{7}{8}$ was showing an income yield of 9.6 per cent it gave a redemption yield of about 10.5 per cent.

With **low coupon stocks**, possibly but not necessarily issued many years ago in periods of low interest rates, the difference between income yield and redemption yield will be greater. Take Treasury 3 per cent 1992. At $83\frac{9}{16}$ it offered an income yield of 3.6 per cent and a redemption yield of 9.17 per cent. But if the stock is standing above its par value of 100, the redemption yield will be lower than the income yield, because there will be a loss rather than a gain when the stock is repaid at 100. **Treasury 14 per cent '96**, for example, stood at $115\frac{3}{4}$ early in 1989 to yield 12.10 per cent on income and only 10.67 per cent to redemption.

How tax affects the returns

The difference between income yield and redemption yield is very important to investors, though slightly less so than when the highest income tax rates were well above 1989's 40 per cent. For capital gains on gilt-edged stocks are tax free. So a high-tax-paying investor might keep only 60p for every pound of income a stock provided him with, but he would keep the whole of every pound he received by way of capital gain. Look again at Treasury 3 per cent 1992 and see what the return is to an investor paying the top tax rate. He is getting 3.6 per cent of income and a notional 5.57 per cent of capital gain to provide the combined 9.17 per cent redemption yield. Tax affects the sums as follows:

	What the investor gets	
	Gross	Net of 40% tax
Income yield	3.60%	2.16%
Gain to redemption	5.57%	5.57% (no tax)
Total return	9.17%	7.73%

So the **net return** is 7.73 per cent. The higher-rate taxpayer would have needed a **gross income yield** of just under 13 per cent to give him the same net return if the whole of it was taxed. Look at the Treasury 9 per cent 1994 we examined earlier and do the same sums:

	What the investor gets	
	Gross	Net of 40% tax
Income yield	9.60%	5.76%
Gain to redemption	0.90%	0.90% (no tax)
Total return	10.50%	6.66%

Though this stock offers a gross redemption yield of 10.5 per cent against only 9.17 per cent for the Treasury 3 per cent, it actually provides a lower net income for the high-rate taxpayer because more of the income comes in the form of highly taxed interest and less in the form of capital gain. It was quite common in the past for the government to issue low-coupon stocks at a substantial discount specifically to appeal to high tax payers. However, with the reduction in top income tax rates and with a technical change in the tax treatment of deep-discounted issues in the 1989 Budget, we may not see this type of issue in future.

Remember that redemption yields of any kind are, to an extent, notional. The redemption yield is relevant to the investor if he **holds the stock to redemption**. In the interim its price will be determined by the interplay of buyers and sellers, though on balance it will obviously move closer to 100 as the redemption date approaches. This is known as the **pull to redemption**.

The examples underline an important aspect of the gilt-edged market. No one government stock is quite like another. Different stocks are worth different amounts to different classes of investor.

Cum-dividend and ex-dividend

Interest on gilt-edged securities is paid twice a year. So between dividend payments it is **accruing** — building up — until the moment it is paid. Prices for gilts are now quoted **clean** (they exclude **accrued income**). But a buyer normally pays for (and receives the right to) any income that has accrued since the last dividend date, in addition to the price he pays for the stock itself. However, if he buys it once the stock has gone **ex-dividend** (see Chapter 4), the seller keeps the right to the forthcoming interest payment. Yields on gilt-edged stocks are always calculated on **clean prices**. If the tax laws permitted, it would benefit a higher-rate taxpayer to buy a stock just after it had gone ex-dividend and sell it shortly before the next dividend payment was due. In this way he receives no income, on which high rates of tax would be payable, but receives the benefit in the form of untaxed capital gain.

This practice, known as **dividend stripping,** has now been outlawed and the interest is normally taxed as income whether in fact it is received as interest or as capital gain. However, an exception is made for investors whose gilt-edged holdings total less than £5,000 at nominal values. These are taxed on an 'income received' basis.

Influence of the redemption date

The other important point the example demonstrates is the influence of the **redemption date**. If you are betting on a general reduction in interest rates in Britain and therefore expect the market price of fixed-interest stocks to rise (see Chapter 1), you would generally buy a **long-dated** or **undated** stock. Their prices will generally move most for a given change in interest rate expectations. If you want to limit your exposure to movements in interest rates as far as possible, you would buy a **short-dated** stock. The reason for this is the **pull to redemption**. When a stock is due to be repaid at £100 in the fairly near future, redemption is the dominant influence and its price will not fluctuate so widely in response to movements in interest rates. However, short-term interest rates can nowadays fluctuate very widely (perhaps by more than long yields), and since these affect short-dated stocks more than the long-dated ones, the price fluctuations can still be quite marked even at the **short end** of the market. Market reports will often highlight the different magnitude of price movements at the long and short end of the market. Investors switch between stocks of different maturities according to the way they expect long-term and short-term interest rates to move.

Index-linked stocks

So far we've been talking of fixed-interest stocks. But there are, and have been, other types of government stock. **Variable-rate** stocks, with the interest rate changing in line with interest rates elsewhere in the financial system, have been tried but did not prove popular, though they are more widely used by borrowers in the **eurobond market** (see Chapter 16). However, **index-linked stocks**, which provide protection against inflation (act as an **inflation hedge**), soon caught on. They were initially introduced in 1981 for the pension funds, then made available to any type of investor.

With an **index-linked stock**, both the income and the price at which it will be repaid at the end of the day are adjusted to take account of the movement in **retail prices**. In other words, both income and capital retain their **real value**. The price you pay for this protection is a much lower nominal coupon rate. Say an index-linked stock is issued at its par value of 100, with a coupon of 2.5 per cent. Over the next five years, retail prices rise by 30 per cent in total, meaning that it would cost you £130 to buy goods and services you could have obtained for £100 five years earlier. So the price at which the stock will be redeemed rises to 130. The interest it pays must also rise by 30 per cent to maintain a real interest rate of 2.5 per cent. So the interest rate after five years will be 2.5 per cent on the new £130 redemption value (equivalent to 3.25 per cent on the original £100 nominal value).

Of course, if retail prices were to fall in year six, the redemption value could be adjusted down again from 130 and so could the interest. But in the more likely event that retail prices continue rising (though at different rates in different climates) the redemption value of the stock will continue to rise.

In practice, the redemption value of an index-linked stock does not match the movement in retail prices (as measured by the **retail prices index**) quite as closely as in the example because there is a time lag of eight months built in so that the size of the dividend is known before the start of the interest period. The *Financial Times* quotes two possible real redemption yields, one on the assumption of 5 per cent inflation and the other on the assumption of 10 per cent. The *Financial Times* also shows (in brackets after the name of each index-linked stock) the **base date** for the indexation sum.

The market price of the index-linked stock is, as with a fixed-interest stock, not directly determined by the redemption value, though this will begin to exert more influence as redemption comes close. Real redemption yields are low (in the 3.5 to 3.75 per cent range early in 1989) partially reflecting the fact that most of the return comes in the form of untaxed capital appreciation. Index-linked stocks are not at their most attractive when **real rates of return** on conventional gilt-edged are high: in other words, when the nominal yields are well above the inflation rate. Index-linked stocks are more popular when inflation fears rise.

'...attention was diverted to the index-linked sector. Election and inflation possibilities, which received a good deal of publicity in the weekend press, touched off renewed hedge buying....'
(*Financial Times*, 17 February 1987)

Indexes for government stocks

Price movements in the fixed interest market are measured on a number of indexes. Separate **Financial Times-Actuaries indexes** are published for **short, medium** and **long-dated stocks** as well as for the **irredeemables,** for **index-linked stocks** and for **industrial debentures**. There is also an **All Stocks Index** for gilt-edged as a whole. The *Financial Times* also publishes its own longer-established **Government Securities Index** with a base of 100 in 1926. Market reports talk of price movements of a **point** or fraction of a point in individual stocks: a point in this context is one pound per £100 nominal.

New issues and dealing mechanisms

The mechanics of issue and subsequent dealing for gilt-edged stocks have, as with equities, undergone some changes with the Big Bang. Traditionally, when a **public offering of stock** is made, a minimum price is usually set and **tenders** are invited at or above that figure. All accepted bidders at tender pay a common price. The price might be due as a single payment, or payment might be made in instalments (see Chapter 8 for a description of **partly-paid stocks** in the equity market, where the procedure is similar).

Stock that does not find buyers at a tender is placed with the Issue Department of the Bank and subsequently made available to the market as and when there is a demand for it and when it suits the authorities to make further sales. Stock available for issue in this way is described as a **tap stock** because the supply can be turned on and off as required. A second source of stock that can be used as a **tap** is small **tranchettes** of stock — possibly of a range of different stocks — which are issued to the Bank and thus available for sale to the market in the same way. Sales of tap stocks to the market are made via the Bank's dealing room.

> 'The Bank of England's tender offer of £1 billion of new gilt-edged stock drew a lukewarm reception in the market yesterday, with only a small proportion of the issue taken by primary dealers and investors. Most of the issue of 10 per cent Treasury loan 1994 was left in the hands of the Bank of England to be operated as a tap stock.' (*Financial Times*, 8 January 1987).

The third method of marketing gilt-edged stocks is new. In 1987 the Bank introduced an experimental series of **auctions** for selling large amounts of stock as a supplement to the tender method. The main difference between the auction and the tender is the implication, in the auction method, that there is the intention to sell all the stock on offer. Also, competitive bidders are allocated stock at the price at which they bid, rather than at a common **striking price** as in a tender (see Chapter 8 for a description of the tender mechanism). But for small bids the facility exists for stock to be allocated non-competitively at the average of the accepted competitive bids.

New stocks are created to satisfy the government's financing needs and the market's need for a balance of short, medium and long dates and index-linked stocks. However, with the government becoming a net repurchaser of stock in 1988 and 1989, shortages of certain kinds of stock have begun to emerge, particularly at the long end of the market. As part of the repurchase programme the Bank of England has insituted **reverse auctions** under which holders can offer to sell stock back to the authorities, who accept the stock offered at the most favourable price. As with the ordinary auction, facilities also exist for small offers of stock.

Before Big Bang, gilt-edged stocks — once issued — were traded on the stockmarket via the **jobber/broker mechanism** as with equities. Under the new order the **marketmaking function** is undertaken by a new breed of **primary dealers** known as **gilt-edged marketmakers**. They include former gilt jobbing and broking firms but also offshoots of banks and other financial institutions including a number of American and Japanese firms. These primary dealers — there were 27 of them immediately after the Big Bang, though there have been some departures and new entrants since then — have an obligation to maintain a market in all government stocks and have the right to deal direct with the Bank of England. They can bid for available tap stocks when required.

> 'Government bonds started well, and the authorities took the opportunity to sell more of the 1994 tap stock issued last week. This checked the market's advance....' (*Financial Times*, 13 January 1987).

The new market mechanism is eased by **inter-dealer brokers**, via whom the gilt-edged marketmakers can effectively deal with each other without disclosing their positions to their competitors. The primary dealers have access to a **price information system** via the

SEAQ screens, but this is more rudimentary than the SEAQ equity service and they rely more heavily on screen-based price information supplied by the inter-dealer brokers. In order to cover their short positions, marketmakers can also borrow (rather than buy) stock from **Stock Exchange money brokers**, who have increased in number since Big Bang.

Dealing in gilt-edged stock is for **cash settlement** (payment the next day), and major institutional investors are likely to deal direct at **net prices** with a primary dealer rather than going through an **agency broker**. Small private investors will go through a broker as before (though **commissions** are lower than on equities) or can buy through the National Savings Stock Register (see below).

However, the new more competitive gilt-edged marketmaking system has not brought unalloyed joy for the primary dealers, a few of whom have already abandoned the market. In the two years or so after the Big Bang their cumulative losses totalled £190m — almost one third of the total capital with which the post-Big Bang gilt marketmakers started business.

Post Office Register

The public also has an opportunity to buy certain gilt-edged stocks without going through a broker at all. A selection of stocks is included on the **National Savings Stock Register** and these can be bought through a Post Office. The cost will be less than the commission payable if you go via a broker, though transactions take longer and the price at which you buy will not necessarily be that ruling at the moment you apply. Stocks bought through the Post Office Register also pay interest **gross**, whereas interest on government stocks is normally paid **net** of basic rate tax to UK investors, as with the dividend on a share. But those who are liable still have to pay the tax at the end of the day.

Corporate bond market

The shortage of long-dated gilt-edged stocks, which began to emerge in 1988 and 1989 as a result of the authorities' repurchase programme, has had implications for the market in companies' long-term IOUs — the corporate debt market. During the 1970s British companies had issued relatively little long-term debt because they were worried about committing themselves to high interest rates for 25 or 30 years.

However, the shortage of long-dated gilts forced interest rates down at this end of the market, reinforcing an existing revival in debt issues by companies and increasing companies' willingness to issue long-dated fixed-interest **industrial debentures** or **corporate bonds**. These work in a similar way to government stocks, though they do not carry quite the same degree of security and must therefore offer somewhat higher yields. They have found ready buyers among insurance companies and other traditional purchasers of government stocks. Other company bond issues have been made in the form of fixed-interest sterling eurobonds. In practice, in the case of sterling bonds, many of the differences in issue and trading techniques between the domestic stockmarket and the euromarkets have now broken down. Dealers tend to talk of the two markets almost interchangeably (see Chapter 16).

13

Banks, borrowers and bad debts

Banks occupy a special place in the economic and financial system. Industrial companies may be allowed to go to the wall or come under the control of foreigners. Banks are normally viewed with a more protective eye by the authorities.

Why? First, there are not many aspects of economic life that can function without a stable banking system. Secondly, banking is a business that depends on confidence. Allow the confidence to be destroyed and you are a fair way to destroying the banks. Thirdly, banks play a vital role in the creation of money: something that governments like to keep within their control.

Deposits, advances and liquid funds

The best way to understand what is written about banking is to start by looking at what a bank is. At its simplest, a bank takes **retail deposits** from private individuals and others and lends money (makes **advances**) to borrowers. A certain proportion of the money it takes in as deposits is held in **liquid** or **near-liquid** form: as cash or in a form in which it can readily be turned into cash. This is a safeguard in case **depositors** want their money back. Another proportion will normally be held in the form of investments which are a little less liquid. The remainder can be lent to customers.

Borrowed money and shareholders' money

The detail may vary, but the principle is much the same for most **deposit-taking institutions**, including **building societies** which are really just a specialist form of bank whose business in the past has been to lend almost exclusively to homebuyers. In practice, banks are not completely dependent on retail deposits because they also borrow **wholesale funds** in the money markets, which add to the money they have available to lend.

Like any company, a bank needs some money of its own — shareholders' funds — as well as the borrowed money it obtains from depositors. But banks are very much more **highly geared** than most industrial and commercial companies. They use a lot of borrowed money and relatively little of their own. Let us see how this structure translates into a (simplified) bank balance sheet:

ASSETS

Liquid assets	£100
Investments	£250
Loans to customers (Advances)	£750
	£1,100

Financed by:	
Current and deposit accounts	£1,000
Share capital and reserves (shareholders' funds)	£100
	£1,100

The bank in this example has only £100 of its own money against £1,000 of borrowed money from depositors. Its total resources are thus £1,100. It holds £100 (equivalent to 10 per cent of its deposits) in liquid form, a further £250 as investments and lends the remaining £750.

The money creation process

How do banks create money? Assume that the bank in our example attracts a further £100 of deposits. It will hold £10 of this as cash and lend the remaining £90. The customer who borrows the £90 spends it on, say, a piece of office equipment. He pays the £90 to the office equipment supplier, who deposits it in his own bank. This increases the deposits of the supplier's bank by £90 of which the bank will lend £81, holding back £9 in cash form for safety. And so on. Since the money finds its way back into the banking system at each stage, that original £100 of extra deposits in the first bank actually generates — in this case — a further £1,000 of spending power in the economy.

If the proportion of their deposits that banks held in liquid form were lower (8 per cent, say) each additional £100 of deposits would create proportionately more spending power. One of the ways central banks sometimes try to control expansion of the **money supply** (see below) is by varying the permissible ratio between deposits and the amount held as **reserve assets**, which covers cash and certain other near-cash items (**reserve assets ratio**), though this system is no longer used by the Bank of England.

The most commonly quoted measures of money supply in the press in Britain are M_0 ('M nought'), which comprises notes and coins in circulation plus banks' balances at the Bank of England. The broader M_3 measure covers notes and coins plus private sector current and deposit accounts with the banks.

A bank works on the principle that no more than a small proportion of depositors will want their money back at any one time and this calculation affects the proportion of deposits held in liquid form (the **liquidity ratio**). And a glance back at the simplified bank balance sheet shows the main ways a bank can get into trouble. If depositors suddenly lose confidence in a particular bank, they may all try to get their money back at the same time and a **run on the bank** develops. The bank will not be able to get back rapidly the money it has advanced to customers and if it runs out of cash it may be forced to close its doors.

Whatever his problems, a banker is virtually obliged to maintain that his bank is totally sound until he is forced to close the doors. Any admission of difficulties will worry depositors and make them more likely to withdraw their money. So statements from bankers that everything in the garden is rosy must be treated with a large dose of salt. It may be true, but the banker would be equally obliged to say it if it wasn't.

Rescues, recycling and lifeboats

To prevent a run if the bank is basically sound, the central bank will often organize a **recycling** operation. Banks which are not under any pressure from depositors will be persuaded to make deposits with the troubled bank to replace its vanishing deposits from the public. Such a rescue for third-tier money-lending institutions — euphemistically referred to as **secondary banks** — was organized in the 1973-75 period of **financial crisis** or **secondary bank collapse** in Britain. The clearing banks were dragooned into forming a **lifeboat** via which they made money available to secondary banks which had seen their normal deposits melt away.

Capital adequacy requirements

In reality, most of the secondary banks were not sound — their liabilities (what they owed) exceeded the real value of their assets (the money they had lent, much of which they lost). And this brings us to the second way a bank gets into trouble. The bank in our sample balance sheet could not lose more than £100 of the money it has lent without becoming insolvent. If it loses £100 of its £750 of advances, this completely wipes out the £100 of shareholders' money in the business. Any further losses and it will not be able to cover what it owes to depositors.

Again, a banker has to judge what 'cushion' of shareholders' money he needs to allow for any likely losses on loans he has made. And the central bank normally makes doubly sure by imposing certain **capital adequacy ratios** which stipulate the amount of its own money a bank needs relative to its total assets. This **capital ratio** or **solvency ratio** is not a simple calculation: the Bank of England will look at the make-up of a bank's business and decide that the risks that need to be covered are higher for some types of business than others. And it will take into account some **off balance sheet risks** that do not appear in the accounts: forms of **guarantee** and **underwriting commitment** the bank may have undertaken. Nor are shareholders' funds the exact measure of the bank's own money that the authorities adopt — in calculating its **capital base** to arrive at a figure for **primary capital** a bank may be able to include certain **subordinated loans** (see glossary) but will have to make deductions for other items. A **risk asset ratio** shows primary capital as a proportion of risk-weighted assets. Capital ratios are part of what are normally described as **prudential ratios**: ratios dictated by banking prudence rather than by the central bank's need to control the money supply via the banking system.

The Third World debt crisis

Prudential ratios lead us into the burning issue of international banking in the 1980s: the problem of **Third World debt** of which the **Latin American debt crisis** is the most visible manifestation. Aspects of the debt crisis are likely to surface regularly in the financial pages for some years to come.

In the 1970s the major commercial banks, particularly in the United States, drew in deposits from oil producing countries which had generated massive revenue surpluses from the oil price increases of that decade. Much of the money was lent to Third World countries — **less developed countries** or **LDCs** in the common banking euphemism — which seemed good business at the time. The total debt of the Third World was put in the mid-1980s at over $1,000 billion. For a variety of reasons — including high interest rates and low prices for basic commodities — many of these borrowers found themselves unable to **service** their loans (meet interest charges and capital repayments).

The outcome was an excellent illustration of the old banking adage that you are at your banker's mercy if you owe him £5 and he is at your mercy if you owe him £5m. A game of poker — for somewhat larger sums — ensued. If the banks admitted they would not get their money back and wrote off their loans, they would be shown to be insolvent or at least they would fail the capital adequacy tests. So they attempted to maintain the fiction that the loans were sound. To do so they frequently arranged a **rescheduling** of the original loans. At best this meant extending the terms of the loan to give the debtor countries more time to pay. At worst it meant lending them more money (which they were unlikely to be able to repay) to meet the instalments of capital and interest (which they could not otherwise pay) on the original loans. Without rescheduling, the debtor countries would be forced to **default** on the loans (fail to keep to the terms) and the lending banks would then be forced to classify the loans as **nonperforming** in the American terminology.

The debtor countries in their turn had a difficult choice. If they simply defaulted, they would find it difficult to borrow again in the international capital markets. But the threat of default was a powerful weapon in bargaining with the lending banks.

The game of make-believe that rescheduling made possible was somewhat disrupted in May 1987 when Citicorp, one of the major

American lenders, announced a $3 billion **provision** or **reserve** against its Third World loans. This meant it was not writing down the value of specific loans but was accepting that it stood to lose at least $3 billion of its Third World lending. Citicorp could afford to make the provision but it posed problems for some other lenders with less capital who were forced by Citicorp's action to acknowledge realities. The major British banks made similar provisions in due course. The banking emperors were not seen entirely without clothes, but were left looking distinctly chilly in their underpants. They will almost certainly have to write off further large amounts before the debt crisis is resolved.

Banking supervision in Britain

For the first half of the 1980s, banking institutions in Britain (with the main exception of building societies which had their own regulatory structure) divided between banks and **licensed deposit takers** or **LDTs,** which comprised mainly the less established or second-tier concerns. The distinction was abolished by a new **Banking Act** in 1987 which allowed all but the smallest deposit-taking institutions to call themselves banks provided they satisfied prudential requirements as to the way the business was run. A **Board of Banking Supervision** took on the supervisory role, adding some outside representatives to the Bank of England's traditional supervisors.

14

The money markets

Money market reports are an acquired taste. Few readers who are not in the money business will come completely to grips with their technicalities. But when the **money markets** are giving an important signal about likely trends in **interest rates**, a less technical interpretation of what is going on will probably appear elsewhere in the financial pages.

Money markets are the responsibility of the **Bank of England**. The Bank is **lender of last resort** to the banking system. The level

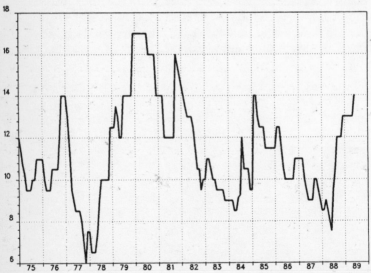

Figure 14.1   Volatile bank base rates. The very high rates of the early Thatcher years contributed to the over-valuation of sterling in the early 1980s. Source: *Datastream International*.

at which it is prepared to lend, and the terms, can be used to influence the level of interest rates across the economy.

Both in money markets and in the **foreign exchange market**, which also comes under the aegis of the Bank of England, a curious guessing game is under way much of the time between the Bank and the market professionals. Echoes of this emerge in the press reports which refer frequently to the various forms of subtle signal the Bank gives to indicate how it might like interest rates to move or not to move — in addition to the very specific **signals** which are given at other times.

Why the subtlety? In theory, interest rates nowadays are determined by market forces with the Bank occasionally giving guidance. But where the Bank does have a clear view of how far and when it considers interest rates should change, it needs to play its cards close to its chest, otherwise it is offering a one-way bet to the market. If the professionals know in advance how rates are going to move, they can buy or sell as appropriate, with an assured profit on the operation.

Functions of the money markets

Why are money markets needed? They are a form of short-term counterpart to the long-term investment markets of The Stock Exchange. The Stock Exchange funnels long-term savings into long-term investment. The money markets allow money which is available for shorter periods to be directed to those who can use it, and also have the virtue of transmuting very short-term deposits into money which can be lent for longer periods. Despite their name they are not just a market in deposits but also in a variety of forms of short-term IOU or **financial instrument** which are close to money because they can be turned quickly into money. We will look at these later.

The money markets fulfill several functions. First, at any one time there will be some banks which have a very temporary shortage of money and others which have a surplus: money has been withdrawn from one bank and deposited with another. A mechanism is needed so that banks which are temporarily short can borrow the funds they need, and those with a temporary surplus can put it to work.

Secondly, banks will in any case want to hold a proportion of their funds in a form which allows them to get at it quickly if

171

needed. This means putting it on deposit with other institutions or buying short-term financial instruments. Thirdly, while banks derive a large proportion of their sterling funds from the accounts of individual depositors (**retail deposits**), they also borrow in very large amounts from companies, financial institutions and local government bodies which have short-term surpluses of cash to put to work (**wholesale funds**). Likewise, these bodies borrow in the money markets when short of cash.

Finally, a mechanism is needed to iron out imbalances in the supply of money between the **banking system** as a whole and the government. There will be times when the commercial banking system is short of money because, for example, individuals or companies are withdrawing funds from their bank accounts to pay their tax bills to the government. But the government can also influence the amount of money available by buying securities from or selling them to the **non-bank private sector**: to individuals and organizations other than banking institutions or government bodies.

These **open market operations** can create a shortage of money in the banking system. For example, when the Government was still a net borrower, it would issue gilt-edged stock to the public via the Bank of England. To pay for, say, £500m of stock the public would have to withdraw £500m from its deposits with the banking system. Therefore this money would leave the commercial banks and be paid to the government. All else being equal, a shortage of cash would be created in the banking system which the Bank could use to increase its influence on the commercial banks.

The money markets provide mechanisms to cope with all these differing requirements. They fall into two main parts (we are talking now of the sterling money markets — a market in foreign currency deposits exists alongside them). There is the traditional **discount market** and there are the **parallel money markets**, of which the main constituent is also known as the **inter-bank market**.

The discount market

Although comparable arrangements can be found elsewhere, the **discount houses** are uniquely British institutions which act as a buffer between the Bank of England and the commercial banks. In practice, they operate as specialist banks which make a living by borrowing surplus short-term money from the commercial banks and using it to buy **financial instruments** such as **Treasury bills,** commercial **bills of exchange** and **sterling certificates of deposit** (these are all forms of short-term IOU which we look at later).

The money the commercial banks lend to the discount houses is **at call**. In other words, the banks can ask to have it back when they need it. This could pose a problem for the discount houses if they have already used the money to invest in bills of exchange. So the Bank of England steps in. When the discount houses are short of cash they have the right to sell bills of exchange, Treasury bills and local authority bills to the Bank (**rediscount** them with — sell them at a discount to — the Bank). This amounts to lending by the Bank to the discount houses and provides them with the cash they need. Until recently, this facility was only available to eight discount houses. In 1988 the Bank opened the way for other institutions to enter the discount market and enjoy the same facilities. The newcomers could take the form of traditional discount houses or, alternatively, gilt-edged marketmakers would be permitted to apply to extend their activities to include a money market dealing relationship with the Bank.

The Bank of England does not now normally publish in advance the rates of discount at which it will buy bills of exchange from the discount houses, though it has the power to do so. Traditionally the Bank used to publish its lending rate as **Bank Rate** and subsequently in a rather different form as **Minimum Lending Rate** or **MLR**, which can still be invoked if needed to underline the Bank's wishes on interest rates. But now that interest rates are meant to be determined by the balance of borrowers and lenders in the market, most of the time the Bank will intervene in the money markets to iron out imbalances between the commercial banking system and the government without pushing interest rates decisively one way or another.

Each working day the Bank of England estimates first thing in the morning the likely size of the shortage or surplus in the money market on that day (a **shortage** is the amount by which the commercial banking system is likely to be short of money and will therefore have to borrow from the government) and may revise this estimate at midday and again at 2 p.m. if necessary. Its estimates go out on the Reuters and Telerate screen information systems. It also publishes during the day the details of how it dealt with the shortage. It may have bought bills of exchange from the discount houses (these are listed in four different **bands**, according to their maturity date). It may have lent money to the discount houses. It may have entered into arrangements to buy securities and sell them back later (**repurchase agreements** or **repos**) which act as a short-term loan. These details are usually reproduced in the press's technical money market reports, which make rather dry reading except at times when the Bank of England is positively influencing interest rates.

An example illustrates this mechanism at work. Towards the end of February 1987, good economic news in Britain and the feeling that interest rates would not need to be kept high to support the pound pointed to a reduction in rates. But the Bank of England clearly did not yet want to see rates drop, possibly because there was political pressure to try and delay a fall to coincide with the Budget on 17 March.

At this point in February the major commercial banks were quoting **base rates** of 11 per cent. Base rate is the rate to which they gear the interest they pay to retail depositors and the rate they charge for overdrafts and personal loans, and is the most commonly quoted yardstick for interest rates on personal or small business borrowing (LIBOR — see below — is the more popular yardstick for larger-scale borrowings). There was pressure for base rates to come down. Since there was a shortage in the market, the discount houses were forced to borrow from the Bank of England. But they were not prepared to do so by selling bills of exchange to the Bank of England in any quantity because they felt the Bank was offering too low a price (in other words, charging too high an interest rate: see below). So instead the houses were invited in a public announcement to borrow from the Bank at rates and on terms which were also made public. The Bank charged them a then penally high interest rate of 11.5 per cent on seven-day loans, thus influencing interest rates throughout the system and making it clear the Bank did not want them to come down yet.

Reporting these events on Friday 20 February the *Financial Times* headed its money market report 'Bank resists cut' and explained:

> 'The Bank of England gave its message that the market is pushing too hard for an immediate cut in base rates by inviting the discount houses to borrow funds to relieve nearly all of yesterday's credit

shortage, and setting the interest rate at a level to underpin the present rate structure. This followed the reluctance of the market to sell bills to the authorities at the present intervention rates.'

Bills of exchange

The discount houses got their name because they **discount** bills of exchange: they buy them at a discount to their face value. To see how this market works we need to examine the mechanism more closely.

Bills of exchange are a form of short-term IOU widely used to finance trade and provide credit. The work like this. Company A sells £1m worth of goods to Company B. It 'draws' (writes out) a bill of exchange for £1m which it sends to Company B. This bill is an acknowledgement by Company B that it owes the £1m, and Company B signs it to show that it accepts the debt. The bill may state that the money is not payable until some date in the future: perhaps in three months. The bill returns to Company A.

Company A then has a choice. It can hold on to the bill, in which case Company B will pay it the £1m in three months. Or, if it needs the cash sooner, it can sell the bill to somebody else. Whoever holds the bill when the three months are up gets the £1m from Company B.

Bills of exchange do not pay interest. But if Company A sells the bill before it is due for payment, it will receive less than face value. In other words, it **sells at a discount**. So if the bill is due for payment in, say, three months, the buyer might pay only £97.50 for every £100 of face value. The buyer is thus getting a profit of £2.50 per £100 when the bill is repaid at face value, which is equivalent to receiving interest and the discount is usually expressed as an annual rate of interest. When the Bank of England is said to have bought bills at $10\frac{3}{4}$ per cent, it means that the Bank bought them at a discount to their face value. Thus if interest rates generally come down, the prices of bills will rise (the discount will be smaller). This is why discount houses may be reluctant to sell them when they think interest rates should come down.

The bill described above is a **trade bill**, issued by one company to another. But a bill may be **accepted** by a bank, in which case it becomes a **bank bill**. By putting its name on the bill, the bank agrees it will pay the amount of the bill on maturity, even if the company which acknowledged the debt should default: it is therefore a form of guarantee. Accepting bills in this way was an important part of the business of the merchant banks in the past, hence the term **accepting houses** for the top-tier merchant banks. A bill accepted by a bank, because of the security it offers, sells at the very lowest interest rates. Any monetary sector institution can accept bills, but the Bank of England only buys or lends against bills accepted by **eligible banks**, hence the term **eligible bills**. The Bank maintains a published list of eligible banks; in general these are banks which have a substantial and broadly-based sterling acceptance business.

Bank bills also provide a substitute for overdrafts in big company financing. A company arranges an **acceptance credit** with a bank, which allows it to issue bills up to an agreed limit. Each bill is accepted by the bank in return for a fee and can be sold at a discount to raise cash for the company. The effective rate of interest may be lower than on other forms of borrowing.

Treasury bills

Treasury bills work in much the same way as commercial bills of exchange, but are issued by the government as a method of raising short-term money. They are sold at a discount, with an implicit rate of interest. In recent years the amounts raised this way have been comparatively small. Each Friday the discount houses, banks and others **tender** for the bills on offer — the discount houses are obliged to tender for the lot, so that the government is sure of getting its money even if others do not tender. The *Financial Times's* money market report on a Saturday will give the results of the tender: the amount of money tendered and the lowest price at which tenders were accepted. The Treasury bills allocated are taken up over the following week.

A recent innovation is for the government to make regular monthly issues of Treasury bills denominated in **ECU** (the **European Currency Unit**). The main purpose of this programme is to assist with the management of the UK's foreign exchange reserves. At the same time it will encourage the development in Britain of a market in ECU-denominated instruments.

Certificates of deposit

Certificates of deposit (CDs) are a method of **securitizing** bank deposits. A company with spare cash deposits £500,000 with a bank. It agrees to lock the money away for a year, thus getting the best interest rate. The bank issues the company with a certificate of deposit for the £500,000, stating the rate of interest payable and the date when the deposit will be repaid. If the company needs its cash before the year is up, it can sell the certificate of deposit in the money market. The buyer acquires the right to receive repayment of the £500,000 bank deposit (plus interest) when the year is up. The discount houses make a market in certificates of deposit and hold them as investments alongside bills of exchange.

The virtue of the certificate of deposit is that the bank (in our example) has acquired a deposit for a year and knows it will have a year's use of the money. But the company which lent for a year and received the CD can in practice have its money back at any time by selling the CD.

The parallel money markets

We started with the discount market because it illustrates how the Bank of England can influence interest rates. But banks wanting to borrow and lend money in the wholesale markets are not confined to dealing with the discount houses. They also operate in the **parallel money markets** — the markets in which banks, local authorities, institutions and companies can borrow from or lend to each other without going through the discount house mechanism. The most important of these markets is the **inter-bank market**, where banks and others deal with each other, often through a money broker who puts the parties together in return for a commission. The market divides further into the sterling inter-bank market and the inter-bank market in foreign currencies, particularly the dollar.

There has been enormous expansion in the use made of the money markets by large companies in recent years. And the 1989 Budget introduced changes which will help to break down the distinction between money markets and the established debt securities markets (Stock Exchange and euromarket) by allowing the issue of commercial paper with a life of up to 5 years. Thus a company wishing to borrow for five years should in future have the choice of following the securities market route or the money market route. Whereas the securities markets are open to private investors, the wholesale money markets are very definitely a 'professionals only' area.

Commercial paper market

Commercial paper is an example of the **securitization** process. For companies it offers an alternative to bank borrowing or to an existing form of short-term security: the bill of exchange.

In essence, commercial paper is just another form of unsecured short term IOU, issued in bearer form. It is normally issued at a discount rather than paying interest. Until the 1989 Budget changes mentioned above, issues were only permitted with a maturity of up to a year. In Britain the average life of commercial paper has been close to 40 days hitherto.

The sterling commercial paper market got under way in London in May 1986 and initially was open only to very large established companies. These conditions, too, were relaxed in the 1989 Budget, opening the way for medium-sized companies to tap the market.

The issue process goes as follows. A company wanting to tap the market gets a bank to set up a programme for it: say, £200m. This defines the maximum amount that the company may have outstanding at any one time. At the same time **dealers** are appointed. When the company wants to raise cash it alerts the dealers, or the dealers may take the initiative by telling the company that there is demand among investors for paper of a particular maturity. The dealers, who are constantly in touch with potential investors, find buyers for the paper. The paper is sold at a discount to its face value which provides the equivalent of a rate of interest. The buyers may be institutions or companies looking for a short-term investment

When the original issue falls due for repayment, further issues can be made to replace it. Thus, though it is a very short-term market, by **rolling over** issues in this way companies may use it as a medium-term source of finance.

Multiple option facility

The **multiple option facility** or **MOF** is another recent form of arrangement for tapping the money markets. It can emerge in various shapes but a typical arrangement might be as follows.

A company gets one particular bank to put together a panel of banks who agree to make available a certain amount of loans — say £150m — for a period of five years. The rate of interest is set at the outset at such-and-such an amount above the benchmark rate of interest at the time the loans are taken up (say, 20 basis points over LIBOR — see below). This £150m is what is known as the **committed facility** or **standby facility**.

Another group of banks is put together, comprising the original banks plus others which are recruited. They form a **tender panel**. When the company decides it needs cash, the tender panel banks are invited to bid to provide the funds. Those that are flush with cash at the time will respond, and the bank or banks bidding the lowest rate of interest will make the loans to the company. If none of the tender panel banks bids at a rate below that on the standby facility, the company will resort to raising the money via this standby. Thus it is sure of getting its cash when needed.

The loans made under this arrangement will probably be short-term: say, for three months. But as one loan falls due for repayment new loans can be arranged, so for the company it provides the equivalent of medium-term borrowing at a competitive rate of interest. The 'multi-option' refers to the fact that the arrangement allows for the money to be raised in a number of different forms, which might include straight loans, acceptances (bills of exchange), foreign currency loans and so on.

Risk hedging

The money markets are also the home of many different types of instrument for limiting exposure to interest rate movements (**hedging** the interest rate risk). A **cap** is really an interest rate option. Say the benchmark interest rate is currently 9 per cent and you reckon a rise to over 11 per cent would seriously damage your business. You can buy a cap from a bank, under which you will be reimbursed for the effects of any increase in the interest rate above 11 per cent.

A **floor** is an option that works the other way. Suppose you agree with your bank that you will pay a minimum interest rate of 7.5 per cent, even if market rates drop below this level. The bank will pay you for agreeing this floor, in the same way as you pay the bank for providing a cap. So the proceeds from selling a floor can be used to offset at least part of the cost of a cap. An arrangement that includes both a cap and a floor is known as a **collar** or **cylinder** — it can be used to limit the interest you might have to pay within fairly narrow bands. Companies use these and similar instruments quite extensively to limit their interest rate exposure.

Perhaps **swaps** or **interest rate swaps** should be included in the same category of hedging instruments. For a description of how they work, see Chapter 16.

Interest rate indicators

You will find in the *Financial Times* a list of the interest rates for deposits and different types of short-term financial instruments under the heading of **London money rates**. For each, a range of maturities is covered. Thus, in the case of inter-bank deposits there is a rate for overnight money, for money deposited at seven days' notice, for a month, three months, six months and a year. You can plot the rates quoted for different maturities to produce a **yield curve**. Typically, this is a rising curve, showing that money deposited for short periods earns lower interest than money deposited for six months or a year. But when interest rates are expected to drop, there may be a **negative yield curve** with a lower rate of interest on money deposited for a year than money deposited for a month.

The money rates table shows the rates of interest on **inter-bank deposits, sterling certificates of deposit, local authority deposits** and **bonds, discount market deposits, company deposits, finance house deposits, Treasury bills, bank bills, trade bills,** and some non-sterling instruments or deposits. In many cases both buying and selling rates are given. A bank will borrow money (or sell

LONDON MONEY RATES

July.6	Overnight	7 days notice	One Month	Three Months	Six Months	One Year
Interbank Offer	15	14	$13\frac{15}{16}$	14	14	$13\frac{13}{16}$
Interbank Bid	12	$13\frac{5}{8}$	$13\frac{13}{16}$	$13\frac{7}{8}$	$13\frac{7}{8}$	$13\frac{3}{4}$
Sterling CDs.	-	-	$13\frac{7}{8}$	$13\frac{15}{16}$	$13\frac{15}{16}$	$13\frac{3}{4}$
Local Authority Deps. ...	$13\frac{3}{4}$	$13\frac{3}{4}$	$13\frac{3}{4}$	$13\frac{15}{16}$	$13\frac{7}{8}$	$13\frac{7}{8}$
Local Authority Bonds ..	-	-	-	-	-	-
Discount Mkt Deps.	$13\frac{7}{8}$	$13\frac{3}{4}$	$13\frac{5}{8}$	$13\frac{5}{8}$	-	-
Company Deposits	-	-	$13\frac{13}{16}$	$13\frac{31}{32}$	$13\frac{31}{32}$	$13\frac{15}{16}$
Finance House Deposits .	-	-	$13\frac{7}{8}$	$13\frac{15}{16}$	$13\frac{15}{16}$	$13\frac{15}{16}$
Treasury Bills (Buy)	-	-	$13\frac{1}{2}$	$13\frac{7}{16}$	-	-
Bank Bills (Buy)	-	-	$13\frac{5}{8}$	$13\frac{15}{32}$	$13\frac{1}{32}$	-
Fine Trade Bills (Buy) ...	-	-	$14\frac{1}{4}$	$14\frac{3}{32}$	$13\frac{31}{32}$	-
Dollar CDs	-	-	9.25	9.07	8.87	8.73
SDR Linked Dep Offer ...	-	-	$8\frac{9}{16}$	$8\frac{9}{16}$	$8\frac{9}{16}$	$8\frac{9}{16}$
SDR Linked Dep Bid	-	-	$8\frac{5}{16}$	$8\frac{5}{16}$	$8\frac{5}{16}$	$8\frac{5}{16}$
ECU Linked Dep Offer ...	-	-	$9\frac{1}{8}$	$9\frac{1}{4}$	$9\frac{3}{8}$	$9\frac{1}{2}$
ECU Linked Dep Bid	-	-	9	$9\frac{1}{8}$	$9\frac{1}{4}$	$9\frac{3}{8}$

Table 14.1   Interest rate information. Source: *Financial Times*.

financial instruments) at the lower rate and lend (or buy financial instruments) at the higher rate. The margins between the two rates in these wholesale markets are generally very fine.

Note that the **inter-bank rate** is a far better measure of short-term swings in interest rates than the **bank base rates**. These change (more accurately, are changed) relatively infrequently and as a conscious decision, to reflect trends that have already emerged in the inter-bank market. The inter-bank rate is the constantly changing measure of the cost of money in large amounts for the banks themselves.

The rates of interest on **floating rate bonds** are often related to the inter-bank **offered** rate: the rate at which banks will lend wholesale to each other. A bond might carry a rate of interest of, say, 50 **basis points** above the inter-bank offered rate. A hundred basis points is equivalent to one percentage point, so 50 basis points is 0.5 per cent. But the rate on an overdraft to a private individual will be related to base rate and expressed as so many **points** above base rate. A point in this case is a full **percentage point** so five points over base means 16 per cent when base rates are 11 per cent.

Thus the **London Inter-Bank Offered Rate** or **LIBOR** (see Chapter 16) is the usual benchmark rate of interest for wholesale funds, and is the rate in relation to which other rates are set. A different LIBOR will be quoted for dollar funds, sterling funds, and so on. The *Financial Times* shows a calculation of three- and six-month dollar LIBOR under the heading of **FT London interbank fixing**. **LIBID** is the equivalent **bid** rate or rate at which banks will borrow. **LIMEAN** (pronounced 'lie-mean') is the rate mid-way between the bid and offered rates.

15

Foreign exchange

If stockmarkets sometimes behave irrationally, they are a model of sanity compared with the **foreign exchange** or **forex** markets in which currencies are bought and sold. Not only are the swings in the value of one currency against another both frequent and dramatic. They also have vital implications for the economic prospects of the countries concerned and often for the prosperity of the whole free world economy. It is no surprise that currency stories migrate so frequently from the detailed and technical **foreign exchange reports** to become lead items in the financial pages.

Precisely because the influences that move currency values are often so irrational, these stories can be difficult to understand without some knowledge of the background. Perhaps the easiest approach is to look on the major trading countries as if they were companies quoted on the stockmarket and on their currencies as if they were company shares.

Official intervention

As with shares, the value of each currency is determined by the balance of buyers and sellers in the market, at least since **floating exchange rates** were adopted in the early 1970s. But just as share prices may be **supported** by friends of the company, the value of currencies can be affected by **official intervention**: buying and selling by **central banks** to try to strengthen or weaken a currency. Where a currency is ostensibly floating but in practice being kept close to a particular value or **parity** by central bank intervention, commentators talk of a **dirty** or **managed float**.

But there is a limit to how far a currency value can be manipulated against the trend of market forces. If the central bank is using its **foreign exchange reserves** to support its country's currency when most other participants in the market are selling because they conclude from economic fundamentals that it should go down, the central bank will in due course run out of money, be forced to abandon the support operation and the value will then drop in any case. The market forces predominate. Successful intervention often requires concerted action by the central banks of a number of countries (see below). But even this will ultimately fail if the economic fundamentals are out of line.

The market forces

What are these market forces? Again, there is a parallel between a company and a country. If a company is trading successfully and increasing its earnings, all else being equal its share price will rise. Successful countries which run a **current account balance of payments surplus** — sell more goods and services to other countries than they buy from abroad — and which keep inflation at a low level will also usually see their own currency strong or rising in value over time.

The effect of interest rates

Even if it is not trading spectacularly well, a company can try to make its shares more attractive to investors by increasing the dividends it pays. A country can also try to increase the attraction of its currency to international investors by increasing its **domestic interest rates**. This increases the returns investors can earn by depositing money in the country concerned or by buying bonds in that country. Suppose Britain is increasing its interest rates to attract overseas investors. To invest in Britain they will need to convert whatever currency they hold into pounds to deposit in Britain or buy British bonds. So they will be buying pounds, and when there are more buyers than sellers the currency should rise.

So far so good. But investors in the stockmarket will not buy a share if they are certain its value is going to drop, almost regardless of the income it offers. The income is of little use if the benefit is going to be wiped out by capital losses on the shares. The same applies to a currency. If international investors think the pound is going to fall, they will be more inclined to sell it than buy it and the interest rates Britain is offering will only have limited effect. Interest rate changes can and do influence the value of a currency and much of what the press writes about currencies is concerned with the way countries are adjusting — or being pressured to adjust — domestic interest rates to adjust the value of their currency. But interest rates are only one factor.

Swings in market sentiment

Increasingly, the vital factor is that indefinable element: **market sentiment**. If investors become enthusiastic about a share, they will buy it. Its price will rise and those who bought will show profits. This in turn may attract other investors to buy, the price rises still further and the process becomes self-fuelling. The same thing happens with currencies. Investors become enthusiastic about the dollar and buy it. Its value rises, which encourages still more investors to put their money in the dollar, so it rises still further. And the process can be self-perpetuating — until something happens to change sentiment or encourage investors to take their profit. When this happens, international investors can sell just as frantically as they previously bought, and the value of the currency can fall as fast as it had earlier risen.

The result is that currency swings can go much too far in one direction or another, creating havoc for businesses which trade internationally: they can never be certain what price they will receive for their goods when translated into their own currency. Here the analogy between stockmarkets and currency markets breaks down. In the stockmarket individual share prices can be carried ridiculously high or ridiculously low by swings in market sentiment. But at the end of the day there are some reasonably objective yardsticks: what the company earns and is capable of earning; the dividends it pays and therefore the yield it offers. Ultimately these **fundamentals** tend to reassert themselves and bring investors back to earth.

In the currency markets the fundamentals frequently exert less influence in the short term, so that the currency moves much further than is needed merely to adjust to trading realities: a process known as **overshooting**. In the very long run the fundamentals will reassert themselves, but before this happens serious damage may be done to a country's trading prospects.

How do we measure currencies?

There is another important difference to allow for before we can look more closely at the way currency questions are covered. In the British stockmarkets we measure share prices in standard units: pounds and pence. But a currency is measured in terms of other currencies and all are moving relative to each other. The pound may be strengthening against the dollar but weakening against the German mark — which was the case in 1986. These **exchange cross rates** — values of each of the major currencies in terms of each of the others — are listed daily in the **currencies, money and capital markets** pages of the *Financial Times*, as are the values of major currencies in terms of the pound and of the US dollar, in somewhat more detailed form. Note one complication: by convention the markets always talk of 'so many dollars to the pound' rather than 'so much of a pound to the dollar', even when talking of the value of the dollar rather than the pound. So the dollar's value in sterling terms is expressed as, say, $1.6235 to £1 rather than £0.6160 to $1.

In reports of currency movements there are two main ways currency values are expressed. In terms of another specific currency or in terms of a **trade-weighted index** where they are measured against a **basket of currencies**. In the second case, taking the value of the pound as an example, an index is constructed of the currencies of the main countries with which

EXCHANGE CROSS RATES

July.6	£	$	DM	Yen	F Fr.	S Fr.	H Fl.	Lira	C $	B Fr.
£	1	1.622	3.068	226	10.39	2.630	3.455	2220	1.932	64.15
$	0.617	1	1.891	139.3	6.406	1.621	2.130	1369	1.191	39.55
DM	0.326	0.529	1	73.66	3.387	0.857	1.126	723.6	0.630	20.91
YEN	4.425	7.177	13.58	1000.	45.97	11.64	15.29	9823	8.549	283.8
F Fr.	0.962	1.561	2.953	217.5	10.	2.531	3.325	2137	1.859	61.74
S Fr.	0.380	0.617	1.167	85.93	3.951	1	1.314	844.1	0.735	24.39
H Fl.	0.289	0.469	0.888	65.41	3.007	0.761	1	642.5	0.559	18.57
Lira	0.450	0.731	1.382	101.8	4.680	1.185	1.556	1000.	0.870	28.90
C $	0.518	0.840	1.588	117.0	5.378	1.361	1.788	1149	1	33.20
B Fr.	1.559	2.528	4.783	352.3	16.20	4.100	5.386	3461	3.012	100.

Yen per 1,000: French Fr. per 10: Lira per 1,000: Belgian Fr. per 100.

Table 15.1   Exchange cross rates. Source: *Financial Times.*

CURRENCY MOVEMENTS

June.28	Bank of England Index	Morgan°° Guaranty Changes %
Sterling	90.8	-20.0
U.S Dollar	71.8	-6.4
Canadian Dollar	103.8	+0.2
Austrian Schilling......	106.4	+9.5
Belgian Franc	105.8	-6.1
Danish Krone	103.0	-1.9
Deutsche Mark	112.5	+20.3
Swiss Franc	107.4	+16.4
Guilder	110.1	+13.2
French Franc	99.0	-15.7
Lira	98.8	-19.1
Yen	140.0	+71.5

Morgan Guaranty changes: average 1980-1982=100. Bank of England Index (Base Average 1985=100)°°Rates are for June.28 .

Table 15.2 Trade-weighted indexes. Source: *Financial Times.*

Britain trades, each weighted according to its importance in trade with Britain. This is expressed not as a monetary value but as an index with a base of 100 in 1985. Thus on a particular day the pound might rise against the dollar from $1.6200 to $1.6300 (you get more dollars for a pound, so the pound has strengthened) but fall from 95.0 to 94.9 on the trade-weighted index. Overall, the pound was a little weaker against all currencies, but the dollar was weaker still so sterling improved against the dollar. Again, the *Financial Times* shows sterling's value on the trade-weighted index (also known as the **sterling index** or the **Bank of England index**) and similar indexes for other major currencies. Dollar, yen, deutschmark, Swiss franc and French franc values are frequently quoted.

The fundamentals

We have seen that the value of a currency might be expected — all else being equal — to rise if the country concerned is earning more from abroad than it is spending abroad. Other countries are having to buy its currency to buy its goods and it is adding to its **foreign exchange reserves**, which are roughly equivalent to a country's bank balance, which may be held in the form of other currencies, **special drawing rights** (see glossary) or gold.

In theory, as the value of a country's currency rises its goods become more expensive for foreigners to buy. So gradually it sells less abroad, earns less foreign exchange, and — all other things being equal — the currency begins to weaken until its goods become cheaper again and the cycle recommences. A country earning a surplus may also take deliberate steps to prevent its currency from rising too high: reducing interest rates to make the currency less attractive to foreign investors and to stimulate domestic demand so that more goods are consumed at home, more are imported and fewer exported.

In practice the phenomenon of **overshoot** means that self-correcting mechanisms may be rendered ineffective or only work with considerable delay. The problem is that there is no such thing as the 'right' value for a currency against any other currency. It can be argued that if the exchange rate is $1.60 to £1, an item which costs £1 in London should cost $1.60 in New York: the **purchasing power parity** argument. But such considerations have clearly not applied in the 1980s when the value of £1 has fluctuated between more than $2.40 and little more than $1.00, which clearly did not reflect movements in the relative prices of goods in New York and London. Instead, when the dollar stood at $2.40 to £1 American goods were very cheap for the British and at just over $1.00 to £1 they were exceedingly expensive. Currency

Figure 15.1   The pound against two major currencies, in index form. In 1985 and 1986 the pound's rise against the dollar (solid line) and fall against the Deutschmark (dotted line) was much what the authorities wanted at the time. Source: *Datastream International.*

Figure 15.2 From more than 2.4 dollars to the pound to little more than one — and then up again as the dollar collapse gathered momentum. The chart shows the number of dollars to £1. Source: *Datastream International.*

volatility exaggerates trade imbalances which in turn increase volatility.

The problem of the American deficits

For most of the first half of the 1980s the dollar was a strongly **appreciating** (rising) currency despite a large and growing United States balance of payments deficit on **current account** (the current account records the difference between imports and exports of goods and services; the **capital account** reflects the flow of capital funds — loans, investments and so on — into or out of the country).

Why? Because the American government was spending more than its income and needed to borrow to cover this rapidly rising **budget deficit**: over $200 billion by 1985. It offered relatively high interest rates to attract the funds. The Japanese, with a surplus of funds to invest, invested heavily in the United States. The flow of money into the dollar helped the dollar to rise, and the profits earned by investors in the dollar attracted still more buyers of dollars. The trade-weighted value of the dollar rose around 70 per cent between 1980 and 1985, making American goods very expensive and making it still more difficult for America to sell abroad.

Then in 1985 worries about the escalating American balance of payments deficit took over: it had passed the $100 billion mark in 1985. The dollar began to fall even faster than it had previously risen, helped by an agreement among the major trading nations — the Plaza agreement — to curtail its strength. It had dropped well over 30 per cent by early 1987. From February 1987, following the Louvre accord, the major trading nations began trying — initially without success — to stem the dollar's fall by intervening to sell other currencies and buy the dollar and by persuading the strong currency countries, Japan and West Germany, to reduce their domestic interest rates and stimulate their economies. Japan in particular was under pressure to open its markets more widely to foreign goods, and a major trade row threatened. In 1988 the dollar's fall tailed off and began to be reversed, but the very limited action taken in the US to correct the twin deficits still left the currency looking vulnerable over the long term.

Much of what is written about currencies in an international context concerns the problem of the American balance of payments and budget deficits and in particular the trade imbalance between the United States and Japan, the effects on their respective currencies and the efforts of the major trading nations to agree a solution. These countries — The United States, Japan, West Germany, France and Great Britain — are referred to as the **Group of Five** or **G5** and become the **Group of Seven** or **G7** with the addition of Canada and Italy.

Sterling and the oil factor

The history of sterling over the 1980s has been complicated by one particular factor: **oil**. As an oil producer from the North Sea, Britain sees its revenues and the government's tax take rise when the oil price is high. The 1979 doubling in oil prices (combined with the high interest rates the incoming Conservative government imposed for domestic reasons) caused sterling to rise very sharply to above $2.40 to £1 by 1980 and to over 100 on the trade-weighted index. British goods became uncompetitive overseas, exacerbating the unemployment in export-orientated industries.

By early 1985, with a much lower oil price coupled with a strong dollar, sterling dropped to almost $1.00 to £1 and to around 91 on a trade-weighted basis. After a recovery, its trade-weighted value was knocked again by a low oil price later in 1985 and in 1986. But early in 1987 it was responding to buoyant government revenues in the UK and a lower-than-expected government borrowing requirement (**public sector borrowing requirement** or **PSBR**). Britain was being **re-rated** by international investors. Soon the Bank of England was allowing interest rates to fall and selling sterling in the foreign exchange markets to prevent its value from rising too far and thus making British goods uncompetitive. By 1989 other factors had intervened. An over-buoyant UK economy was sucking in imports, threatening a current account balance of payments deficit of over £15 billion. Fears of a serious fall in sterling helped to dictate a policy of high interest rates.

The central problem posed by the American deficits — helping to destabilize the world currency scene — will not disappear in a hurry. But such is the volatility of mood in currency markets in the short term that it is anybody's guess which currencies will be in need of support and which will need holding down even a month or so from the date of writing.

Figure 15.3 Graphic view of currency turmoil. Plummeting dollar (solid line) and soaring Japanese yen (dotted line) posed problems for America, Japan — and plenty of others. Source: *Datastream International.*

Figure 15.4 Sterling's trade-weighted value (value against a basket of currencies). High oil prices and high interest rates led to serious over-valuation at the start of the 1980s. Source: *Datastream International.*

The European Monetary System

Concerted action to stabilize currencies between a group of countries is the thinking behind a formal linking of European Community currencies: the **European Monetary System (EMS)**. The **Exchange Rate Mechanism (ERM)** of the EMS is the framework in which the values of most of the EEC currencies (though excluding sterling, at the time of writing) are linked. Each currency within the ERM is accorded an exchange rate expressed in terms of the **ECU**: a hypothetical currency unit created from an amalgam of the European Community currencies (including sterling). Each of the ERM currencies is allowed to diverge by a given percentage from this central exchange rate: the permitted divergence is larger in the case of the volatile Italian lira and Spanish peseta.

If a currency looks like diverging beyond the permitted limits, the central banks will intervene to bring it into line, while the country in question may have to amend its economic policies to tackle the underlying cause of the divergence. If this does not work, the currency in question may need to be revalued or devalued against the ECU, adopting a new central exchange rate. The whole structure can move up or down in value relative to other currencies such as the dollar or the yen. Britain has been under pressure to link the value of sterling to the EMS Exchange Rate Mechanism but in mid-1989 was still outside.

Forward markets and hedging

Now that governments have only limited control over the value of currencies, it is up to businesses to protect themselves against the effect of wild swings as best they can. There are various ways they can **hedge** the **currency risk**.

There is a **forward market** in currencies as well as a **spot market**. In the spot market currencies are bought and sold for immediate delivery — in practice, delivery in two days' time — whereas in the forward market they are bought and sold for delivery in the future. You will see that the *Financial Times* table of the value of the pound against major currencies lists a spot price and prices for delivery in one month and three months.

The forward price relative to the spot price reflects the **interest rate differential** between the countries concerned. Suppose, say, you hold sterling and are due to pay for goods in German marks in three months' time. You are worried the value of the mark will rise, in which case you will have to pay more in sterling terms. So you might buy German marks today for delivery in three months' time, which means you are **locking in** to a known exchange rate.

Suppose also that you can deposit money in Britain to earn 10 per cent and in Germany to earn only 4 per cent. For three months you have the benefit of the higher sterling interest rate, whereas if you had bought the German marks immediately you would have been depositing the money at the lower German interest rate until it was needed. So the price you pay for the deutschmarks for delivery in three months will be higher than the spot price by an amount that reflects this interest rate advantage — in other words, at the three months' price you will get fewer deutschmarks for your pounds than at the spot price. But if the currency you want to buy forward offers higher interest rates than in Britain, the forward price will be lower than the spot price (at a **discount** rather than a **premium**). These premiums and discounts for currencies in the forward market are shown in the *Financial Times*, together with the annual interest rate differential they reflect.

POUND SPOT- FORWARD AGAINST THE POUND

July.6	Day's spread	Close	One month	% p.a.	Three months	% p.a.
US	1.6145 - 1.6260	1.6215 - 1.6225	0.62-0.60cpm	4.51	1.85-1.81pm	4.51
Canada	1.9250 - 1.9360	1.9310 - 1.9320	0.28-0.21cpm	1.52	0.78-0.68pm	1.51
Netherlands	3.44¾ - 3.46	3.45 - 3.46	2-1⅞cpm	6.73	5⅝-5½pm	6.44
Belgium	63.95 - 64.20	64.10 - 64.20	31-29cpm	5.61	88-83pm	5.33
Denmark	11.89¼ - 11.91½	11.90 - 11.91	4⅜-3⅞orepm	4.16	12⅜-11⅞pm	4.07
Ireland	1.1440 - 1.1480	1.1440 - 1.1450	0.40-0.35ppm	3.93	1.15-1.05pm	3.84
W. Germany	3.05¾ - 3.07	3.06½ - 3.07	1⅞-1¾pfpm	7.09	5⅛-5pm	6.60
Portugal	255.90 - 257.25	256.25 - 257.25	3-37cdis	-0.93	91-174dis	-2.06
Spain	192.45 - 193.80	193.05 - 193.35	1-15cdis	-0.50	8-35dis	-0.45
Italy	2214 - 2222¼	2219½ - 2220½	4-3lirepm	1.89	10-8pm	1.62
Norway	11.21¾ - 11.25¼	11.24 - 11.25	3-2⅝orepm	3.00	8½-7⅝pm	2.87
France	10.37 - 10.39¾	10.38¾ - 10.39¾	3⅞-3¾cpm	4.40	11½-11⅛pm	4.35
Sweden	10.45¼ - 10.48	10.46 - 10.47	2⅛-1⅞orepm	2.29	6⅛-5⅝pm	2.25
Japan	224½ - 226½	225½ - 226½	1⅝-1½ypm	8.30	4¾-4⅝pm	8.30
Austria	21.50 - 21.59	21.55 - 21.58	11⅜-10⅝gropm	6.12	34⅛-30½pm	5.99
Switzerland	2.62 - 2.63½	2.62½ - 2.63½	1½-1⅜cpm	6.56	4⅜-4⅛pm	6.37
ECU	1.4780 - 1.4835	1.4780 - 1.4785	0.60-0.57cpm	4.75	1.00-1.67dis	3.61

Commercial rates taken towards the end of London trading.Belgian rate is convertible francs. Financial franc 64.20-64.30 . Six-month forward dollar 3.78-3.73cpm 12 months 7.08-6.98cpm

Table 15.3 Spot and forward rates. Source: *Financial Times*.

In practice, hedging strategies in the foreign exchange markets may be a great deal more complex than simply buying or selling a currency forward, though this illustrates the principle. Currencies may be **swapped**, too (see Chapter 16). Those wanting protection against currency risk can also buy **currency contracts** or **currency options** on the **London International Financial Futures Exchange (LIFFE)** and movements in the values of these contracts may be quoted in the foreign exchange reports as a sensitive indicator of currency trends. Banks also market a range of currency-hedging products.

Who deals in the forex markets?

Foreign exchange is dealt in by the major banks and by specialist **foreign exchange brokers**, with the traders operating from the screen-cluttered trading floors familiar from many film and television reports. Dealing is via these screens and telephones: there is no central marketplace.

London, conveniently placed between Tokyo and New York in the time zones, is the largest foreign exchange market. A Bank of England survey of 347 banks and deposit takers and 8 recognized foreign exchange brokers in 1986 estimated the average volume of the London market at $90 billion per day, with US dollar/sterling and dollar/deutschmark business accounting for over half of the total. The market is likely to have shown further substantial growth since then.

Was there really $90 billion of cross-border trade per day that required currency transactions in London? Of course not. Banks' direct business with customers accounted for only 9 per cent of turnover. The great bulk of the turnover is purely speculative — dealing for a quick profit — though the Bank pointed out that each trade-backed transaction may in practice require a number of separate transactions on the exchanges: almost all business between sterling and the German mark, for example, takes place via the US dollar. **Arbitrage** (see glossary) evens out temporary disparities between rates for different currencies and ensures that interest rate differentials are reflected in forward rates. Currency dealers justify this vast speculative activity with the argument that it results in a highly liquid market in which necessary trade-backed transactions can be carried out with ease.

While the economists at the banks may seek to make rational forecasts of likely trends in a particular currency, the dealers have a much shorter-term view, taking advantage of temporary swings and anomalies. In the absence of rational reasons for currency swings, they may enlist the help of **chartist** techniques (see Chapter 7) which indicate likely trends purely on the basis of recent movements. It adds to the volatility of the market.

16

International money: the euromarkets

By far the biggest **capital market** centered on London is the **eurocurrency market**. You do not read a great deal about it day-to-day — except in the *Financial Times* and a few specialist publications — because it is a market for professionals, it has no central marketplace and does not directly impinge on many private investors in Britain. Yet the $179 billion raised, according to Euromoney Capital Markets, in the eurobond market in 1988 completely dwarfs The Stock Exchange as a source of capital.

As our starting point, what is a **eurocurrency**? It is a currency held outside its country of origin. Dollars deposited in a London bank are **eurodollars**. Japanese yen on deposit in Switzerland are **euroyen**. There are 'euro' versions of the Japanese yen, German mark, French franc, Dutch guilder and British sterling among others. Dollars were the original eurocurrency and are still the most common.

Origin of eurocurrencies

How does a eurocurrency arise? A British exporter, say, sells goods to the United States and receives payment in dollars. He may decide to convert them into sterling. But if, instead, he deposits them as dollars in a bank outside the United States, they become eurodollars. As America runs a massive trade deficit, it is effectively exporting the dollars it uses to pay for the goods it buys from abroad. Banks around the world accumulate deposits of these dollars.

In one way or another, these deposits of currencies held outside their country of origin are going to be put to work: they will be lent. And there can be advantages both for lenders and borrowers in dealing in eurocurrencies. Since they are 'stateless' money, transactions are not circumscribed by the local rules and regulations of any particular financial centre. London is the biggest centre for eurocurrency transactions, but the eurocurrency market is not a domestic British market neither is it run mainly by British institutions; the biggest players in London were traditionally the American banks and their offshoots, but Japanese institutions have been challenging for the lead.

How eurocurrencies are lent

The eurocurrency market is also known as the **euromarket** or **international money market**. And it mirrors most of the facilities and forms of security available in domestic financial markets. Eurocurrencies can be deposited and borrowed for very short periods or for many years. Borrowers can take out the equivalent of a term loan in a eurocurrency. They can issue various forms of IOU or bond to raise money in a eurocurrency. And because the eurocurrency market is largely unfettered by national restrictions, many of the more innovative forms of financing are first devised in the eurocurrency market and often copied subsequently in domestic financial markets.

It is important to note the difference between borrowing a eurocurrency and simply borrowing in an overseas financial market. A euroyen loan is a borrowing of yen that are held outside Japan whereas a **samurai** bond is a yen bond issued by a foreigner in the Japanese domestic market. A **yankee** bond is a dollar bond issued by a foreigner in the United States and a **bulldog** bond is a sterling bond issued in Britain by a foreigner. The samurai, yankee and bulldog are not eurobonds.

Syndicated loans

Out of the original short-term market in eurocurrency deposits — the **inter-bank market** — grew the **syndicated loan** market. **Syndicates** of banks would get together under a **lead bank** to provide medium-term or long-term loans running into hundreds of millions of dollars — though the currency in which the money was borrowed would not necessarily be dollars; it could equally well be German marks or Japanese yen. By each contributing part of the loan, the individual banks avoided too large a commitment to any one customer.

Securitization of debt

Securitization of eurocurrency lending was the next step. While this initially took the form of the **eurobond**, shorter-term forms of IOU are now issued. The **euronote** is an IOU with a life of under a year but it can be transmuted into longer-term borrowing. Borrowers arrange with a bank or dealer to sell or take up the notes they issue under arrangements such as the **revolving underwriting facility (RUF)** or **note issuance facility (NIF)**. The borrower can thus issue further notes as he needs the money or as the earlier ones fall due. **Eurocommercial paper** is another form of short-term IOU issued by companies which has been gaining ground rapidly (see Chapter 14 for a description of commercial paper in the domestic market).

Eurobonds

For long-term borrowing the **eurobond** is the answer. It is much like the bonds that governments and companies issue in their domestic markets, but it taps the 'euro' pool of stateless money. Once the bond has been issued in the **primary market** it can be traded in the **secondary market** in eurobonds, conducted by dealers over the telephone and television screen. It can at times be a volatile market partly because dealers (unlike marketmakers on The Stock Exchange) have not had an *obligation* to make a market. If times got tough in a particular sector they might temporarily pull in their horns and the market would lose its liquidity. In the move towards securitization of debt, tradable eurobonds have gained ground at the expense of syndicated loans. Eurobonds are issued in **bearer** rather than **registered** form which gives them attractions for investors who do not intend being over-frank with the tax man.

The bank which arranges a eurobond issue is usually paid its **fees** in the form of a discount to the issue price. So if the issue price was 100 and the fees were 1.5 per cent the bank would be losing money if the bond did not sell at a price of at least 98.5. Hence statements in reports of eurobond issues that a bond 'was quoted slightly outside its 1.5 per cent fees' (the bank lost money) or 'was quoted at 100.25, well within its 1.5 per cent fees' (the bank got the pricing right and made money on the operation).

Variations on the bond theme

Eurobonds can carry a fixed rate of interest, or they may be issued in the form of **floating rate notes (FRNs)**. Some banks have issued **perpetual floating rate notes** or **perpetuals** which are never required to be repaid, though the value of these suffered a dramatic market collapse a few years back. Traditional fixed-interest eurobonds with a redemption date and without conversion rights or other peculiar features are known as **straights**.

The complexities arise in the many variations of these basic themes, introduced to make eurobonds more attractive to issuers or investors (or both). First the borrower must choose what currency he will borrow in; the interest rate would be lower in a hard currency such as the German mark than it would be in sterling, but if the mark rises, the debt could be a lot more expensive to repay. Some bonds (**dual currency bonds**) reduce the currency exposure from the point of view of the investor: he puts up the money in one currency but is repaid in another at a rate of exchange fixed in advance.

Some eurobonds issued by companies incorporate an **equity sweetener**. Either the bond can be **converted** (wholly or in part) into the shares of the issuing company or it comes with **warrants** to subscribe for the company's shares. The principles are the same as those outlined in Chapter 5 in the context of convertibles and warrants issued by domestic British companies. And, as in the domestic bond market, eurobonds may be issued at a **deep discount** instead of paying a rate of interest (**zero-coupon bonds**) or may initially be issued in **part-paid** form.

The real complexities, however, concern the interest rate and the compromises evolved to obtain some of the advantages of both fixed-rate and floating-rate bonds. Floating-rate notes are issued which can **convert** into fixed-rate at the option of the investor (the **debt convertible**) or may become fixed rate if interest rates drop to a predetermined level (the **droplock**). Or there may be an upper limit (a **cap**) to the interest rate payable on a floating rate note (a **capped floating rate note**) and sometimes a lower limit or **floor** as well.

Euro and domestic markets in Britain

Of late the distinctions between the domestic market and the euromarket in sterling-denominated bonds have been greatly eroded. Much the same firms deal in securities in both markets, and the rules for the issue of domestic sterling bonds on The Stock Exchange have been relaxed to bring them closer in line with those applying in the euromarket. Many major British companies have issued **convertible loan stocks** and **convertible preference shares** in the euromarket, and for larger companies the choice between the two markets often depends mainly on questions of tax, issue costs and the type of investor they are trying to attract.

While the domestic market is the main one for the issue of **secured loans** (eurobonds are usually unsecured) recent years have seen rapid expansion of euromarket issues of **mortgage-backed securities** by British-based **specialist mortgage lenders** who now compete with the building societies and banks to provide housing finance. Large numbers of individual residential mortgages — typically a thousand or so — are 'pooled' in a special-purpose company which then issues floating rate notes or bonds to investors at large, thus recouping the money originally lent to homebuyers. The payments of interest and capital by these homebuyers provide for the interest on the notes and for their eventual repayment. The process is a prime example of **securitization**: mortgage loans are transmuted into traded securities.

Setting the interest rate

The *Financial Times* carries a table of **eurocurrency interest rates**. These follow but do not necessarily exactly match domestic rates within the countries concerned. Rates are given for a range of eurocurrencies for deposits ranging from very short term to periods of up to a year. Needless to say, rates are lowest for the strongest currencies.

The key rate is three-month or six-month **LIBOR**, which stands for **London inter-bank offered rate** (see Chapter 14). This is the rate at which banks will lend in the inter-bank market, and is adopted as the benchmark rate of interest. The interest on floating rate notes is usually set by reference to the average rate of LIBOR and expressed as 'so many **basis points**' (hundredths of one percentage point) above LIBOR.

EURO-CURRENCY INTEREST RATES

June.28	Short term	7 Days notice	One Month	Three Months	Six Months	One Year
Sterling	$13\frac{1}{2}-13\frac{3}{8}$	$13\frac{1}{2}-13\frac{3}{8}$	$13\frac{3}{4}-13\frac{11}{16}$	$14-13\frac{7}{8}$	$14\frac{1}{16}-13\frac{15}{16}$	$14-13\frac{7}{8}$
US Dollar	$9\frac{1}{2}-9\frac{3}{8}$	$9\frac{9}{16}-9\frac{7}{16}$	$9\frac{1}{2}-9\frac{3}{8}$	$9\frac{3}{8}-9\frac{1}{4}$	$9\frac{3}{16}-9\frac{1}{16}$	$9\frac{1}{16}-8\frac{15}{16}$
Can. Dollar	$11\frac{1}{2}-11\frac{1}{4}$	$11\frac{5}{8}-11\frac{3}{8}$	$11\frac{7}{8}-11\frac{5}{8}$	$11\frac{15}{16}-11\frac{11}{16}$	$11\frac{3}{4}-11\frac{1}{2}$	$11\frac{5}{16}-11\frac{1}{16}$
D. Guilder	$6\frac{7}{8}-6\frac{3}{4}$	$6\frac{7}{8}-6\frac{3}{4}$	$7-6\frac{15}{16}$	$7\frac{3}{16}-7\frac{1}{16}$	$7\frac{3}{8}-7\frac{1}{4}$	$7\frac{7}{16}-7\frac{5}{16}$
Sw. Franc	$7\frac{1}{4}-7\frac{1}{8}$	$7\frac{5}{16}-7\frac{3}{16}$	$7\frac{3}{8}-7\frac{1}{4}$	$7\frac{5}{16}-7\frac{3}{16}$	$7\frac{1}{8}-7$	$7-6\frac{7}{8}$
Deutschmark	$6\frac{11}{16}-6\frac{9}{16}$	$6\frac{3}{4}-6\frac{5}{8}$	$6\frac{3}{4}-6\frac{5}{8}$	$6\frac{7}{8}-6\frac{3}{4}$	$7\frac{1}{16}-6\frac{15}{16}$	$7\frac{3}{16}-7\frac{1}{16}$
Fr. Franc	$9\frac{1}{8}-9$	$9\frac{1}{8}-9$	$9\frac{1}{8}-9$	$9\frac{1}{8}-9$	$9\frac{1}{8}-9$	$9\frac{3}{16}-9\frac{1}{16}$
Italian Lire	11-9	$13\frac{1}{2}-12\frac{1}{2}$	$12\frac{3}{4}-12\frac{1}{4}$	$12\frac{3}{8}-11\frac{7}{8}$	$12\frac{3}{8}-12$	$12\frac{7}{16}-12\frac{1}{16}$
B. Fr. (Fin)	$8\frac{13}{16}-8\frac{11}{16}$	$8\frac{1}{2}-8\frac{3}{8}$	$8\frac{7}{16}-8\frac{5}{16}$	$8\frac{1}{2}-8\frac{3}{8}$	$8\frac{1}{2}-8\frac{3}{8}$	$8\frac{1}{2}-8\frac{3}{8}$
B. Fr. (Con.)	$9-8\frac{5}{8}$	$8\frac{5}{8}-8\frac{1}{4}$	$8\frac{3}{4}-8\frac{3}{8}$	$8\frac{3}{4}-8\frac{3}{8}$	$8\frac{11}{16}-8\frac{5}{16}$	$8\frac{5}{8}-8\frac{1}{4}$
Yen	$5\frac{1}{4}-5\frac{1}{8}$	$5\frac{7}{16}-5\frac{5}{16}$	$5\frac{3}{8}-5\frac{1}{4}$	$5\frac{3}{8}-5\frac{1}{4}$	$5\frac{7}{16}-5\frac{5}{16}$	$5\frac{7}{16}-5\frac{5}{16}$
D. Krone	$9\frac{3}{8}-9\frac{1}{4}$	$9\frac{3}{8}-9\frac{1}{4}$	$9\frac{1}{4}-9\frac{1}{8}$	$9\frac{3}{8}-9\frac{1}{8}$	$9\frac{9}{16}-9\frac{7}{16}$	$9\frac{13}{16}-9\frac{9}{16}$
Asian $Sing	$9\frac{9}{16}-9\frac{7}{16}$	$9\frac{5}{8}-9\frac{1}{2}$	$9\frac{9}{16}-9\frac{7}{16}$	$9\frac{3}{8}-9\frac{1}{4}$	$9\frac{1}{8}-9$	$9\frac{1}{16}-8\frac{15}{16}$

Long term Eurodollars: two years $9-8\frac{7}{8}$ per cent; three years $9-8\frac{7}{8}$ per cent; four years $9-8\frac{7}{8}$ per cent; five years $9-8\frac{7}{8}$ per cent nominal. Short term rates are call for US Dollars and Japanese Yen; others, two days' notice.

Table 16.1 Eurocurrency interest rates. Source: *Financial Times*.

Euroequities

The distribution networks used by major eurobond dealers to market loan and bond issues to investors have also been used on a smaller scale to market ordinary shares in major internationally-known companies. It may suit a company to raise cash by selling shares outside its domestic capital market when this is too small for its needs. Other companies may wish to attract shareholders in overseas countries where they trade. Such operations are known as **euroequity** issues. Some $2bn worth of shares in the Italian Fiat car group were sold via the euromarket network in 1986, though the sale was not an unqualified success.

Interest rate and currency swaps

The form in which borrowers can most easily raise money is not always the form best suited to their purposes. Company A, say, finds it can easily raise fixed-interest money when it really needs floating-rate funds. Company B, on the other hand, has no problem in raising a floating-rate loan but its real need is for fixed-interest money.

The solution may be a **swap** — in this case an **interest rate swap**. Company A issues its fixed-interest bond and Company B issues a floating-rate loan. They then agree to swap their interest payment liabilities. Company A pays the floating-rate interest due on Company B's loan and Company B pays the fixed rate of interest on the Company A borrowing. By this mechanism each ends up with money in the form in which it needs it.

This is the principle. The mechanisms are in reality more complex. One of the original borrowers may first negotiate a swap with a bank which can either find a counter-party for the deal or may act as counter-party itself. And swaps, once set up, may subsequently be traded or adapted as conditions change in the market.

The second type of swap is the **currency swap**. Company A may be able to borrow on the most advantageous terms in German marks, because its credit rating is high in Germany where it is known. But it needs US dollars. Company B can most easily raise money in US dollars, but it needs German marks. So Company A issues a German mark loan and Company B borrows dollars. They then swap the currencies so that each ends up with what it needs. Since each is borrowing where its credit is best, both end up with cheaper funds than if they had borrowed direct in the currency they needed. Again, a bank probably acts as intermediary. With many swaps both interest payments and currencies are exchanged.

It has been estimated that at times that as much as 80 per cent of the funds raised in the euromarket are immediately swapped.

Ranking of borrowers

The interest rate paid by a borrower in the euromarket depends partly on the borrower's standing. The main borrowers are governments, public bodies and internationally known companies, and companies known only in their domestic markets may be less well received.

Several organizations, including **Standard & Poor** and **Moody** in the United States, provide **bond rating services** which attempt to quantify the credit-worthiness of a borrower. The highest rating is AAA, hence the term **triple-A-rated** for the very safest borrowers.

Tombstones

Banks which are active in the euromarkets like to advertise their success in raising funds for clients. They do so partly by taking **tombstone** advertisements in the financial pages, particularly (in Britain) in the *Financial Times* and the magazine *Euromoney*. These advertisements announce that they appear 'as a matter of record only' (in other words they are not a solicitation to buy securities) and give the name of the borrower and brief details of the loan facility or bond issue arranged plus the names of the participating banks. The lead bank or banks which put the deal together appear at the head of the list and the remainder are normally listed in alphabetical order. The distinctive layout of these advertisements makes it clear why the term 'tombstone' is appropriate.

Press coverage

On Mondays the 'Companies & Markets' section of the *Financial Times* carries an extended round-up of international capital markets, including the euromarkets, and there is an extended list of **eurobond market prices**. On Tuesdays to Fridays the **international capital markets** page includes a daily eurobond market report plus comment on new issues, and a smaller table of market prices for recently issued eurobonds. Other serious dailies carry less frequent notes on the euromarkets. The monthly magazine *Euromoney* was set up specifically to cover the international capital market. And a variety of euromarket newsletters and news services are aimed mainly at the market professionals.

17

Futures, options and commodity markets

Every financial market involves risk for the market user, but there are some markets whose main function is the **redistribution of risk**. On the one hand, they are the riskiest markets of all. On the other, they are markets in which risks can be reduced or eliminated. These are the **options** and **futures** markets.

The customers who use these markets fall into two main categories: those who want to **hedge** (guard against) a risk to which they are exposed. And those who are prepared to accept a high risk in return for the possibility of large rewards: the **traders** or **speculators**.

Options on shares

The principle is clearest in the case of traditional **options** on shares. An option in this case is the right to buy or the right to sell a share within a stipulated time period at a price that is fixed when the option is bought. Say that you decide at the beginning of January that the shares of XYZ Holdings are likely to rise sharply within the next month or so. The current price is 100p and you think it might well rise to 130p by the end of March. You could, of course, buy 10,000 of the shares for £10,000, and if you are right your 10,000 shares will be worth £13,000 within three months: a profit of £3,000, or 30 per cent on your outlay. But you need to have £10,000 to do it, and though the value of the XYZ shares is unlikely to fall to nothing, you are in theory putting the whole £10,000 at risk.

Instead, you might consider it was worth paying, say, 10p per share for an option that gave you the right to buy a share in XYZ for 100p at any time over the next three months. If the XYZ share price stays at 100p, the option has no value and you lose the 10p **premium** you paid. But this is the most you can lose. If the share price does rise to 130p, then your option clearly has a value and is worth **exercizing**: you have the right to buy for 100p a share that you could resell for 130p.

Suppose you had bought options on 10,000 XYZ shares. The total cost at 10p per share would have been £1,000. If you exercise your option to buy the 10,000 shares at 100p and immediately resell them at 130p, your profit is £13,000 less £10,000. So you make £3,000 but against this you have to offset the £1,000 cost of your options. But this still leaves a profit of £2,000 on an outlay of only £1,000, or a profit of 200 per cent: considerably better than if you had simply bought the shares. The point to note is that options are a very **highly-geared investment**. A comparatively small movement in the share price results in a proportionately far larger movement in the value of the option.

But there is another side to the bargain. Who was prepared to agree to sell XYZ shares at 100p if you exercised your option? It was probably an owner of XYZ shares who took a different view from you of what the price was likely to do. He took the view that XYZ shares were fairly fully valued at 100p and that he would be prepared to sell at this price or a little above. But instead of selling at 100p, he could create or **write** an option at 10p per share: the option you bought.

If the price of the shares fell below 100p, the option would not be exercised and he would hang on to them; but he would have an extra 10p per share in the kitty to set against the fall in the share price. If the price rose above 100p and the option was exercised, he would be obliged to part with his XYZ shares at 100p. But he would really be getting 110p, because he has the 10p premium as well. So by getting 10p for the option he has reduced by 10p his possible paper loss if the XYZ share price falls. He has also limited his possible profit if the XYZ price rises, because the maximum he gets is 110p: 100p for the share and 10p for the option. He has written options as a way of hedging his risk: limiting his possible loss but also restricting his possible profit.

Hedging with futures

The buyer of an option always knows exactly what money he is risking: the price he pays for the option and no more. **Futures**

contracts also redistribute risk, but the mechanism is rather different and the possible loss is not necessarily limited to the amount of money put up in the first instance.

A futures contract is a contract for delivery of a standard package of a standard commodity at a specific point in the future but at a price agreed when the contract is taken out. The 'commodity' may be a commodity in a traditional sense such as copper or cocoa, or it may be a currency, a bond, a hypothetical package of equities or even an interest rate (don't worry if this sounds confusing: the principle is clearer when we come down to examples).

The principle is easiest to illustrate if we take a physical commodity such as a metal. Today's price for a ton of metal to be delivered in three months' time is £1,000. A producer of the metal knows he will have metal available for sale in three months. He does not know what the price will be at that point. So he may decide to reduce his risk by selling a contract for a ton of metal to be delivered in three months. This means he contracts to deliver the metal in three months. He knows what price he is getting: £1,000. If in three months' time the price for a ton of metal for immediate delivery — the **spot** price — has fallen to £900, he will have done better than if he had waited till then to sell his production. If in three months the spot price has risen to £1,100, he will have lost some extra profit because he will have to sell at £1,000. But at least the uncertainty had been removed. He knows what money he will get.

The buyer of a contract for delivery of a ton of metal in three months' time might be an engineering company which knows it will need the metal in three months to satisfy a particular order. Instead of taking the risk that it might have to pay a lot more for the metal in three months, it prefers to 'lock in' to a known price today so that it can cost its order effectively. By buying a contract at £1,000 for delivery in three months, it knows exactly where it stands. If the spot price is £900 in three months time, it will have lost by buying the future. If the spot price is £1,100, it will have saved itself money. But the uncertainty has again been eliminated.

This is the theory of **futures markets**, and they undoubtedly serve a valuable function by allowing both suppliers and consumers to plan ahead on the basis of known prices. But it ignores two very important points. First, contracts to buy and sell a commodity in the future are not necessarily made between consumers and producers and do not necessarily result in physical delivery of the commodity when the time has elapsed — in some futures markets, physical delivery is very rare. Secondly, the buyer of a contract does not have to put up the full price of the contract at the time of purchase. He pays a deposit — a **margin** — which might be ten per cent of the value of the contract, but could be a lot less in some **financial futures**. This is where the gearing and the risk come in.

Suppose a speculator rather than a producer buys a contract for a ton of metal for delivery in three months. He pays £1,000 and thinks the price will rise. He only has to pay £100 today. If he is right and the spot price has risen to £1,100 at the end of the three months, he has the right to a ton of metal at £1,000 and can immediately sell it for £1,100: a £100 profit on the £100 margin he had put up. In practice he does not take delivery of the metal and then sell it, but instead he sells a contract for a ton of metal at £1,100. The contract he bought and the one he sells cancel each other out, and he pockets the difference of £100.

But what if the price of metal falls? He has again bought a contract for £1,000 for delivery in three months and put up £100 margin. But in the first month the price falls to £900. He has a loss of £100 on paper, which wipes out the whole of the margin he had put up. If he still thinks that the price will rise before the three months are up, he will have to provide further money as margin. If he does not, the position will have to be **closed** by sale of a contract that cancels out his original purchase, and he will have lost the whole of the money he put up.

Note that in futures you *buy* a contract if you are betting on a price rise and you *sell* a contract if you are betting on a fall. The contract itself is the same in either case. With options, too, you can bet on rising or on falling prices. But in both cases you *buy* an option: it is the option itself that is different. If you are **bullish** you buy a **call** option which gives you the right to buy shares at a predetermined price. If you are **bearish**, you buy a **put** option which gives you the right to sell shares at a pre-determined price. Now for the detail.

Traded options

Traditional options to buy or sell shares are arranged with one of the stockbrokers specalizing in this business. You can take out call or put options, or **double** options which give you the right to buy or sell. The *Financial Times* gives in its market reports section an indication of current prices.

More prominent, however, is the London market in **traded options**. This **Traded Options Market** was founded in 1978 and is part of The Stock Exchange. The traded options pitch is the only active area of the Stock Exchange floor now that the trading in equities and gilt-edged stocks has moved to the telephones and the screens away from the market floor — though the traded options market and the financial futures market have talked about getting together.

The principle of traded options is clear enough if we go back to the example of XYZ Co. You paid 10p for the right to buy an XYZ share at 100p within the next three months. You exercized the option if the XYZ price rose. If it did not rise, the option **expired** valueless and you lost the whole of your money.

A traded option differs from the traditional type in that you can buy and sell the option itself, much as if it were a share. Suppose after a month the XYZ share price rose from 100p to 110p. The option for which you paid 10p now has **intrinsic value**, because it gives you the right to buy a share at a price below its current value. So the option itself is now worth more than the 10p

Option		CALLS Jul	Oct	Jan	PUTS Jul	Oct	Jan
Alld Lyons	420	47	64	71	1½	5½	10
(°462)	460	13	32	44	11	17	21
	500	3	15	22	40	41	55
Brit. Airways	180	30	36	39	1	1½	3½
(°207)	200	11	20	26	3	7	9
	220	2½	11	15	15	18	18
Brit Com	140	22	30	32	4	6	8
(°158)	160	10	18	22	9	12	15
	180	4	9	13	24	24	26
Beecham	550	97	118	130	1	4	7
(°642)	600	48	75	90	4	12	16
	650	14	41	58	18	30	33
Boots	260	43	54	62	1	3	4½
(°300)	280	24	37	45	1½	6	10
	300	9	23	32	7	12	15
B.P.	260	44	50	57	½	1½	4
(°302)	280	25	31	38	1	4½	8½
	300	10	20	26	4½	9½	15
British Steel	70	8¾	13¼	17½	1¼	2¾	3¾
(°78)	80	1¾	7	11	5	5¾	8
	90	½	4	6¼	13	13	13¼
Bass	950	85	117	132	3	10	18
(°1022)	1000	42	82	95	11	22	32

Option		CALLS Jul	Oct	Jan	PUTS Jul	Oct	Jan
Shell Trans.	390	51	58	73	1½	6	9
(°434)	420	22	33	46	5	10	15
	460	5	14	26	29	33	35
Storehouse	140	16	20	24	4	6½	8
(°155)	160	5½	9½	16	16	18	20
Trafalgar	347	18	32	39	5	11	18
(°355)	377	4	17	23	24	26	32
Utd.Biscuits	300	70	82	88	1½	3	4
(°366)	330	4	54	62	2	5	9
	360	14	32	42	8	13	18
Unilever	500	98	116	128	1	1	3
(°594)	550	50	72	88	1½	7	11
	600	13	37	53	16	22	26
Ultramar	280	44	54	66	1	4½	7
(°319)	300	26	42	50	4	9	12
	330	6½	82	30	17	22	24

Option		Aug	Nov	Feb	Aug	Nov	Feb
Brit Aero	600	92	74	102	12	26	30
(°680)	650	50	74	102	12	26	30
	700	21	48	75	35	50	55

Table 17.1 Traded option information. Source: *Financial Times.*

you paid for it. Reflecting the rise in the share price, it might now be worth, say, 19p. So you could sell it at this point and take your profit without needing to exercise it. If the XYZ share price had fallen, the value of the option would also have fallen, but you would have had the chance of selling and recouping some of your outlay.

The 10p you paid originally for your XYZ traded option was all hope value or **time value**. There was no intrinsic value initially in an option giving the right to buy a share at 100p (the **exercise price**) when the share price was 100p. In the market jargon, the option was **at the money**. If it had been a call option to buy an XYZ share at 100p when the share price was 90p, it would have been **out of the money**. An option to buy a share at 100p when the share price is 110p is **in the money** — it has intrinsic value. With put options this works the other way round; the option is in the money when the market price is below the exercise price.

The time value in an option erodes throughout its life. It may be worth paying 10p for the chance that a share price will rise by more than this amount some time in the next three months. It would probably not be worth paying the same if the option only had a week to run. So the market price of an option will usually drop gradually unless the market price of the underlying share moves the right way (up for a call option and down for a put).

The London Traded Options Market offers options on the shares of over 60 companies, including the major privatization stocks, British Telecom and British Gas. It also offers options on a few French shares and on the FT-SE ('Footsie') index. The latter is an index of 100 leading shares and the option is a way of betting on the movement of the market as a whole.

For each company there are options with different **exercise prices** (the exercise price is shown in the *Financial Times* in the column immediately following the name) and there are call and put options at each price. The idea is to have at least one **out of the money** and one **in the money option** for each company. And at each price there are options with differing lives. They normally run initially for three, six or nine months. Once the life of the three-month option has expired, the six month option will only have three months life left, the previous nine months option will only have six months and a new nine month option will be created. Options in Allied Lyons, say, have expiry dates in January, April, July and October — only three being available at one time. Others follow a different cycle to prevent all options having the same expiry dates. FT-SE options work rather differently with lives of one to four months.

The Financial Times gives middle prices for traded options, listed under the expiry date. In practice, as with shares, marketmakers quote a spread of **bid** and **offer** prices. The price quoted is for an option on a single share, but deals are in **contracts** which normally consist of options on 1,000 shares. Under the name of the company is shown the previous day's price for the shares themselves.

Because of the gearing, price swings in traded options can be very large and can happen very fast. There are theoretical models for calculating what the price of an option should be relative to the underlying share price, and professionals deal actively to take advantage of small anomalies. Activity is sometimes very heavy in options of companies in the news — particularly takeover candidates. The *Financial Times* normally comments on options market activity in its London market report. More specialist investment publications such as the *Investors Chronicle* discuss option market strategy.

Financial futures

The **futures market** most closely related to the securities markets is the **London International Financial Futures Exchange** or **LIFFE** (pronounced 'life'). It provides a market for futures contracts in **long-dated**, **medium-dated** and **short-dated gilt-edged stocks**, **American**, **German** and **Japanese government bonds**, **short-term sterling and euro interest rates**, the **FT-SE Index** and a variety of **currencies**. In addition it offers options to buy or sell futures contracts and options on cash instruments. It is modelled on the American futures markets: Chicago and New York are the home of futures trading, which is now spreading worldwide.

The members of LIFFE are mainly subsidiaries of financial institutions — banks, discount houses, stockbrokers — plus individual traders or **locals** who trade on their own account. Trading works on the **open outcry** system. Traders yell and signal to each other on the floor, creating bedlam during the busy periods.

As with options, financial futures can be used to hedge an existing risk or to accept a higher risk in return for large potential profits. Each contract is structured differently from the others; the long gilt contract is probably easiest to understand.

The size of this contract is a nominal £50,000 and the price is expressed in terms of a notional 9 per cent long-dated stock. If the price were 93$\frac{20}{32}$ it would be shown as 93-20. The minimum step by which the price can move (a **tick**) is a 32nd of one per cent. Expressed as a proportion of the £50,000 contract value, this is £15.625. The buyer of a contract is theoretically buying a nominal £50,000 of gilt-edged stock for delivery in the future.

If interest rates fall, the value of the contract is likely to rise because gilt-edged stocks will rise in value. If the price rose to 96-18, the investor could sell a contract at 96-18 to cancel the contract he had bought at 93-20. This would represent a profit of 94 ticks or £1,468.75. The initial margin on the long gilt contract is £500, so anyone who had bought a contract would have a profit of 294 per cent. Financial futures contracts very rarely result in physical delivery. The purchaser of a contract simply closes his position by selling an identical contract and taking his profit or his loss.

The contract can be used in a number of ways. A trader might simply buy a contract as a bet on a reduction in interest rates. An insurance company which knew it would have £50,000 coming in in three months to invest in gilt-edged stocks might be scared that prices would have risen by the time it had the money to buy. So for an initial outlay of £500 it could buy one long gilt contract. If it had to pay a higher price for its gilt-edged stocks when the £50,000 was available, it would have a profit on its futures contract to offset the higher cost. Someone who thought interest rates would rise and gilt-edged values would therefore fall would sell the long gilt contract in the hope of buying a contract more cheaply later and pocketing the difference in the price.

The same principle applies to the contracts in currencies, interest rates or the FT-SE equity index. By using futures it is

LONDON (LIFFE)

20-YEAR 9% NOTIONAL GILT
£50,000 32nds of 100%

	Close	High	Low	Prev.
Sep	94-09	94-24	94-08	94-26
Dec	94-10	94-16	94-10	94-28

Estimated Volume 9787 (12309)
Previous day's open int. 25256 (25335)

Table 17.2   Prices for the long gilt contract. Source: *Financial Times*.

LONDON METAL EXCHANGE			(Prices supplied by Amalgamated Metal Trading)		
	Close	Previous	High/Low	AM Official	Kerb close	Open Interest
Aluminium, 99.7% purity ($ per tonne)					Ring turnover 15,625 tonne	
Cash	1835-45	1810-5	1840/1838	1835-8		
3 months	1775-80	1778-80	1790/1775	1775-80	1780-3	32,418 lots
Copper, Grade A (£ per tonne)					Ring turnover 28,650 tonne	
Cash	1473-5	1494-6	1479/1478	1477-8		
3 months	1461-2	1479-80	1476/1450	1462.5-3.5	1460-1	75,119 lots
Lead (£ per tonne)					Ring turnover 4,825 tonne	
Cash	414-5	420-0.5	415/411	413-5		
3 months	397.5-8	403-4	402/396	396.5-7.5	397.5-8	9,456 lots

Table 17.3 Metals prices. Source: *Financial Times*.

possible to lock into a known exchange rate or hedge against a rise in interest rates: the value of an interest rate contract falls if interest rates move up, much as with a gilts contract. So you buy a contract if you are betting on a fall in interest rates and sell if you expect a rise. The techniques available to the futures trader can be highly complex. But the most important point in terms of press comment is that price movements in the futures market will sometimes give advance warning of likely price trends in the stockmarket itself (the **cash** market) or the foreign exchanges.

Commodity markets

London's main commodity markets divide between the **metals** and the **soft** (foodstuff) commodities. Metals are traded on the **London Metal Exchange (LME)** and the soft commodities on the **London Futures and Options Exchange** (the former **London Commodity Exchange**), also known as **London FOX**.

The main non-ferrous metals — **copper, lead, zinc, nickel** and **aluminium** — are traded on the LME. **Tin** is now traded again after a longish hiatus (see below). Trading is carried out by the **ring-dealing members** who transact their own or their clients' orders on an **open outcry** basis in trading sessions that last five minutes for each metal and take place four times a day. The official price for the metal for the day is the price ruling at the end of the session, though there is also extensive dealing on the telephone before and after the official sessions.

In addition to the ring-dealing members, there are **commission houses** which offer a brokerage service to would-be investors or speculators in commodities. They channel their business through a ring-dealing member (in some cases they may own one).

Trading on the LME is a mix of **physical** and **futures** business. A price is established for each metal for immediate delivery (the **cash** price or **spot** price) and also a price for delivery in three months. Prices may also be agreed for any period between, and nowadays it is also possible to deal up to fifteen months ahead. The futures price is for a standard contract (25 tonnes in the case of copper) of metal of a defined grade and there are also official LME options on futures contracts. The *Financial Times* shows both the cash and three months prices for the LME metals and the movement on the day. Usually the three months price is higher than the cash price (**contango**) because the buyer is avoiding financing costs for three months. **Backwardation** is the situation where the cash price exceeds the three months price.

Tin was traded actively until a disastrous collapse in the price destroyed the market and left a legacy of litigation that rumbled on. The **International Tin Council**, consisting of major producer and consumer countries, operated a **buffer stock** system whereby the buffer stock manager would buy tin for stock when the price was low and release it to the market when the price was high, thus evening out extreme price and supply fluctuations. Or that was the theory. It emerged in 1986 that sustained buying at high prices had resulted in a totally artificial tin price, which then collapsed when the buffer stock manager ran out of money and could buy no more. Following a recovery in the price, tin trading has now resumed.

The London Futures and Options Exchange offers futures contracts (and options on futures) in **cocoa**, **coffee** and two grades of **sugar**. It works on an open outcry system, except that there is an automatic trading system for one of the sugar contracts. Prices can move sharply on reports or rumours of glut

COFFEE £/tonne			
	Close	Previous	High/Low
Jul	860	870	880 856
Sep	866	880	900 865
Nov	884	896	905 880
Jan	905	912	921 900
Mar	925	932	930 919
May	942	952	953 939
Jul	965	966	970 965

Turnover: 5937 (9393) lots of 5 tonnes
ICO indicator prices (US cents per pound) for
Jul 5: Comp. daily 85.78 (88.35). 15 day average
97.97 (99.07)

Table 17.4   Coffee market report. Source: *Financial Times*.

or crop failure in the producer countries. The **International Petroleum Exchange**, which is located in the same building, offers futures contracts in **gas oil** and other petroleum products.

The **Baltic Exchange** houses futures markets in a number of agricultural products as well as shipping freight.

18

Lloyd's and insurance

Lloyd's of London, the international insurance market, is one of the oldest of the City's institutions and a major contributor to Britain's foreign earnings. In 1987 its net contribution to Britain's **invisible earnings** was put at £2.4 billion.

But the 1980s have not been its finest decade. Traditionally, Lloyd's minded its own business and expected the world outside to do likewise. The interest the press began to take in Lloyd's in recent years was viewed initially as an impertinent intrusion and an unwarranted attack on one of the very pillars of City life. Lloyd's was beyond reproach, particularly from outsiders. But this attitude proved impossible to sustain as news of a variety of scandals percolated through Lloyd's walls and led to heated debate in parliament as well as the press. At the heart of these scandals was strong evidence that some at least of the market's professionals were enriching themselves at the expense of the outside **names** — the non-working 'investors' whose wealth allowed the market to function. And in a few cases this process constituted outright theft rather than merely time-hallowed market custom and practice. The debate on Lloyd's is far from over yet.

Underwriting profits and investment income

In outline, the business of insurance is not unduly complicated. We're talking here about **general insurance** — **underwriting** the risk of damage or destruction to ships, aircraft, property and so on — rather than **life assurance**, which is a different kind of business. The insurer charges a **premium** commensurate with the risk he is underwriting, and hopes that all the premiums he receives will exceed all the **claims** he has to pay out. If he is right, he makes an **underwriting profit**. But he does not rely on the **premium income** alone. The money he receives as premiums is earning interest until it has to be paid out in claims, so in addition he is receiving an **investment income** which can help to offset any losses he makes on the underwriting side. Insurance claims often take a number of years to finalize, so he may have use of the money for some considerable time (business where claims may arise a long time after the insurance was arranged is known as **long-tail business**).

Where an insurer is worried by the size of a risk he is underwriting, he can lay off part of his bet (rather like a bookie) by **reinsuring** it with another insurer. Thus the original insurer may say 'I'll bear the first £10m of any loss, the **reinsurer** will take the next £10m, and I'll accept any excess over that'. Part of the original premium obviously has to be handed over to the reinsurer.

The principle is much the same whether the original insurer is a company or a Lloyd's **syndicate**. The greater part of insurance business in the UK is undertaken by insurance companies, particularly the more standard types of business such as household and car insurance. Lloyd's is best known for marine insurance and for insuring the more unusual types of risk.

How names' wealth is put to work

An insurance company relies on the premiums plus the company's own funds to cover the risks it underwrites (though it may also reinsure part of its risk). Lloyd's, though its members also use reinsurance, works on a different principle. It has over 6,000 working members who underwrite the business, and some 25,000 non-working members who are also, confusingly, underwriters but are usually known as **names**. These rich individuals derive various tax advantages from underwriting at Lloyd's.

The names do not have to put up vast amounts of money. Instead, they stand surety for the risks that are underwritten at Lloyd's. In other words, they pledge the whole of their wealth to meet claims, should this be necessary. They hope that premiums and investment income will outweigh claims and that they will never have to stump up. But if the worst comes to the worst, they might have to sell everything they own — though it is possible to insure against this risk, too.

The beauty of the system is that wealth can be made to work twice over, and sometimes more. To become a name the individual has to be able to show a minimum amount of wealth (excluding his home and certain other assets): £250,000 at the time of writing. But the amounts he has to hand over in cash are very much smaller. So his £250,000 or more of wealth can be, say, invested in stocks and shares and earning a return for its owner. At the same time it is providing the necessary back-up for the risks that are being insured.

However, the reduction in the top rate of income tax to 40 per cent in the 1988 Budget has somewhat eroded the advantages of being a Lloyd's name and, taken together with heavy losses faced by some members and the increase in wealth required (it was previously £100,000), has resulted in a modest decline in the number of non-working underwriters.

The syndicate structure

In theory, all members of Lloyd's trade as individuals. In practice they are grouped into **syndicates** — over 400 of them — and one name may spread his risk by belonging to several syndicates. A **working underwriter**, who is a Lloyd's profesional, accepts insurance risks on behalf of the syndicate. The business will be brought to him by a **Lloyd's broker**, who represents the client seeking insurance and whose duty is to arrange it on the best terms. The name is introduced to his syndicate or syndicates by a **members' agent** who looks after his interests. A **managing agent** looks after the organizational side of the syndicate's business. **Underwriting agencies** sometimes combine managing agents and members' agents in one organization. Accounts are drawn up three years after the year to which they relate, because of the length of time required for claims to be assessed.

Scandals and regulation

Lloyd's regulates its own affairs under an Act of Parliament. It does not come within the scope of the Financial Services Act (see Chapter 21). The most recent legislation is the Lloyd's Act 1982, introduced in response to the scandals of the late 1970s and early

1980s. The governing **council of Lloyd's** was to include non-working members and nominated members from outside, and a new office of Chief Executive was created (the incumbent to be approved by the Bank of England). Previously, many large Lloyd's brokers (with their duty to the client) had also owned **underwriting agencies** (with a responsibility to members of the syndicates they managed). The brokers were required to dispose of such interests to avoid the obvious **conflicts of interest**. And greater disclosure of outside interests was required of working members.

The scandals these measures were intended to deal with fell into several categories. Brokers were accused of excessive pressure on syndicates to settle dubious claims. Some underwriting agents took on more business than the syndicate was entitled to underwrite, thus exposing it to excessive losses. Reinsurance was arranged with **offshore companies** in which working underwriters had interests they had not declared to the names and which could be highly profitable. There were suspicions of **baby syndicates**, whose members were Lloyd's professionals, to which the most profitable business might be channelled. And many underwriting agents managed **parallel syndicates** — two syndicates alongside each other, with a risk that one might be favoured at the expense of the other.

There were also cases of taking on business which was suspected to be fraudulent, and still worse cases of straightforward theft of names' money. The problem for names who lost heavily in some of these scandals was in establishing that they had suffered as a result of breaches of Lloyd's rules or fraud (in which case they might be entitled to compensation from Lloyd's) rather than poor underwriting alone (in which case they would have to bear the losses). In the biggest of these affairs — the case of the PCW syndicates — names were faced with losses running into the hundreds of millions of pounds.

Lloyd's has maintained that the scandals that rumble on relate to events that took place before 1982, and that its regulatory house is now in much better order. Sir Patrick Neill, reporting early in 1987 on regulation at Lloyd's, recognized that progress had been made but suggested that there was still a great deal to do and that the market was still weighted far too heavily in favour of working members. His recommendations included a call for more outside nominated members on the council and an

Ombudsman to whom names could appeal — both of these measures have been implemented. However, there is still occasional political pressure to bring Lloyd's within the scope of the Financial Services Act.

19

Commercial property investment

Commercial property — office buildings, shops, factories and warehouses — is one of the major avenues for investment by the **insurance companies** and **pension funds**. Together, they hold properties valued at around £60 billion. There is, however, no central marketplace in commercial property. The 'market' is largely organized by the major firms of **chartered surveyors** or **estate agents** which include a 'Big Four': Jones Lang Wootton, Richard Ellis, Healey & Baker and Hillier Parker. These firms provide a range of property investment services. They advise on property portfolios, often manage portfolios on behalf of institutions, provide valuations, negotiate lettings, purchases and sales and assist in arranging finance for developments.

There are really two **commercial property markets**. There is the **letting market** in which landlords let buildings to tenants. And there is the **investment market** where completed and revenue-producing buildings are acquired by financial institutions as long-term investments. The two markets overlap and increasingly the larger institutions are involved in both aspects. They create investments by undertaking **property developments**, letting the completed buildings and holding on to them for the rent they provide.

Property journalists write about both markets: how rents are moving for particular kinds of property, and the prices investors are prepared to pay for revenue-producing properties.

Property as an investment

A commercial property tends to be regarded as a growth investment rather like an ordinary share, though the income

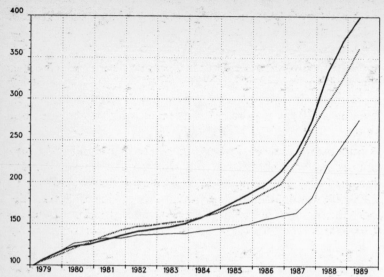

Figure 19.1 Investors Chronicle Hillier Parker rent indexes for shops (upper solid line), offices (dotted line) and industrial buildings (lower line). Shops have shown the greatest growth in rents. But for all classes of property rents began to rise very fast in 1987, after a dull five years. Source: *Datastream International.*

comes in the form of **rent** rather than dividend and it requires more management by the investor. However, properties in Britain are often let on **full repairing and insuring leases** which put much of the responsibility for maintenance on the tenant.

Commercial properties are often let on very long **leases** — 99 years used to be common — but nowadays the rent the tenant pays is normally reviewed every five (or even three) years. The owner of the building obviously hopes that the **rental value** of the building (the rent it would fetch if let today in the open market) will rise consistently, but he only collects these increases at three- or five-year intervals when **rent reviews** occur or when the lease comes to an end and is renegotiated.

Properties are normally **valued** as a **multiple** of the rent they produce. Take an office building in London with 10,000 square feet of lettable area and producing a rent of £20 per sq. ft. per year. The total annual income will be £200,000. An investor might be prepared to buy the building at a price which showed him a return of five per cent on his outlay. He is prepared to accept a fairly low initial return because he expects the income to increase in the future, as with an ordinary share.

He is therefore prepared to buy the investment at £4m, which is the price that would show him a five per cent return and is 20 times the rent it produces. This is effectively the 'PE ratio' of the investment, though the property world would talk of buying the building at 20 **years' purchase** of the rent, which means the same thing.

Suppose the first **rent review** is due in five years, and as this time approaches the rental value has risen to £30 per sq. ft.. The income from the building if let at its market rent would now be £300,000, though the tenant is still only paying £200,000. But once the rent is reviewed at the end of the fifth year, it jumps to £300,000, which then holds good for the next five years.

Because rent reviews only come at intervals, it is clear that for much of the time the tenant may be paying a rent below the current market value. The rent will revert to its market value when the lease runs out and a new one is negotiated or when the rent review in the existing lease occurs. Property journalists thus talk of a landlord expecting large increases in revenue as 'rent reviews and **reversions** occur over the next few years'.

Freeholds and leaseholds

The pattern of property ownership in Britain is complex. The example above is of a **freehold** building, which for most purposes is owned outright by the landlord. But often the interests in the building are split. The original owner of the land may only have granted a lease — for 99 years, say — to the developer who put up the building and who now 'owns' it. In this case the freeholder is the owner of the land, and he charges the developer an annual **ground rent** which used to be a fixed amount but nowadays will probably be adjusted upwards at intervals. The developer becomes the **leaseholder** and his building is **leasehold**. He lets the building to a tenant at a market rent or **rack rent**, and from this he has to pay the ground rent to the freeholder. In practice, ownership of property can be considerably more complex than this with several layers of lease before you get to the tenant who pays the market rent.

Valuation

Valuation of properties — but particularly of leasehold buildings or of **reversionary properties** (properties currently let below the market rent) — can be very complex and is usually undertaken by a chartered surveyor. Since no one property is quite like any other property, he has to work from recent precedents. Suppose investors seem to expect a five per cent return from standard office buildings of the type he is valuing; he adjusts for the different special factors that apply to this building and works out what price would provide a comparable return.

If a property is reversionary — the rent it currently produces is, say, £200,000 but this will jump to £300,000 in a year's time when the rent review occurs — the yield based on the current rent may be very low. However, this yield is often adjusted to produce an **equivalent yield**, which shows what yield the valuer would be working on if the building were let at the market rent.

Finance for developers

We have talked about both investors and **developers** in the property business, though the financial institutions may now fulfill both functions. But long before they got into the development business on their own account, they were the traditional source of long-term finance for property development because they had large-scale funds looking for a long-term home. The 'developer' was usually an entrepreneur with an eye for a good site who would carry out the development but use mainly other people's money to finance it.

In the immediate post-war years, developers of commercial buildings (mainly property companies) normally obtained their long-term finance by **mortgaging** the development to a financial institution when it was completed and let. Insurance companies and pension funds would, typically, provide a loan of two-thirds of the value for 25 years or more at a fixed rate of interest.

As interest rates rose, this became less practicable and various forms of partnership between institution and developer evolved. The most common was the **leaseback** or **sale and leaseback**. The developer identified the site and the possibility of putting up a building. The institution bought the land and provided finance for the development, which was managed by the developer. On completion, the institution granted a lease to the developer, who in turn granted a lease to the tenant at a rack rent. The developer paid a ground rent of, say, 70 per cent of the rental value of the building to the institution. The remaining 30 per cent **top slice** belonged to him. There were numerous variations on this theme, and the developer's rent to the institution would normally rise as the rental income of the building rose. Clearly, if the developer was unable to let the last 30 per cent of space in the building, he had no profit.

Subsequently, various other forms of partnership financing arrangement evolved which split the risk more equitably between the provider of finance and the developer — these may be referred to as **side-by-side** or **partnership** arrangements. But increasingly the bigger institutions began to cut out the developer altogether by undertaking their own projects, possibly with the help of one of the large firms of surveyors.

The **sale and leaseback**, incidentally, has also been widely used as a financing method for commmercial companies, particularly retailers. Company A might take over Company B, which owns the shops from which it carries out its trade. The shops can then be sold for a lump sum to an institution but Company B continues to occupy them, now paying a normal commercial rent as a tenant.

The property companies

Apart from the institutions, **property companies** are also significant property owners. These are often stockmarket-quoted companies which either simply hold properties as an investment (**property investment company**) or undertake developments (**property development company**). Many of them do both. An investment and development company provides a very secure income, since its revenue comes mainly from recurring rents. A development company whose profits come from selling buildings on completion (a **property trading company**, sometimes known as a **merchant developer**) can be more erratic, since profits can fluctuate widely.

Many of the longer-established investment or investment and development companies were originally built up by entrepreneurial developers after the war. Property investment companies tend to be valued on the stockmarket by reference to the **asset backing** for their shares. As with investment trusts, the shares

223

usually stand at a discount to the NAV, except at times of temporary market euphoria. Trading companies which make their profit from selling properties are more likely to be rated on a PE ratio basis and the shares often stand above the asset value.

Unitized property

Apart from the shares of property companies, there are a few other avenues for investment in commercial property. There are specialist **property unit trusts** which own a range of properties. Pension funds or charities can invest in these units to obtain a stake in a portfolio of commercial property as an alternative to owning properties outright. But these vehicles are not open to the public.

The public can, however, acquire a stake in commercial property by investing in **property bonds**. These are unit-linked life assurance contacts (see Chapter 20) where the link is to the value of a portfolio of commercial properties rather than shares. It is also proposed to allow **authorized unit trusts** (those in which the general public may buy units) to invest directly in property. Hitherto this had been prohibited.

There are plans to extend the principle of **unitization** — dividing the ownership of properties among a number of investors — to single properties. The reason is that some individual buildings are now so valuable that it is difficult to find even an institution that will buy or finance one by itself. If the ownership can be divided, however, the problem is eased. The ownership of the £20m building could be divided, say, into 20,000 units of £1,000 each, and both institutions and private investors could take a stake. By the beginning of 1989 one form of unitized property scheme — **Property Income Certificates** or **PINCs** — had surmounted the regulatory hurdles and was ready to launch. PINCs would be traded on The Stock Exchange.

Property indexes

In writing about property there are several yardsticks that journalists and others use. For **property shares** there is a **property company sub-index** of the Financial Times-Actuaries indexes. And a number of firms of estate agents produce **indexes of rental values** of different types of property, of **movement in capital values** and of the yields on which **prime properties** (the best property investments in their category) or average investment-grade properties are changing hands. The other end of the scale from prime property is **secondary property** which may not be of investment grade for the institutions. Normally **shops** show the lowest yield (are the most highly valued), **offices** come next and **industrial properties** which covers factories and warehouses are valued on the highest yields.

Property performance

Commercial property values tend to follow a pronounced cyclical pattern, and often move counter-cyclically to shares (and also sometimes to residential property). The period 1982 to 1986 (while the stockmarket was booming) was very dull in the commercial property market with values showing comparatively little growth. Then in 1987 and 1988 rents and values rose very sharply and were virtually untouched by the October 1987 crash on the stockmarket. By 1989 some worries over the level of bank lending to property companies were beginning to surface: it had reached £22 billion.

20

Savings and unit-linked investment

The public flotations of British Telecom, Trustee Savings Bank and British Gas attracted millions of first-time investors to the stockmarket. But these issues could give a misleading impression of how the bulk of the British public invests its money.

Direct ownership of shares, in the traditional wisdom, is for those with enough spare cash to afford holdings in a spread of companies, thus reducing the risk if any one of them falls on hard times. Savers who are not yet in this happy position are almost invariably given the following advice: start buying your own home and take out **life assurance**, both as a means of saving and to protect your family. Make suitable **pension** arrangements if you are not part of an **occupational scheme** (a scheme run by your employer). Smallish amounts of spare cash may be invested for safety, convenience and a reasonable return with your **building society**. Only when you have spare cash after taking care of the necessities should you become more adventurous in your investment policy.

This advice is backed by considerations of tax efficiency as well as safety. Interest on (in 1989) up to £30,000 of a **mortgage** taken out to buy your main home can be offset against both basic and higher rate income tax. Profits on the sale of your main home are free of capital gains tax. Home ownership is often regarded as an investment as much as a comfort of life.

Life assurance used to offer tax benefits until 1984. There was partial tax relief on the premiums, and there still is for anyone with a pre-1984 policy. New policyholders do not get tax relief.

Pensions, however, remain the best tax bargain of all. Up to approved limits, there is tax relief on premiums. And once the premiums are invested by the pension fund it pays no tax on either income or capital gains. The sums invested to provide a pension can thus compound in value far more rapidly than most other forms of investment where income would be taxed.

How the British invest their money

This pattern of investment is confirmed by the official figures. By far the largest single item in the wealth of individuals is **housing**, with an estimated value of £739 billion in 1987 before deducting the amounts owed under house purchase loans.

Next look at the **financial assets** of individuals: how they hold and invest their money. In the third quarter of 1988, total gross financial assets of the **personal sector** were estimated at £921 billion. The most important items were:

	£ billion
Cash and sterling bank balances	105
National savings	37
Government stocks	28
Building society shares and deposits	143
Shares in UK companies	137
Equity in insurance and pension funds	386

Thus the value of individuals' stakes in life assurance and pensions far outweighs any other form of investment. Building society investment comes next and **direct shareholdings** in companies at £137 billion come third. This figure for shareholdings has risen in recent years, partly because of privatization issues which attracted many first-time investors to the stockmarket and partly because of the rise in share prices up to October 1987. Even so, up to 1987 private investors had regularly sold more UK shares than they bought each year. And though in 1989 there are nine million or so direct shareholders, many of them simply have a few hundred pounds' worth of shares in British Telecom or British Gas.

It remains to be seen whether the government's programme of nationalized industry sales will permanently reverse the trend of net sales by private individuals and persuade them again to be a significant direct force in the stockmarket. Employee share ownership schemes as well as privatization issues may help. But for the time being, saving via the financial institutions is the order of the day, though the **unit trusts** grew faster than other forms of collective savings during the market boom and in mid-1989 managed investments of over £50 billion.

The basic personal finance guidance in the press follows the pattern of individuals' savings preferences. The main areas covered are **life assurance, pensions, house purchase** and **unit trust investment**, with a fair helping of **tax advice**. The schemes on offer from the major life assurance companies are compared. The investment performance — where applicable — of different life assurance savings schemes and of individual unit trusts is recorded. Following changes to the terms of Personal Equity Plans (PEPs) in the 1989 Budget (see below) we can also expect greater press coverage of this investment medium.

Financial intermediaries in the savings market

This information is aimed at insurance brokers as well as the public. Much life assurance and related savings products is sold through **financial intermediaries**, which in practice normally means **insurance brokers** who frequently also operate under the title of **investment advisers** or **financial consultants**. These are the middle-men between the public and the insurance companies or savings institutions. Since they live from the commission on the products they sell there is an inevitable temptation for them to be swayed in favour of the product paying the highest commission, and the independence of their advice is sometimes called into question. As an indirect result of the City's new regulatory system, an increasing number of them are in any case tying themselves to one particular insurance company or provider of investment products.

Traditional life assurance

The basic life assurance theme has an infinite number of variations. **Term insurance** is a straight bet with the insurance company: you pay premiums for an agreed period, and if you die during that time the insurance company pays the sum for which your life was insured. If you survive, you've lost the bet (or won it, depending on your outlook) and you get nothing at the end of the period. **Whole life** insurance pays a lump sum when you die, at any age. So your family gets something even if you live to 90.

Endowment asssurance is a savings vehicle for you as well as a protection for your dependents. You pay the premiums, and at the end of the term of the insurance you get a lump sum. If you die earlier, your dependents get a lump sum, as with whole life. The life assurance aspect of the contract is not too complicated: insurance company actuaries can calculate pretty accurately from mortality tables the risk of your dying before such-and-such an age (though new dangers such as AIDS cause problems) and provide for it in the premium they charge. The premium income goes into the **life funds** of the insurance company, where it is invested and this is where the main uncertainty arises: the return the insurance company will earn on its investments. In the case of a **with-profits policy** the policyholder is entitled to a share of the profits from the growth of the fund.

Company and individual pensions

Pensions are an extension of life assurance, and the major insurance companies provide them: both company schemes and schemes for individuals. Take the company schemes first. These may be **insured schemes**, where the insurance group tells the company what premium it needs each year to provide the eventual level of benefit required. Or the company may hand over the contributions to be invested in a **managed fund** run by the insurance group; the pension scheme is allocated units in the fund pro rata with its contribution, and the value of the units depends on the investment performance of the fund. Or the pension fund may simply employ the insurance company as an **investment manager**, to manage its assets as a separate fund: a field in which merchant banks, brokers and other fund management groups compete fiercely.

Alternatively the pension fund can, of course, manage its own investments, as many of the larger ones do. With a buoyant stockmarket and high real returns on investment, many pension funds were showing **surpluses** in the mid-1980s. The value of their investments exceeded what was needed to meet expected liabilities. These surpluses were being reduced in a number of ways and were also being 'raided' by the sponsoring company and by takeover practitioners.

In the past employees of a company which ran its own pension scheme were normally forced to join that scheme. From 1988 they have been free to make their own arrangements, sometimes known as **personal portable pensions** because they can be taken from job to job. The self-employed already do this if they do not wish to rely on the fairly meagre benefits of the **state pension schemes**. To build up bigger pensions, those in pension schemes may make **additional voluntary contributions** or **AVCs**.

Pensions are increasingly used to provide security for loans to an individual or a business. Since part of a pension may be paid as a lump sum and the remainder as a continuing income, the pension terms are designed so that, on retirement, the lump sum repays the loan.

Repayment and endowment mortgages

Buying a house with the help of a **mortgage** is usually regarded as a form of savings and mortgages, too, can have a life assurance element. The homebuyer can take out either a **repayment mortgage** or an **endowment mortgage**. With the **repayment mortgage** the amount borrowed is repaid via monthly instalments of interest and capital (more interest and less capital in the early stages and more capital and less interest in the later ones). Repayments are calculated so that the whole of the sum will have been repaid by the end of the term: usually 25 years, though because people move house the average life of a mortgage in practice is much shorter. But since the interest rate on mortgages is normally variable, payments may have to be adjusted up and down as interest rates change. Changes in the rates are always hot news.

The **endowment mortgage** introduces the life assurance. The money to buy the house is borrowed, usually from a **building society**, and interest is paid to the lender in the normal way. But no capital is repaid. Instead, the borrower takes out an endowment life assurance policy which, when it matures, will provide a lump sum large enough to repay the loan from the building society. Instead of repayments of capital, the borrower is paying premiums to the life assurance company. These policies can again have a with-profits element so that, on maturity, the loan is repaid and there is an additional sum for the policyholder. There are many variations on this theme, and the relative tax advantages of the repayment and endowment mortgage are periodically aired in the personal finance columns.

```
M & G Securities (y) (0915)H
Three Quays, Tower Hill, EC3R 6BQ
Cust Services 01-626 4588      Unit Dealing 0245 266266
Amer & General .....5 255.3₁  255.4   270.1  -0.9 1.12
(Accum Units) .......5 306.97  307.0   324.7  -1.2 1.12
Amer Recovery ......5 286.91  289.4   306.0  -2.2 0.93
(Accum Units) .......5 320.22  322.9   341.5  -2.5 0.93
Amer Smllr Cos .....5  58.50   59.90   63.30  -0.3 0.04
(Accum Units) .......5  59.62   61.00   64.50  -0.3 0.04
Australasian ........5 101.24  101.3   107.1       1.60
(Accum Units) .......5 113.30  113.3   119.8  -0.1 1.60
Charifund ...........1 570.74  580.4   586.3  -0.8 5.89
(Accum Units) .........1777.81 1808.2  1826.3 -2.6 5.89
Commodity .........5 260.55  260.6   275.6  -0.6 1.68
(Accum Units) .......5 354.95  355.0   375.4  -0.9 1.68
Compound Growth ..5 621.38  621.4   657.1  -0.8 3.22
Conversion Growth ..5 543.78  559.4   591.6  -1.2 4.02
Conversion Income ..5 280.16  285.6   302.0  -0.1 5.56
Dividend ...........5 605.96  615.5xd 650.9  -1.0 5.02
(Accum Units) .......5 1986.70 2018.2  2134.2 -3.2 5.02
European ..........5 290.61  293.5xd 310.4  -1.5 0.76
(Accum Units) .......5 352.63  356.1   376.6  -1.8 0.76
Extra Yield ........5 345.29  350.4   370.5  -0.8 5.35
(Accum Units) .......5 827.90  840.2   888.5  -1.8 5.35
Far Eastern ........5 185.87  187.8   200.9  -0.5 0.58
(Accum Units) .......5 233.55  236.0   252.5  -0.6 0.58
Fund of Inv Tsts ..5 366.67  371.6xd 393.9  -0.7 2.55
(Accum Units) .......5 611.86  620.1   657.3  -1.2 2.55
General ...........5 922.33  922.4xd 975.4  -1.6 3.83
(Accum Units) .......5 2123.40 2123.4  2245.5 -3.8 3.83
Gilt Income ........5  56.38   56.50   59.30       9.62
(Accum. Units) .....5 105.25  105.4   110.7  -0.1 9.62
Gold ..............5  44.49   45.1xd  48.3  +0.5 1.49
(Accum Units) .......5  49.47   50.20   53.70 +0.5 1.49
High Income ........5 443.55  451.2xd 477.1  -0.6 5.44
(Accum Units) .......5 1359.90 1383.4  1462.9 -1.6 5.44
Internatnl Growth ..5 987.73  988.7   1057.9 -0.2 1.28
(Accum Units) .......5 1633.02 1634.6  1749.0 -0.3 1.28
International Inc. ..5  68.16   68.80   72.80 -0.2 4.97
(Accum Units) .......5  78.37   79.10   83.70 -0.3 4.97
Japan & General ..5 1133.65 1134.2xd 1202.3 -1.9 0.00
(Accum Units) .......5 1216.41 1217.0  1290.0 -2.1 0.00
Japan Smaller Cos .5 133.86  134.6   142.7 +0.1 0.00
(Accum Units) .......5 134.80  135.6   143.7 +0.1 0.00
Midland ...........5 1035.56 1059.3  1120.2 +0.2 4.14
(Accum Units) .......5 2795.29 2859.4  3023.8 +0.6 4.14
Pension ex ........2 685.05  685.1   702.2 -1.2 4.31
Recovery ..........5 630.08  640.7xd 677.5 -1.3 4.08
(Accum Units) .......5 878.53  893.3   944.7 -1.8 4.08
Second General ....5 993.70  1013.1xd 1071.3 -4.5 3.78
(Accum Units) .......5 2121.65 2163.1  2287.5 -9.5 3.78
Smaller Cos .......5 1170.54 1208.2  1277.7 +1.7 2.92
(Accum Units) .......5 1940.64 2003.2  2118.4 +2.9 2.92
Trustee ...........5 664.88  669.7   716.6 -2.2 4.49
(Accum Units) .......5 2112.99 2128.5  2277.5 -7.0 4.49
```

Table 20.1   Unit trust price information. Source: *Financial Times*.

Unit-linked investment vehicles

Move beyond the basic insurance and loan products, and you are next likely to meet the **unit-linked** investment vehicles. These give some of the benefits of stockmarket investment while spreading the risks.

It is inappropriate, as we have seen, for an individual with modest savings to risk them all on the vagaries of one share price — except when the Government is off-loading previously nationalized industries, we are asked to believe. But it makes sense for those with small amounts of capital or no knowledge of the stockmarket to invest in a spread of shares rather than the shares of a single company. Hence **unit trusts** and **unit-linked assurance.** Look at the pages of tables at the back of the *Financial Times*, just ahead of the stockmarket prices, and headed **FT unit**

trust information service, with the sub-headings **authorized unit trusts, insurances** and **offshore and overseas**. They occupy over three pages and have grown enormously in recent years. These are the products that the investment management community is offering the public.

Principles of unit trust investment

Despite the variety on offer, the principle of **unitized** or **pooled** investment is simple. Suppose you and ninety-nine other people each stump up £1 for investment in a new **unit trust**. The managers thus collect £100 in total and use it to buy shares in a variety of companies. Over a period the value of the trust's investments rises by, say, 20 per cent. The original £100 of investments is now worth £120. You own one of the hundred units in issue, so the value of your unit is one hundredth of the total value of the fund. In other words its value has risen from £1 to £1.20 (the actual calculations, allowing for costs, are more complex — see below). How would you sell your unit if you wanted to cash in? You would sell it back to the managers of the unit trust, who will then try to sell it to somebody else. If they cannot do so, they may have to sell some of the trust's investments to raise the money to pay you.

Unit-linked insurance incorporates a similar collective investment mechanism, where the value of the unit is linked to the value of a specific fund or sub-fund of investments, but technically it is a life assurance contract. You hand over your money to the managers. A small proportion of it goes to provide a minimal amount of life assurance cover. The remainder is invested in units of what is technically a **life fund**. If the value of the fund rises, the value of your investment rises, too. What is the point of unit-linked insurance, when you can invest in unit trusts? In the past, there were tax advantages in investing in a life assurance contract. Also, a life fund could invest direct in property (unit-linked schemes invested in property are called **property bonds**) and the scheme could be sold door to door, which was not allowed in the case of unit trusts. The treatment of the two types of investment is now being brought closer in line and property-owning unit trusts are on the way.

Pricing of unit trusts

The operations of a unit trust are not, of course, quite as simple as in the example. There are charges for the service: typically, an initial charge of 5 per cent or 6 per cent (it has been rising rapidly) of the value of your investment and an on-going annual charge of 1 per cent or more. So, as with shares, there is not a single price for the units. There is a buying price and a selling price: you buy the units from the managers at the higher 'offer' price and receive the lower 'bid' price when you sell them back. The price spread partially reflects the fact that the unit trust itself has to pay a higher price when it buys shares, gets a lower price when it sells them and will incur dealing expenses. But the spread also includes the initial charge by the managers and various other costs. If a unit trust suffers a large outflow of funds it has some leeway to move bid and offer price down to a lower pricing basis, known as a **bid basis** or **liquidation basis**.

Note that performance figures for unit trusts should always allow for the spread. So if the quotation for a particular trust has moved up from 100p-107p to 120p-128p over the year the calculation should allow for the fact that the investor would have bought at 107p and sold at 120p: a gain of 13p or 12.1 per cent, not 20p.

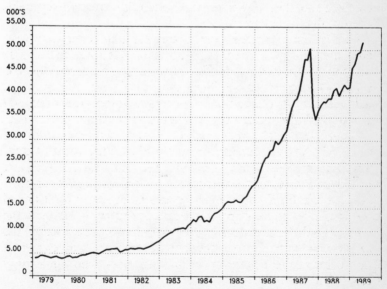

Figure 20.1   Value of funds managed by unit trusts. This rose sharply during the boom years, both because of new money coming in and because share prices were rising. The total has picked up well after the sharp setback caused by the October 1987 crash. Source: *Datastream International.*

Features of unit trust operation

A unit trust which is marketed to the public needed in the past to be **authorized** by the **Department of Trade and Industry**, though responsibility for authorization has passed to the **Securities and Investments Board**. There are also **unauthorized** trusts which some stockbrokers run for their clients and **unauthorized property unit trusts** are permitted to offer a form of collective investment in property to the pension funds. Advertisements for unit trusts are fairly closely monitored and must contain a **health warning** — a reminder that the unit price can go down as well as up.

When they first launch, and sometimes occasionally thereafter, unit trusts make a **fixed price offer** for a limited period — you will see the advertisements in the financial pages of the national papers, usually on a Saturday or Sunday. At this time you can apply for units at a known price. The rest of the time you pay the price ruling around the time your application is received. Fund management groups also frequently provide the opportunity for regular savings plans: you arrange to pay so much a month, the money being invested in units when it is received.

Unit trusts may pay out the income they receive on their investments to their unitholders, pro rata with their holdings. But sometimes the investor has a choice between **income units** (where he gets his share of the dividends) and **accumulation units** (where his share of the income is added to the value of the units). This second option is a convenience but does not offer any tax saving: the income is reinvested net of basic rate tax. An alternative is for the investor to be credited with additional units representing the reinvested net income.

Who offers unit-linked investment?

The *Financial Times* lists around 170 fund management groups offering unit trusts and well over 100 offering unit-linked assurance. Variations of the same name frequently crop up in both categories: most of the larger fund management groups offer the whole range of unit-linked products.

Computers make it easy to calculate the value of a trust's investments each day, and hence the unit price. The *Financial Times* listings show, for unit trusts, both **bid** and **offer prices** and the price movement over the previous day, plus the **gross yield**. In many cases separate prices are shown for income units and accumulation units: the latter will be higher, because of the reinvested income.

Specialist investment policies

The original idea of unit trusts was to offer a spread of investments across most areas of the stockmarket. Then came more specialist funds, investing according to particular philosophies or in particular areas. Have a look at the trusts run by **M & G Securities**, the doyen of the unit trust business. There is a **general fund**. Then there are funds investing for **high income**, in **smaller companies**, in **recovery stocks** (companies down on their luck whose share price should improve dramatically if they pull round) and so on. And there are trusts investing in specific geographical areas: America, Australia, Japan and Europe.

The same range of investment policies is evident in the unit-linked assurance funds, normally known as **bonds** (though not to be confused with government bonds). In fact, many unit trusts have a **bondized** equivalent: an insurance fund which invests in the relevant unit trust. The prices for the bonds, under the heading of **insurances**, follow the same pattern as those for unit trusts, except that no yield is shown since no income is distributed. With unit-linked assurance, the income from the fund's investments is automatically reinvested in the fund after deduction of tax at the life assurance rate.

Managed funds and switching facilities

Two aspects of 'bond' investment attract a lot of press comment. First, most groups run a **managed fund**. This means that the fund invests in the group's other bond funds and the manager can make a strategic decision to switch the emphasis of the managed fund's investments from one area to another as conditions change. If the London stockmarket looked too expensive he might get out of the group's general UK funds and into, say, its property fund. Second, the individual investor may be given some of the same flexibility. He might buy, say, the property fund, but have the right to switch his investment into another of the management group's funds without incurring the full costs of selling one investment and buying another. This degree of flexibility is, because of the different charging structure and tax position, more difficult to build into unit trust investment.

Note that some insurance brokers will concoct their own investment packages for clients, putting together their own mix of the products offered by the fund management groups.

Offshore and overseas funds

After the **insurances** in the *Financial Times* come the prices for **offshore** and **overseas funds**. These are not authorized unit trusts, though they operate on the unit principle and many operate under the umbrella of one of the fund management groups that offers authorized unit trusts in the UK. Many of the offshore funds are technically located in the Channel Islands and managed from there, the UK parent group being described as 'adviser' to the fund. Hence management group names with 'C.I.' in the title.

The **offshore funds** operate under the tax regime of the country where they are located: usually more liberal than in Britain. But for a British investor living in Britain there is no tax advantage in investing in them. He will be treated for tax according to the UK rules. Expatriate Britons working, say, in the Middle East and paying little if any UK tax may do better in an offshore fund than in one registered in the UK. The offshore funds do, however, offer a range of investments in money market instruments and currencies which could not in the past be provided by an authorized UK unit trust.

Monitoring performance

Performance statistics for unit trusts and bonds are closely followed. The monthly magazine **Money Management** provides a comprehensive list, showing the value of £1,000 invested over periods ranging from six months to seven or ten years. Performance can vary very markedly, particularly over the shorter periods, and picking the right country is often more important for the managers than picking the right share, especially at times of wild currency swings. In 1986 the best performing unit trust turned £1,000 into £2,122 and the worst reduced £1,000 to £794. Most of the winners were specialist Japanese and Far Eastern trusts; many of the losers were trusts investing in North America. It was the year of currency gains and losses. The Japanese yen soared and the dollar plummetted.

But an investment policy that was precisely right one year could equally well be precisely wrong the next.

Investment trusts

There is one other — and much older — form of collective investment vehicle which crops up frequently in the personal finance pages: the **investment trust**. An investment trust is a company whose business — rather than making widgets or running laundries — is simply to invest in other companies. It holds a portfolio of investments in the same way as a unit trust or a life fund, thus providing professional management and a **spread of risk**. But you cannot buy 'units' in an investment trust. You buy its **shares**, in the same way as you would buy the shares of an industrial company. Investment trust share prices are thus listed in the share price pages of the *Financial Times* rather than on the unit trust or insurance fund pages.

The value of shares in an investment trust is determined in exactly the same way as the value of the shares in any other company, by the balance of buyers and sellers in the stockmarket. But in making their buying and selling decisions, investors naturally look at the value of the investments the trust owns, usually expressed as a **net asset value per share**, or **NAV** (see Chapter 4) and for technical reasons the share price of an investment trust nowadays is normally below the value of the assets backing the shares. In other words, it stands at a **discount** to the NAV. The size of the typical discount varies with stockmarket conditions.

This poses a considerable problem for anyone wanting to launch a new investment trust. Say he proposed to offer 100 shares to the public at £1 each and invest the £100 he received across a range of companies. The investment trust would have a portfolio of investments worth £100 and the NAV of each of its own shares would thus be £1. But the chances are that the shares would trade in the stockmarket at 80p or so: a discount of 20 per cent to the NAV. And few investors want to put up £1 for something which shortly afterwards will be worth only 80p.

Geared and split-level trusts

There are various ways an investment trust can try to reduce or eliminate the discount to the asset value. It may offer special investment expertise in a particular area, which encourages investors to rate its shares more highly, or may attempt to cash in on a current stockmarket fashion. It might have considerable **gearing** — investment trusts can use borrowed money as well as shareholders' money — which means the asset backing for the shares would rise faster than the value of the investment portfolio in a rising market. Or it might organize itself as a **split-level trust**. There are a number of variations on this theme. The principle is that the investment trust's own share capital consists of **income shares** and **capital shares**, the income shares being entitled to all the income from its investment portfolio and the capital shares being entitled to the whole of the rise in capital value of the portfolio.

Unitizing investment trusts

But the surest way for an existing investment trust to increase its total worth is to be taken over or to **unitize** itself. **Unitization** simply means that the investment trust turns itself into a unit trust, substituting units for shares. The unit price is then calculated directly from the value of its investments (and fully reflects this value, which the share price did not). An investment trust is a **close-ended** investment vehicle, because it has a finite share capital. A unit trust is **open-ended** because the managers can create new units or cancel existing ones as demand and supply dictate.

Personal equity plans

In the 1986 Budget the way was paved for a new type of personal investment vehicle: the **Personal Equity Plan** or **PEP**. These PEPs were launched from the beginning of 1987 and attracted much advertising and a commensurate volume of editorial comment in the personal finance pages. The 1989 Budget doubled the amounts that could be invested each year via a PEP.

The idea of the PEP is to encourage investment in the stockmarket, much as the **Business Expansion Scheme** encourages high-earning individuals to invest in shares of unquoted companies. However, the tax incentive comes in a different way and the sums involved are still much smaller.

Individuals are entitled to one PEP each year and can invest £4,800 in each PEP, which is simply a vehicle for holding shares in

UK companies for the individual. Income on investments held within the PEP is not liable to tax, neither is there tax on any capital gains. If investments are taken out of the PEP these concessions are lost for the future. Up to £2,400 a year of the £4,800 PEP total may be invested in unit and/or investment trusts that themselves hold more than 75 per cent of their investments in UK companies. Alternatively, a maximum of £750 may be invested in unit and/or investment trusts, with no restrictions on which countries the trusts invest in.

As long as the investments remain within the PEP structure they continue to enjoy the tax concessions (within the PEP one share can be sold and another bought with the proceeds without incurring tax liability). Thus investors are expected over the years to build up portfolios consisting of a number of individual PEPs, each started in a different year.

As an exercise in popular capitalism, the scheme is less than ideal. You may not run your own PEP. It has to be managed by a **professional fund manager** approved by the tax authorities. In practice this means more business for the traditional fund managers: stockbrokers, banks and merchant banks and unit trust groups — though building societies are also allowed to compete. Most of these managers either insist on picking the shares themselves or allow the investor to choose from a very restricted list. And the charge for setting up the PEP will probably mop up the first year's income from most equity investments.

Supervising the City

Customers in shops have various forms of redress against unscrupulous traders and shoddy products. Users of the City's services have a similar need for protection. So there are safeguards to prevent the investor from suffering at the hands of unscrupulous financial operators. There are rules regarding the nature of the products on offer. And there are rules to govern the operations of the markets themselves and the professionals who trade in them.

The City's **supervisory systems** feature frequently in press reports. Partly this is because of the new system introduced over the period 1986-1988 (and still far from finalized in some of its detail) which replaces a ramshackle regime that left investors at the mercy of con men like unscrupulous investment advisors and promoters of dubious commodity investment schemes. It is also partly a consequence of the insider dealing and takeover scandals that have highlighted areas of abuse in the City's own workings.

Statutory versus non-statutory supervision

There are two main approaches to regulating financial markets: **statutory regulation** and **self-regulation**. Most financial systems have some elements of both. The American system leans towards statutory regulation. A statutory body, the **Securities and Exchange Commission (SEC)**, monitors the issue of securities to the public and the securities markets in which they are traded and reinforces the work of self-regulating bodies such as the New York Stock Exchange.

It is argued that an SEC would not work in Britain. The

markets must be policed by those who understand their workings. In America the SEC can attract bright young lawyers as a career stepping-stone. In Britain a comparable body would probably submerge under the weight of civil service bureaucracy. There is special pleading here from the City, which hates outsiders watching its workings, but an element of truth as well.

The new British system

In practice, regulation of the financial system in Britain is a mixture of statutory and non-statutory measures, but with a strong bias in favour of self-regulation. The framework for the system, however, is enshrined in legislation — the **Financial Services Act** which entered the statute book in 1986, though its main provisions came into force considerably later, in April 1988. The Financial Services Act developed from a report on **investor protection** produced by a shrewd lawyer and adviser to the Department of Trade and Industry, Professor Jim Gower. Under the Act, virtually any person or body wanting to carry on an **investment business** in the UK has to be authorized to do so. The maximum penalty for operating an investment business while unauthorized is two years in jail. The definition of 'investment business' is drawn very widely. It covers brokers, marketmakers, investment managers, financial intermediaries of various kinds, commodity scheme operators (a previously glaring gap) and even publishers of investment newsletters and tip sheets. But newspapers were excluded from the provisions, despite a stout rearguard action by the Labour party.

Role of the Securities and Investments Board

With whom do you register? This is where the complications begin. At the apex of the system stands a new body, the **Securities and Investments Board** (SIB). The SIB is not a government agency. It is a private company, but with regulatory powers delegated to it under the Financial Services Act. Under this umbrella organization are a series of **Self-Regulating Organizations (SROs)** for different types of financial activity: five existed initially. Many organizations need to register with several different SROs when their activities encompass a range of different investment businesses. Certain professional bodies whose members undertake investment business that is incidental to their main activities — accountants, for example — can apply to be **Recognized Professional Bodies (RPBs)** instead of all their members' needing to join an SRO. The markets in which investments are traded do not need recognition as investment businesses if they obtain recognition from the SIB as **Recognized Investment Exchanges (RIEs)**, though their members still need to be authorized to carry on investment business.

Each SRO had to devise a **rulebook** for members, and has to ensure they observe it. Each rulebook has to be approved by the SIB. The SIB's own rules have to be approved by the Secretary of State for Trade and Industry. Those who do not or cannot join an SRO have the option of applying direct to the SIB for authorization for investment business, though it is hoped that most will continue to follow the SRO route.

The Self-Regulating Organizations

The initial line-up of SROs is as follows:

- The Stock Exchange and the **International Securities Regulatory Organization (ISRO**, which represented those dealing from London in international bonds) merged to form **The Securities Association (TSA)**, whose members cover most aspects of securities trading. The Stock Exchange, under its new guise as The International Stock Exchange of the United Kingdom and the Republic of Ireland, also obtained recognition as a Recognized Investment Exchange.
- The **Financial Intermediaries, Managers and Brokers Regulatory Association (FIMBRA)** covers insurance brokers and independent investment advisers. This is perhaps the most important of the bodies as far as the small investor is concerned.
- Futures and options dealers (other than Stock Exchange share options traders) come under the **Association of Futures Brokers and Dealers (AFBD)**. This covers those operating in the commodity futures markets and the financial futures markets.
- The **Investment Management Regulatory Organization (IMRO)** brings together those managing the main forms of

pooled investment: investment trusts, unit trusts and pension funds.

- The marketing of pooled investment products by the companies which provide them is regulated separately from the investment management side. The relevant SRO is the **Life Assurance and Unit Trust Regulatory Organization** or **LAUTRO,** which therefore covers the retail marketing of life assurance and unit trusts.

Under the new regime, the financial community has to bear the costs of operating its own regulatory systems: a prime appeal for the government but a heavy burden for some financial institutions and ultimately for their customers. The regulators are practitioners with experience of the different businesses involved.

Standards to be applied

What standards does the new system impose? Some are self-evident. Those authorized to carry on investment business must be fit and proper — and of adequate financial standing — to do so. Spot checks on a firm's records can be carried out where necessary and a range of sanctions from a rap on the knuckles to removal of authorization can be meted out.

The basis of an investment business's relationship with its customer normally needs to be set out in writing. The investment business has to deal fairly with its client. There has to be a complaints procedure. Unsolicited calls to sell investments (**cold calling**) are normally prohibited except for insurance (as previously) and unit trusts.

Adequate arrangements for segregating clients' money from that of an investment business are required. Much pain in the past has been caused by investment managers who collapsed taking clients' money down with their own. And — an interesting provision for brokers and tipsheet writers, though one that would be dificult to enforce — published investment recommendations must be researched and be able to be substantiated.

Compensation arrangements

The Stock Exchange had long operated a **compensation fund** so that the public could not suffer from the default of a member.

Since Big Bang it has been replaced by a somewhat watered-down compensation arrangement. Today, all investment businesses must provide compensation arrangements to protect clients' money up to a cetain level should the business go into liquidation. Naturally, neither this provision nor the one requiring research of investment tips insulates the client from losses resulting simply from poor advice.

Where legislation takes a hand

The new self-regulatory structure is designed mainly to supervise those who operate in the investment business. The nature of many of the investments in which they deal is still shaped by legislation.

The affairs of **companies** (both private companies and those whose shares are traded on a market) are largely governed by the **Companies Acts**, of which the latest comprehensive revision is the **Companies Act 1985**. The **Department of Trade and Industry (DTI)** is the ministry responsible for enforcing companies legislation. Companies Acts cover matters such as preparation and submission of accounts, requirements for prospectuses, duties and rights of auditors, safeguards for creditors and shareholders, duties of directors, powers to appoint inspectors into the affairs of a company, and the like. But they also touch on some aspects of securities markets and share trading. **Disclosure** of **5 per cent shareholdings** in a public company (to be changed to **3 per cent shareholdings)** is a Companies Act provision. The prohibition of **insider trading** (dealing in shares on the basis of privileged **price-sensitive information**) is now covered by the **Company Securities (Insider Dealing) Act**, but powers of investigation are beefed up in the Financial Services Act. The Companies Acts prohibit a company from giving **financial assistance for the purchase of its own shares** except with a lengthy process of shareholder approval: the key issue in the **Guinness affair** in 1986-87, which looked like coming to court in 1990.

Unit trusts had been regulated for many years under the **Prevention of Fraud (Investments) Act**. Now they are authorized and supervised under the SIB regulatory structure, though the DTI has responsibility for determining the types of investment they may hold.

Other Acts govern the affairs of specific types of business. **Insurance companies** are governed by the **Insurance Companies**

Acts. **Building societies** come under the **Building Societies Act**.

Banks are regulated under the **Banking Act** — a revised Act reached the Statute Book in 1987 — and supervised by the **Bank of England**, though now with outside assistance on the new **Board of Banking Supervision**. The Bank has a wider supervisory role which encompasses banking, money markets, foreign exchange markets and the gilt-edged market, but it may make its views felt in any of the markets whose health is vital to the functioning of the City.

The **Lloyd's insurance market** governs itself within the powers granted by a specific Act of Parliament. The latest **Lloyd's Act**, which came into force in 1983, tightened up the self-regulatory requirements in response to recent scandals. But Lloyd's fought successfully against being dragged within the scope of the Financial Services Act.

Traditional self-regulating bodies

The Stock Exchange has traditionally regulated its own members, who could be disciplined by the representative **Stock Exchange Council**, and in this respect has probably changed least under the SIB regime. The difference is that the job is now split between The Stock Exchange and The Securities Association. Broadly, The Stock Exchange is responsible for matters relating to the running of the market and The Securities Association for policing the financial health of the market's members. If a stockbroker is 'unable to meet his commitments' (in other words, goes bust), he used to be **hammered** on The Stock Exchange floor. More financially than physically painful, this means the market was told of his default and that he had ceased to trade. Prosaically, the message now goes out on the screens.

The **City Panel on Takeovers and Mergers** (the **Takeover Panel**) was established by City institutions (including The Stock Exchange) in 1968 to police the takeover jungle where most abuses occurred (see Chapter 10). It was not initially intended to be part of the SIB regulatory framework, though with effect from 1988 its powers were beefed up to give its decisions the backing of the SIB's range of sanctions.

Regulatory problems across frontiers

The internationalization of securities markets poses various problems for regulators. First, it is difficult for the supervisors of any one country to monitor effectively the activities of an international securities house, which can switch its 'book' between Tokyo, London and New York in the course of a day.

Secondly, some markets such as the eurobond market are truly international in that they are not attached to any one country (though London is still the major centre for eurobond dealing). There is no official supranational body with the power to enforce rules on all participants: a cause for concern which crops up periodically in press reports of discussions among leading bankers.

Finally, the international nature of today's securities business can frustrate the efforts of the best-intentioned domestic supervisory authorities. The **removal of exchange controls** in Britain, combined with the use of **nominee names,** means that the British as well as foreigners can deal anonymously in British markets via the medium of a **Swiss bank** and run little risk of detection if they flaunt the rules. It is also very difficult to clamp down on dubious investment schemes selling from overseas to investors in Britain.

The new system in practice

It was not until February 1988 that investment businesses had finally to apply for authorization and early in 1989 some were still operating on 'interim authorization' — their applications had been received but a decision had not yet been made. These firms could continue to trade, but clients would not be covered by the compensation system which came into effect in August 1988.

In the meantime a major fund management scandal had arisen. Investors who had handed over more than £100m to be invested by a firm called **Barlow Clowes**, supposedly in safe government securities, discovered that much of the money had been misappropriated and would be lost.

Barlow Clowes investors were a residual casualty of the pre-Financial Services Act regulatory system, when no effective compensation scheme was in force. The SIB emerged with some credit from the affair, having brought it into the open by closing down Barlow Clowes. The SIB also made early use of its powers to close a number of suspect commodity 'investment' firms.

The SIB has nevertheless evoked considerable hostility in the City: particularly in the banking community, which considers its rules and procedures excessively legalistic and bureaucratic. There have been widespread complaints from investment businesses about the costs of complying with the Financial Services Act.

Another bone of contention is the question of **polarization** (see glossary) under which financial intermediaries must decide whether they are independent investment advisers or whether they simply market the investment products of one group. By 1989 the system was encouraging many would-be independents to link with a particular provider of savings products and raising fears that genuinely independent advice would become even more scarce. The insurance industry was also fighting vigorously to avoid having to disclose its costs and commissions to prospective clients.

The authorities responded to City antagonism towards the SIB by appointing a Bank of England executive director to head it and there were signs by 1989 that it was moving in the direction of simplifying and sometimes relaxing certain of its rules. In 1989 it was indicated that a less complex set of rules might be introduced, consisting of a number of general principles and about 50 specific rules applicable to all SROs, supplemented where necessary by further detailed rules applied by the individual SROs.

By then a further conflict had arisen. In the move towards a single market in 1992, the European Community wanted harmonization of securities regulation. But Britain was naturally reluctant to amend or abandon the new system it had introduced so recently. The debate rumbles on.

22

The financial pages

The British have access to a very wide range of financial reading matter. Much of it comes as an adjunct to more general daily reading: the business and City sections of the national daily and Sunday newspapers. At times of boom in the financial markets the national newspapers derive a large portion of their revenue from financial advertising and the editorial pages of the financial sections expand to reflect the heightened interest.

But any review of the financial press has to start with London's *Financial Times* — the 'FT'. It sells almost 300,000 copies a day, the greater part in the UK though it also prints in Germany, France and the United States. It is the City's bible, and on days when the FT fails to appear the City has a rudderless feel. It is international in outlook with a range of overseas correspondents that much of the British press lacks. It covers as a matter of course all the major financial markets of the UK and the more important ones overseas. It is a journal of record for news of UK companies. Its news reporting covers the major political, economic, business and financial events worldwide, and its interests extend to the arts and leisure activities. News is put into perspective with the help of background analysis and feature articles. And its statistical information and price coverage of all major financial markets is far more comprehensive than can be found elsewhere. It is now divided into two sections, with the more general domestic and international business and political news in the first part and the specific news of companies and financial markets in the second.

In fact, the FT is easier to define by what it does not cover than by what it does. First, it does not make investment recommendations as such, though you can read between the lines in the Lex investment comment column and some of the company comment. Secondly, it normally deals in fact rather than speculation. Though its market reporting duly records the rumours that move share prices, it does not always fully mirror the gossipy nature of much City activity. Its nearest American counterpart, the *Wall Street Journal*, is also read in the City: primarily for its coverage of North American business. It has not seriously challenged the FT on its home beat.

Not everybody has the time to read a newspaper of the FT's scope each day. The financial pages of the quality press — the *Guardian*, the *Independent*, the *Daily Telegraph* and *The Times* — offer an alternative, covering the main items of business and financial news and dealing briefly with many of the minor ones. A similar formula — news stories, company results coverage, editorial comment and feature articles — surfaces in different guises. While the *Guardian* has a somewhat ambivalent attitude to specific share recommendations, the other three carry regular investment comment.

On Saturdays these quality dailies — like the FT — change shape and devote much of the available space to personal finance coverage: questions of tax, insurance, pooled investments such as unit trusts and family finance planning in general.

A number of Britain's major regional papers — the *Birmingham Post*, the *Yorkshire Post* and *The Scotsman* — follow a similar pattern to the national dailies, though with a bias towards news of local businesses and events.

Below the level of the 'heavy' dailies, the *Daily Mail* and the *Daily Express* have less space to devote to financial coverage, though the *Mail* in particular has at times had significant influence on the stockmarket. The result is a greater emphasis on one or two major financial 'stories'. Both also provide stockmarket reports, and the *Mail* runs a mid-week personal finance section. The attention to financial news in the *London Standard* shows that this is regarded as a significant selling point in the battle for London readers.

The heavyweight Sunday papers — *The Sunday Times*, the *Observer* and the *Sunday Telegraph* — start with the assumption that their readers will have picked up the main items of the week's financial news elsewhere. Thus the emphasis is on background analysis of current stories and attempts to get in first with the stories that will hit the financial headlines in the coming week. In this they are sometimes helped by financiers (or their public relations advisers) who find it convenient to float a story before the new week's dealings begin in the markets. Not every 'story' necessarily results from journalistic legwork, nor is a partisan approach always entirely absent. All provide personal finance coverage and all at one time or another are active with **share tips**, often of the 'close to the market gossip' variety.

Because of the extensive financial coverage in the national press, Britain supports relatively few stockmarket magazines. The largest and by far the longest established is the *Investors Chronicle*, now wholly owned by the *Financial Times* group. Its strength is its very detailed analysis of company profits and company prospects, useful for those who want to monitor their existing investments as well as pick up ideas for new ones. It does make specific share recommendations, but the bulk of its coverage also contains an element of evaluation or advice. Its feature material contains much that is aimed at helping the newcomer to the stockmarkets. It also carries a regular personal finance coverage. Considerably larger in terms of circulation is the *Economist*, but domestic financial markets now occupy a small proportion of its pages, though its coverage of international business is extensive. *Corporate Money* is a relative newcomer covering companies' capital-raising and takeover operations in the financial markets.

Monthly magazines covering investment and personal financial planning for the individual have launched on the back of the investment boom. Those seen on the bookstalls include *What Investment*, *Money & Family Wealth* and *Money Observer* (an offshoot of the newspaper). For subscribers, *Money Which* provides advice on financial services and products.

These personal finance magazines for the individual should not be confused with the publications aimed primarily at financial intermediaries — insurance brokers and the like — who market investment products to the public. The leaders here include the monthly *Money Management* and *Planned Savings*, both of which provide detailed coverage of the performance of unit trusts, insurance funds and other investment products, and the weekly market is dominated by *Money Marketing*. They overlap with trade magazines for the insurance and pensions industries (insurance magazines are legion).

Banking is served by the *Banker*, a monthly magazine in the *Financial Times* stable, and by *Banking World*, and the eurocurrency market by *Euromoney*.

Britain has a highly developed trade press. The property world is served mainly by the long-established weekly *Estates Gazette*, by *Chartered Surveyor Weekly* and by the more news-orientated weekly free-circulation newspaper, *Estates Times*. Accountancy spawns numerous publications, of which the monthly magazine *Accountancy* and the weekly free newspaper *Accountancy Age* dominate the market.

Newsletters are a publishing market in themselves. Many sectors of the financial community are served by a range of specialist newsletters: taxation, accountancy and eurobond newsletters are prominent. But in addition there is a vast range of stockmarket newsletters — **tip sheets** — promoting themselves directly to the general public.

Some stockmarket newsletters are established, well researched and reputable. But some are distinctly dubious, backed by claims of successful recommendations in the past which may fall down on detailed scrutiny. Promotional costs aside, the newsletter publishing business is cheap to get into — little more than a wordprocessor and a telephone is required — and it attracts its fair share of get-rich-quick merchants. You have been warned.

23

Update for the 1990s

Two years is a long time in finance. The foregoing chapters were revised in the first half of 1989 for the second edition, at a time — as it happened — when signs of an end to the 1980s boom were already apparent. Interest rates had almost doubled over a year, indications of trouble were emerging in the retail sector as the consumer boom faded, residential property prices were heading for the rocks and danger signals were beginning to emerge from the commercial property market. With relatively low turnover on the stockmarket, many securities houses were making heavy losses, and it was becoming apparent that many more of the groupings formed in the lead-up to Big Bang would either slim down drastically or withdraw from the market (see notes on Chapter 6). Inflation was high by recent standards and climbing.

The events those signs predicted have come to pass over the past couple of years, exacerbated in some cases by the uncertainties introduced by the Gulf War early in 1991. Homeowners have been chastened by seeing the value of their houses fall both in nominal and in real terms. Values have plummetted in the commercial property market, not only in Britain but in most of the major economies, causing considerable distress to banks that had lent against inflated values. High interest rates have taken their toll not only on small and young businesses which feel the pinch first, but also on many of the products of financial engineering and takeover fever in the 1980s. Business failures have risen sharply. Lay-offs in the securities business have been a frequent occurrence (see notes on Chapter 6).

In other words, the economic cycle has moved sharply down,

exposing some of the aberrations of the 1980s on its way. But in structural terms, there have been few radical changes in markets or the financial system since 1989. By and large the markets have still been adjusting to the extensive changes of the 1980s. The one important exception is Britain's entry into the **Exchange Rate Mechanism** of the **European Monetary System** in October 1990. We will look at what that means — and doesn't mean — later in this chapter.

The 1980s had been a period of many illusions in the financial markets. First was the illusion that the markets themselves could create value, almost independent of what was happening in the real economy. That illusion was largely shattered by the stockmarket crash of 1987 when share prices, having far outstripped company earnings growth, fell back to earth.

The concept of a **share-owning democracy** was widely promoted but proved more illusory than real. **Privatization issues**, and the launch of former building society Abbey National on the stockmarket, had greatly increased the number of individual **shareholders** since the Conservative Government came to power in 1979. In 1979 there were reckoned to be about 3m individual shareholders while 12 years later there were more than 11m.

However, of the 11m, 54 per cent held shares in only one company, a further 17 per cent in only two companies and 8 per cent in three companies. Only 3 per cent of shareholders, it was reckoned, had more than 11 holdings, which would be about the minimum required for a reasonable spread of risk. The proportion of all shares owned by the institutions had actually increased over the period.

Most of the new shareholders were therefore adding comparatively little to market activity or brokers' commissions. This sparked off a change in objectives. In place of working for **wider share ownership**, the investment community switched the emphasis to 'deeper' share ownership.

Three developments of the 1980s were in particular disrepute by 1991. First, the concept of **leveraged buyouts** or **takeovers** of listed companies, in which a company was bought with a small amount of equity money and massive amounts of bank debt. This fad came later to Britain than the United States and fortunately had not progressed very far before the consumer spending downturn and rocketting interest rates exposed some of the weaknesses of the theory. Lowndes Queensway, the highly-geared carpet and furniture retailer, went into liquidation and other leveraged groups such as Magnet, MFI and Isosceles (the former Gateway supermarkets business) were unable to meet the original terms of their bank loans and were obliged to enter into financial reconstructions.

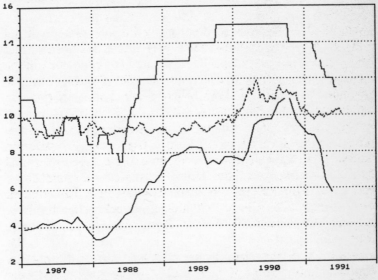

Figure 23.1   The continuous top line shows how bank base rates almost doubled from the Spring of 1988, while the bottom line shows the spiralling inflation rate the Government sought to control. The dotted middle line gives the redemption yield on long-dated gilts. Source: *Datastream International*.

Another feature of the leverage fad, **junk bonds,** never caught on in the UK. In their United States homeland they came into serious disrepute and their protagonist, Drexel Burnham Lambert, was forced to seek protection from its creditors under Chapter 11 of the US bankruptcy laws.

Second, the **takeover** craze as a whole was subjected to more critical scrutiny. Two major companies — British & Commonwealth and Coloroll — collapsed largely as a result of unwise takeovers. As a result of these cases and in the rather more complex circumstances of the collapse of fruit-to-electronics group Polly Peck, the usefulness of published accounts and the role of the **auditor** came under scrutiny. Had published accounts given any warning?

Third, some of the weird and wonderful **hybrid financial instruments** which surfaced towards the end of the 1980s were not looking so clever by 1991. These products of the merchant banks' **financial engineering** techniques often sought to blur the distinction between debt and equity and between the needs of companies and investors. A typical example was the case of advertising group Saatchi & Saatchi, which had issued £176m of **convertible** preference shares with a **premium put** feature (see below). Under the terms of the issue, investors had the right to demand repayment of the issue at £211m in 1993 if conversion did not prove worthwhile. Saatchi's business had hit problems and its share price had collapsed. The obligation to repay this issue at a premium could have brought the group down altogether, and it was only saved by a financial reconstruction which left its original ordinary shareholders with a massively reduced stake in the company.

Finally, before we launch into the detail, the early 1990s were also a time of retribution for some of the individual financial sins of the 1980s. In 1990, three of the key characters in the **Guinness** affair found themselves for varying periods in Ford open prison while a fourth was heavily fined and stripped of his knighthood. Other participants were still awaiting trial. And in mid-1991 the trial of bankers, brokers and lawyers involved in the **Blue Arrow affair** was in full spate.

Chapter 2: Money flows and the money men

By 1991 the government was back to being a net borrower in the **gilt-edged market**, after a period in which it had been a net redeemer of debt.

Chapters 3, 4 and 5: Companies and their accounts; The investment ratios; Refining the figurework

In his 1991 Budget the Chancellor reduced the standard rate of **corporation tax**, which is mainly paid in arrear. The rate charged for the financial year 1990 was to come down to 34 per cent and the rate for the financial year 1991 to 33 per cent.

By 1991 a new quasi-official body, the **Accounting Standards Board**, had taken over the job of setting **accounting standards**. Some of its initial declarations of intent were widely contested. In particular, it proposed to tighten up the way companies account for 'one-off items' (see page 46). It suggested that most items treated as **extraordinary** (ie, deducted or added below the line and therefore not affecting published earnings) should become **above-the-line** items, which would be reflected in the earnings per share figure.

The debate about treatment of **goodwill** continued to attract controversy. As noted on page 79, the practice had been to write off against reserves the goodwill arising from an acquisition. Companies were then threatened with a different treatment, under which they would be obliged to **amortize (depreciate)** goodwill against profits over a period of years. Goodwill usually arises in a takeover when one company buys another at a price above the value of its tangible assets. If Company A buys Company B for £50m and Company B has only £20m of tangible assets, Company A will have paid £30m for the goodwill of Company B's business and will have to account for it as goodwill.

The annual write-off against profits would have the effect of reducing published profits and earnings and would be particularly disadvantageous to some companies that relied heavily on expanding via acquisition. In favour of this treatment was the fact that it would bring the accounts of UK companies closer in line with United States practice. Against the change it was argued that, unless an acquired business actually fell in value after it was bought, there was no reason to make a deduction from profits to write down its purchase cost.

Still more radical accounting changes were proposed which could oblige companies to show their assets not at their **historic cost** but at **current values**. This, too, could depress profits, as the higher values generally resulting would require higher annual deductions for depreciation.

By 1991, as a result of the 1989 **Companies Act** and new accounting recommendations, the definition of a **subsidiary company** had been extensively widened to include companies effectively controlled by a parent even if the parent did not have more than 50 per cent of the shares. This made it more difficult for companies to hide the debt of other companies they effectively controlled by keeping it off their own group balance sheet (see **off balance sheet items** in glossary). But genuine 50:50 **joint venture** companies still did not need to be consolidated in the accounts of either parent.

Two new types of capital-raising instrument for larger companies had come into prominence by 1991. The **convertible capital bond** was really a substitute for **convertible loan stocks** or **convertible preference shares**. It was structured in such a way that it went through a two-stage conversion process: first, it could be converted into preference shares, which would immediately be swapped for ordinary shares. The reason for this complex structure was to produce an instrument that the tax man would accept as debt (so that the interest was tax-deductible) but which companies could treat as part of their capital rather than as debt in their balance sheets.

Convertible capital bonds, like other convertible stocks and shares, might or might not incorporate the **premium put** feature that had become popular in the late 1980s. This is an option for the investor to sell the stock back to the company at a premium over its issue price after, typically, five years if the share price has not risen sufficiently to make conversion worthwhile. Take the example of a convertible capital bond issued by food group Sainsbury. The stock carried a low **coupon** of 5 per cent. But the investor could sell it back to the company at £133.28 per £100-worth after five years to take his total return to 10.26 per cent. The conversion price into Sainsbury shares was 262p but effectively the Sainsbury price had to rise to 349p to make conversion a better option than selling the stock back to the company at £133.28p for every £100 issued. As it happened, the Sainsbury share price rose rapidly and the stock was converted. Saatchi & Saatchi — and others — were less lucky.

The **premium put** feature appeals to euromarket investors who are generally bond-orientated rather than equity-orientated. The disadvantage for the issuer is that he is not sure when issuing the stock whether he is raising permanent capital or whether he will have to find the money to redeem the issue at a premium after a few years.

The second instrument was **auction market preferred stock** or **AMPS**. This was technically preference capital in the accounts of the UK issuing company but was sold in the United States market as a form of money-market instrument. Instead of paying a fixed dividend, it paid a 'dividend' that reflected US money-market rates and which was re-set at regular intervals via an auction procedure. The advantage to the issuer was that it could be shown in the accounts as share capital rather than debt.

By 1991 investors had the use of a new stockmarket index: the **FT-SE Eurotrack Index** of Continental European shares. Denominated in German marks, this index provides the basis of new futures and options contracts.

Chapter 6: Equities and the Big Bang

The post-1989 period has not seen any changes on the **Stock Exchange** of a magnitude to compare with the revolution of the 1980s. Wisely, perhaps, the Exchange — having rejoiced for some time in the full name of The International Stock Exchange of the UK and the Republic of Ireland Ltd — reverted in 1991 to an earlier and simpler title: the **London Stock Exchange**. In the same year agreement in principle was reached for the merger of the **London Traded Options Market (LTOM)** with the **London International Financial Futures Exchange (LIFFE)**. This promised finally to make the Stock Exchange's **trading floor** redundant. Prosaically, the space was destined for conversion into offices.

However, if few major changes had taken place since 1989, one important development was in the air in mid-1991. This related to the less actively traded shares (all except the top five hundred or so companies) where spreads between the **marketmakers'** bid and offer prices were often wide. The Stock Exchange suggested a change to the dealing system under which a single dealer would in future have monopoly rights to deal in a particular share or shares from this 'less active' list. This radical departure from the Stock Exchange's traditional commitment to competitive marketmaking seemed likely to arouse lively debate.

By 1991 the **Third Market** had already been abandoned — it never attracted sufficient support — leaving the **main market** and the **Unlisted Securities Market (USM)**. The **SAEF** system of automatic execution of small share bargains was in place, but not widely used except at times of heightened market activity, such as the trading in the immediate aftermath of a privatization issue.

In theory, the **Alpha, Beta, Gamma** classification of shares was abandoned in favour of a new system of 12 categories which depended on the average size of market dealings in the relevant share. But the *Financial Times*, after some initial hesitation, opted to stick with the earlier system in its share price pages.

On the regulatory front, the **self-regulating body** for the Stock Exchange, **The Securities Association**, merged with the **Associa-**

tion of Futures Brokers and Dealers to form The **Securities and Futures Authority (SFA).** This recognized the close connection between the share market and some of the markets in derivatives.

But life for the **securities firms** remained tough. Revenue of Stock Exchange member firms fell 32 per cent to £2.2bn in 1990 and staff numbers were cut by more than 10 per cent. In aggregate, the industry showed losses of £350m for 1990 and while some firms were in profit, the Stock Exchange reckoned that 'only a few earned more than a bare minimum return on capital'. So much for the high hopes with which the City embarked on the Big Bang changes. But, fortunately, the early part of 1991 was looking considerably better for the securities industry as the equity market turned up.

In mid-1991 two further developments had come closer to realization. Despite many delays, the **TAURUS** 'paperless' electronic share registration system was on course for introduction in 1992. The purpose was to simplify **settlement** procedures and avoid the need for **share certificates** to change hands each time shares were bought or sold.

In a connected move, London's two- or three-week **account system** was again under scrutiny. There were proposals to replace it with a **rolling settlement** system, under which shares would be paid for a specific number of days after purchase. Proposals for the length of time allowed for payment ranged between three days and ten days, with the possibility of a two-tier system under which institutional investors settled within three days of purchase and private investors were given a longer period.

Chapter 8: Stockmarket launches

As noted earlier, the **Third Market** had never proved a success and was closed. In the **main market** and **USM**, rules had been amended slightly to come closer in line with Continental European practice. The number of years' trading record required for a launch on the main market was reduced from five to three and for the USM from three to two.

There has been one significant change in the **new issue** rules since mid-1989. The way has been opened for companies making a medium-sized offer to mix the techniques of an offer for sale and a placing, so that a proportion of the shares can be offered to the general public and a proportion can be placed via intermediaries.

Chapter 9: Rights, placings and scrip issues

The first half of 1991 saw a spate of **rights issues** as over-borrowed companies sought to restore their equity base or raise funds for expansion. By the end of May 1991 over £4.5bn had been raised by the issue of ordinary shares and around £1bn by the issue of convertibles.

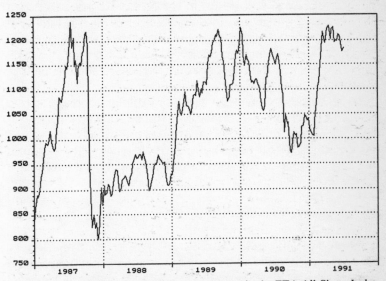

Figure 23.2   The graph shows the movements in the FTA All-Share Index from the beginning of 1987. In 1990 worries about company performance in the recession killed the recovery from the 1987 crash, though the market was in more optimistic mood in 1991. Source: *Datastream International.*

The dangers of the **bought deal** procedure (see page 127) were underlined in 1990 when merchant bank Kleinwort Benson paid £138m (or 99p per share) to Burmah Castrol for its 29 per cent stake in Premier Consolidated Oilfields, hoping to distribute the shares quickly at a profit. Instead, the price fell heavily and Kleinwort eventually got out at 78p for a loss of £34m on the operation.

Chapter 10: Bidders, victims and lawmakers

We have seen that by 1991 highly **leveraged takeovers** of large companies were in some disrepute. Bank finance for such operations had become difficult to obtain, and a period of shaky profits and high interest rates made leveraged operations unpopular.

The biggest attempted leveraged bid for a UK company — Sir James Goldsmith's 1989 attempt to acquire and break up the BATS tobacco-to-financial-services group — was eventually abandoned in the face of regulatory hurdles in the United States and lack of enthusiasm in the UK. But the idea of the very large bid was not, in itself, dead. In May 1991 the Hanson conglomerate surprised the market by spending £240m on a 2.8 per cent stake in the ICI chemicals group — a move that was widely interpreted as a prelude to a takeover attempt.

The level at which a buyer must declare a share stake in another company is now **3 per cent**.

By 1991, European merger control regulations were removing some of the competition-monitoring responsibility from national bodies. The European Community takes an interest in the merger of companies with a worldwide aggregate turnover of 5bn ECU or more, or where at least two of the parties have a turnover in the EC of over 250m ECU.

Chapter 11: Venture capital and leveraged buy-outs

The second half of the 1980s had been a very profitable period for **venture capital firms,** but by the 1990s the prospect was less rosy. The **buy-outs** and **buy-ins** that provided much of the profit were becoming considerably more difficult. First, the most obvious candidates for the buy-out treatment had already been processed. Second, the question of **take-out** had become more difficult. In a less buoyant stockmarket climate, it was rarely practicable to rely on a Stock Exchange launch as a way for investors to get their money back after a few years (the disappearance of the Stock Exchange's Third Market removed one avenue for flotation in the case of smaller companies and those financed on BES money).

Third, the larger buy-outs which relied on sales of part of the group to reduce the initial bank debt looked less attractive. In a recessionary climate it was not always possible to dispose of these surplus businesses at attractive prices. And finally, high interest rates and pressure on profitability made the whole operation appear more risky.

The **Business Expansion Scheme (BES)** rules were revised in the 1990 Budget to increase to £750,000 the amount that could be raised in a year by companies other than those investing in residential properties let on assured tenancies (where the limit is still £5m).

Chapter 12: The gilt-edged market

By 1991 the pendulum of public finance had swung the other way and the government was again a net borrower in the **gilt-edged market**. The Bank of England reactivated its **auction** procedures.

The **gilt-edged marketmakers** were finding life a little better. By 1991 their number had shrunk to 18, but they had recorded profits of £40m in 1990 or roughly a 10 per cent return on funds employed in the market. There was talk of additions to their number in the improved climate.

Chapter 13: Banks, borrowers and bad debts

Hardly had the banking system completed the necessary write-downs of its **Third World lending** before it was faced with losses from another quarter. In their 1990 results, the British clearing banks were forced by the general recession and the collapse in values in the commercial property market to make large **provisions** against loans to small businesses and to property developers.

Losses on **property lending** affected banks in most of the major economies, particularly the United States, and in many cases led to a downgrading of the **credit rating** of the banks' own issues of debt.

In 1991, when bank base rates were finally moving down, the British clearing banks incurred widespread criticism for failing to reduce their interest charges to small businesses by similar amounts. It was claimed that they were trying to recoup from smaller businesses the losses they had made or were likely to make on unwise lending to property companies and to major companies that got into trouble, such as British & Commonwealth and Polly Peck.

The failures of a number of major companies had highlighted another problem in the banking sector. The second half of the 1980s had been a period of **transaction-based** banking. Big companies tended to shop around among a number of banks for the most attractive or cheapest loan package. Often this meant borrowing from a **syndicate** of banks.

This posed problems in the early 1990s when companies got into financial trouble. Any form of bail-out or reconstruction of debt might involve the agreement of a large number of individual banks. This was often difficult to obtain. Individual banks that were simply members of a 30-strong lending syndicate might have little by way of a relationship with the borrower. The temptation was to get out rather than standing by the company.

This was one factor behind a trend back towards **relationship banking** in the 1990s. Some companies took the view that they would be safer relying for their funds on one main bank or a small number of banks, rather than shopping round the market for the deal that looked cheapest in the short term.

The cost of borrowing had, in any case, risen. In the very competitive climate of the 1980s, the **margin** over **LIBOR** paid by large companies had become very thin. In the early 1990s, when recession and problem debts made the banks considerably less eager to lend, the margin over LIBOR paid by companies widened considerably as the banks attempted to restore their profit margins. Companies needing to renew their borrowing facilities usually had to concede a considerable increase in the margin they paid.

Finally, in early July 1991 the banking system itself delivered a major shock when an Abu Dhabi-controlled institution, **Bank of Credit and Commerce International** (BCCI), was closed down at the behest of the Bank of England amid allegations of widespread fraud, and Britain's Serious Fraud Office moved in to investigate. BCCI had many customers among Britain's Asian business community and its collapse seemed likely to impose a severe strain on Britain's **deposit protection** arrangements, under which individual depositors in a failed bank are covered by a **compensation scheme** for 75 per cent of any deposit of £20,000 or less. The banking system as a whole meets the cost of this protection.

Chapter 14: The money markets

The scope of the money markets has been widened a little to allow borrowers to issue 'IOUs' with a life of up to five years (the life of **commercial paper** had originally been limited to one year). However, by mid-1991 few companies had taken advantage of their ability to issue these medium-term IOUs, usually referred to as **medium-term notes** or **MTNs**.

By 1991 the heyday of the **multiple option facility (MOF)** was over, and the terms on those that were renegotiated were generally less attractive to the borrower. Many companies were tending instead to negotiate **bi-lateral credit lines**. In other words, they would negotiate a loan facility direct with a single bank or make a number of different arrangements, each with a single bank (see notes on Chapter 13 above).

Chapter 15: Foreign exchange

On 8 October 1990 the United Kingdom joined the **Exchange Rate Mechanism (ERM)** of the **European Monetary System (EMS)**. Since that date the value of the pound sterling has been formally linked with those of the other European currencies within the **ERM**, and a little more explanation is needed of how the mechanism works.

Start with the **ECU**, the notional European currency constructed from an amalgam of the currencies of all European Community members. Each country's currency is represented in the ECU with a weighting that roughly reflects the country's economic size. Thus Germany has the largest economy and the **German mark** has the heaviest weighting within the ECU. A movement in the value of the German mark against, say, the dollar will therefore have a greater effect on the dollar value of the ECU than a movement in any other currency.

Each currency starts with an exchange rate against the ECU: its **central rate**. Most currencies are allowed to diverge only about 2.25 per cent up or down from this central rate, though some currencies which would have problems with this discipline are allowed a divergence of about 6 per cent up or down (about 12 per cent in total). The **Italian lira** was originally in this wider band but has now come within the 2.25 per cent band. In mid-1991 the **Spanish peseta** and the pound **sterling** were in the wider 6 per cent band.

As well as being limited in the amount they can diverge from their central rate against the ECU, currencies are also limited (within the same percentage bands) in the amount they can diverge from their central rates against each other, and in practice this is often the stricter discipline. Thus if at any time the strongest currency in the system and the weakest one threaten to diverge more than is permitted against each other, the central banks of the two countries will need to take remedial action to bring them back into line.

If this happens, the central banks of the two countries would sell the strong currency and buy the weak one. In practice, a country whose currency is moving out of line may take action before this by buying or selling its own currency or raising or lowering short-term interest rates.

If measures such as these fail to keep a currency within bounds, the EMS members may be forced to agree a formal **revaluation** which re-sets the particular currency's central rate within the ERM. But this is regarded very much as a last resort.

Britain, which has frequently run a considerably higher **inflation rate** than most other EC members, hoped to gain from the discipline imposed by this formal currency linking. To hold its position within the ERM it would need to bring its inflation rate closer in line with that of other EC members, since high inflation normally leads to depreciation of the currency. But the ERM does not provide a substitute for political will, and ultimately a government must still decide to take the action necessary to keep its position in the mechanism.

The hope in Britain has been that membership of a system dominated by the stability of the German mark would ultimately bring the benefits of low inflation that Germany has enjoyed. Ironically, by 1991 the mark had lost some of its traditional strength because of Germany's problems in integrating the former East Germany, and its position as lynch-pin of the ERM was somewhat weakened, at least temporarily.

By mid-1991, membership of the ERM had grown to nine with the arrival of the peseta and the pound. Though the currencies of Greece and Portugal are part of the EMS, they had not yet joined the Exchange Rate Mechanism.

The ERM is meant to be only a stage on the road to full **European Monetary Union** (which gives us yet another acronym: **EMU**). Ultimately EMU could mean closer cooperation in economic and monetary policy between EC member countries, the establishment of a European central bank and possibly the substitution of a single European currency for the existing different currencies. The speed with which this might happen still arouses considerable controversy. Britain has been cautious compared with some of the more gung-ho members of the Community.

London, incidentally, has hung on to its supremacy as a **foreign exchange** dealing centre, ahead of the United States and Japan. A survey published in 1990 showed that the daily volume of business in London had risen to $187bn.

Chapter 16: International money: the euromarkets

Borrowing techniques in the domestic market and the euromarket have continued to move closer in line. A number of UK companies issuing convertible stocks have structured them so that one part was offered in the domestic market and another in the international market.

Chapter 17: Futures, options and commodity markets

Markets in derivative products (or **derivatives**) such as **futures** and **options** have continued to expand. The planned merger between the **London Traded Options Market (LTOM)** and the **London International Financial Futures Exchange (LIFFE)** has been noted earlier.

LIFFE itself has introduced a number of new contracts, including contracts on **ECU bond futures** and (together with LTOM) contracts on the new **FT-SE Eurotrack 100 Index** of Continental European shares.

The **London Futures and Options Exchange (London FOX)**, as well as introducing **property futures** in May 1991 (see notes on Chapter 19), has taken over a number of existing futures contracts formerly traded at the **Baltic Exchange**. These include **grain, soya bean meal, potatoes** and **pigs** as well as **freight futures**. The **International Petroleum Exchange (IPE)**, situated in the same building as London FOX, now offers futures contracts in gas oil, Brent crude oil, Dubai sour crude oil, Heavy fuel oil and, as of April 1991, naphtha. Options are also available on gas oil and Brent crude.

The **London Metal Exchange (LME)** has extended the period for which metals can be traded forward to 27 months in the case of copper, aluminium and zinc and to 15 months for the rest. Traded options on metals with monthly expiry dates are also available.

Chapter 18: Lloyd's and insurance

By 1991 Lloyd's membership was dropping sharply. This did not matter too much near the bottom of an underwriting cycle, but threatened to limit the capacity of the market when business turned up.

Partly the loss of members was because the minimum show of wealth required had been increased to £250,000. But the reduction in income tax rates in Britain had eroded the possible benefits of membership for rich individuals. Even more important were the massive losses with which many Lloyd's **names** were faced.

It was again argued in the 1990s that the remaining scandals at Lloyd's were an overhang from the pre-1982 period, before reforms were introduced. But the dividing line between fraud and incompetent underwriting was often difficult to draw. Many syndicates faced massive losses as a result of a number of large disasters and of asbestosis claims in the United States, while worries were growing about the liability in respect of pollution claims, also in North America.

The system of closing the accounts for a particular year three years after it ended meant that names worried by mounting losses remained at risk for at least three years after they decided to leave. The Lloyds market as a whole posted losses of over £500m for 1988 and 1989 was expected to be considerably worse. Moreover, because of uncertainty as to claims still to emerge, many syndicates were forced to keep accounts open for particular years well beyond the normal three-year cut-off point.

Membership of Lloyd's, which had once carried considerable *cachet* and appeared to offer a safe and relatively high return to the well-heeled, looked a far more dubious benefit in the 1990s. A 'Lloyd's joke' quoted by the *Sunday Times* in May 1991 encapsulated the changed atmosphere. Question: How do you make a small fortune at Lloyd's? Answer: Start with a large one.

In 1991 Lloyd's was lobbying the government for tax concessions to help members absorb their losses. There were suggestions that the market as a whole might abandon its old unlimited liability principle — where names are liable down to their last collar stud — and move towards some structure that limited the maximum loss.

Chapter 19: Commercial property

By 1991 the **commercial property market** was close to the bottom of a slump even more severe, in many eyes, than the property and **secondary banking collapse** of the mid-1970s.

The root of the problem lay in over-development, financed largely by bank money. **Bank lending** to property companies had almost doubled to £40bn over the previous couple of years.

Unfortunately, the new space was coming on the market at a time when high interest rates and the downswing of the economic cycle were forcing businesses to contract rather than expand. Thus there was a severe shortage of prospective tenants.

Coinciding with the lack of tenant demand was a lack of enthusiasm for **property investments** among the traditional long-term buyers: the insurance companies and pension funds. This particularly hit **developer/traders,** who develop buildings with a view to letting them and then selling the revenue-producing investment at a profit. Even if he could find a tenant for his completed property, the trader could not find a buyer for the property as an investment. Until the developer could sell the property, he could not repay the development loan from the banks.

By the spring of 1991 some nine quoted property companies had gone to the wall and the banks were bracing themselves for losses on their property lending likely to run into billions of pounds. Values had dropped heavily — the average yield on property investments had risen from 7.2 per cent to 9.3 per cent. Rents were falling in many areas, and the property world expected recovery to be a long and painful process. To add to the problems, the crash in property values from the inflated levels of the late 1980s was not confined to Britain. Other major markets such as the United States and Japan were also suffering severely, reducing the possibility that the British market would be helped by buying from abroad.

Of the innovations on the horizon a couple of years earlier, the **PINCs** concept of **unitising single properties** had been abandoned as the market turned down. **Authorized unit trusts** investing direct in commercial property were still on the agenda, but had not yet seen the light of day.

One innovation had surfaced: **property futures** were intro-duced by **London FOX** in May 1991. These allowed property owners, developers or speculators to hedge their property market risk or bet on property market movements. They worked in much the same way as futures based on a stockmarket index. Four different contracts were introduced, allowing bets on commercial property values, commercial property rents, house prices and building society mortgage rates. The two commercial property contracts were based on indexes of property values and of rents produced by Investment Property Databank. At the time of going to press, it was too early to judge whether property futures would attract enough two-way business to be viable.

Chapter 20: Savings and unit-linked investment

The 1991 Budget brought one important change for homebuyers. **Mortgage interest** could no longer be offset against the higher 40 per cent rate of income tax. Henceforth, relief would only be available at the basic 25 per cent rate. Meantime, the limit on the size of mortgage on which tax relief could be claimed on the interest remained stuck at £30,000. These two facts underlined the government's intention to continue to phase out the real value of the tax relief subsidy granted to homebuyers.

The savings market has seen some new products over the past couple of years, plus changes to existing ones. The main innovation is the introduction of **TESSAs**, which stands for **Tax Exempt Special Savings Accounts**. From the beginning of 1991, individuals could deposit a maximum of £9,000 over a five-year period in a special account where the interest would be tax-free. Some of the interest can be taken out during the life of the TESSA without incurring a tax liability. The rules at the outset were that you could put £3,000 into the account in the first year and up to £1,800 a year in subsequent years, subject to the overall limit of £9,000. TESSAs were designed as a bank-deposit counterpart to Personal Equity Plans in the stockmarket, providing some tax shelter for relatively modest savings.

The rules for **Personal Equity Plans** or **PEPS** were themselves altered in the 1991 Budget. Each person can now invest £6,000 in a PEP each year. But in addition, the investor can (from the beginning of 1992) also put £3,000 in a **single-company PEP** each year. These are PEPSs designed to hold shares in just one company and are usually promoted by the company itself. Shares that are received under all-employee incentive share schemes may be transferred straight into the single-company PEP without capital gains tax liability.

The investment rules for the PEPs are also being slightly changed to allow investment in shares of all European Community companies, not only British ones, and in unit or investment trusts which are at least 50 per cent invested in such shares. The limit on investment in unit or investment trusts which do not meet these requirements goes up to £1,500 or a quarter of a £6,000 PEP. Not more than half of a £6,000 PEP may be invested even in qualifying unit and investment trusts.

Plans to allow the formation of unit trusts investing in futures and options, and direct in property, have aroused some controversy (see below).

Chapter 21: Supervising the City

The amalgamation of two of the original five **Self-Regulating Organizations (SROs)**, **The Securities Association** and the **Association of Futures Brokers and Dealers**, to form The **Securities and Futures Authority (SFA)** has already been noted. The SRO most frequently in the news has undoubtedly been The **Financial Intermediaries, Managers and Brokers regulatory Association (FIMBRA)**, not only for the number of times it has been obliged to intervene with member firms but also because of its own difficulties in pulling in sufficient membership income to finance itself.

There have been a number of changes in the regulatory structure itself, mainly in the interests of simplicity. The **Securities and Investments Board (SIB)** has published ten principles plus 40 core rules which all the SROs must take on board. The individual SROs then prepare their own third-tier rules appropriate for their areas of activity.

Responsibility for unit trusts has swung further from the **Department of Trade and Industry** to the SIB, which now has total control over their investment and borrowing powers. Plans to allow the formation of unit trusts investing in futures and options have aroused considerable controversy in the unit trust industry. Some of the traditional funds are worried that these higher-risk vehicles could damage the image of the industry as a whole.

***

If the City of London managed to present itself in the 1980s as the symbol of Britain's economic revival, the remainder of the 1990s may be rather different. The first half of 1991 saw lay-offs even among normally cushioned professionals such as lawyers and accountants, while the major securities houses seemed overdue for further staff shedding and many mergers and acquisition experts were twiddling their thumbs.

The post-Big Bang **securities businesses** built their empires on the assumption of high volumes of share dealing in the secondary market. In the long run it always seemed unlikely that the markets would deliver the frenetic levels of activity needed to cover the costs of the much expanded securities industry. Like other businesses, the City is learning that it must tailor its costs to the available revenue rather than expecting revenue to expand to match its cost base.

The result will probably be a lower-key City for much of the 1990s, with attention shifting towards the companies that create the wealth and away from the institutions that service them with finance and provide a market for their shares.

How to read between the lines

Reading the financial pages is one thing. Reading between the lines of the financial pages is a different art. Financial journalists do not always say exactly what they think — often because Britain's very strict libel regime prevents them from doing so. Moreover, they are reporting on a world — the world of finance — which has its own layers of jargon and pseudo-scientific gobbledegook, often disguising the banal nature of what is going on.

To round off our examination of the financial markets, here's a less serious guide to some of the more confusing turns of phrase you might come across in financial reports and the financial press. The interpretations are purely personal and in no way imply that the words and phrases are used in any particular paper or report in the sense suggested here.

The first problem the financial journalist hits is when he wants to put across a warning or express disbelief. Remember, we're talking about money and a surprising number of people take money very seriously: particularly those who hope to make a lot of it or already have a lot of it to lose. Since this definition embraces a high proportion of people in the City, the journalist attacks them at his peril. A casual aside suggesting that the directors of Muggitt Finance put in a bulk order for rose-tinted spectacles before preparing their prospectus profit forecast is enough to have Muggitt's lawyers baying at the gate.

In fact, can a journalist safely suggest that a share is vastly overpriced, even if he is not implying skulduggery on the part of the directors? It's a moot point and he'll often try to find a way round it. 'Muggitt's shares have fallen from 300p to 100p so far this year, and holders should consider taking their profits' is one approach. If he simply thinks they're far too high, without the company necessarily being on the skids, he might say 'On a PE ratio of 35, Muggitt Finance is rated well above the sector average; this anomaly is likely to be ironed out in the near future'. He doesn't mean that shares of the other companies in the sector are due for a rise. He means that Muggitt is heading for a fall. 'With the PE ratio at 35, investors should not ignore Muggitt's downside potential' is another way of saying the same thing. 'Not for widows and orphans' simply means 'highly speculative' and occasionally 'not for anyone in his right mind'. It is rather like the definition of a 'recovery stock'. It can mean a share that is going to rise as the company recovers or a company that won't be around very long if it doesn't recover.

When a journalist suggests shares are 'fully valued' he is almost certainly trying to say 'overvalued' without offending the company too deeply. This is not the same thing as describing them as 'fairly valued', which probably means the writer hasn't a clue one way or the other ('a sound long-term hold' also implies that he is sitting firmly on the fence).

There was a journalist in the pre-decimalization days who spoke his mind and suggested that one company's shares 'standing at 2s 6d' were 'about half-a-crown too high'. His fate is lost in the mists of history.

Comment on individuals is more perilous. For the financial journalist there can be no such thing as a crook, at least until he is safely convicted and behind bars (which, in Britain, he rarely is provided his crime is big enough). The paper's lawyer might just let him get away with 'controversial City financier'. Hence you'll occasionally read pieces like this: 'Speaking from Panama City, Mr Cyril Buck, the controversial financier at the head of the troubled Muggitt Finance group, today strongly criticised the decision by the company's auditors to state that the accounts were prepared on a going concern basis and did not reflect a true and fair view of the company's affairs'. In the vernacular this might be translated as 'Cyril Buck, the spiv at the head of Muggitt, has done a bunk. He's annoyed because the auditors say that the company is bust and the accounts are fiddled.'

Even journalism has had characters of questionable judge-

ment, probably operating at the fringes of the share-tipping end of the market and almost certainly writing for a stockmarket 'newsletter' of the kind that claims divine insight into the future movement of share prices. Be a little careful when you read the following: 'Since Rudyard Sharpe took the helm at the end of last year and injected his private business into Salter Way Holdings it is recognised as one of the most dynamic groups in the financial services sector. The shares are a narrow market, but should be bought at prices up to 200p'.

It may be a well researched and genuine tip. It could equally well mean: 'Ruddy Sharpe flogged his private company to Salter Way at an exhorbitant price and is now ramping the shares for all he's worth. That's why he had me to lunch last week. The company's a load of junk but there aren't many shares around so the price will rocket if a few mugs jump in and buy them on my advice. That's why I bought 20,000 myself at 140p last week. I'll sell the moment my readers have pushed the price up to 190p.'

Crooked writers are rare. Two other types of financial commentator can be dangerous to your financial health: the excessively vague and the excessively precise. How many times have you seen a share described in terms like these: 'The shares stand on a PE ratio of 12, which is generous in today's markets'. What does it mean? That the rating is generous to the investor (the shares are priced below their true worth and should be bought)? Or the rating flatters the company (the shares are over-rated and should be sold)? Take your pick.

Then the over-precise, which is most likely to crop up in the research circulars produced by Porsche-powered stockbrokers' analysts but may well be repeated in the financial press: 'The acquisition of Nuggins should contribute around £2.735m to the pre-tax profits of Bloggins Plc next year. Assuming internally-generated sales growth in the range of 11.7 to 11.8 per cent and a 2.34 per cent improvement in the margins of the timber business, the shares at 393p are on a prospective PE ratio of 14.27 and are a medium to strong buy on a seven month view.' Roughly translated, this might mean: 'Your guess as to Bloggins's profits is as good as mine. But our marketmaking arm has a whole load of Bloggins's shares on its books and told me to help shift them. And it's for writing this sort of junk that they pay me £80,000 a year'.

276

The big institutional investors know which stockbrokers' analysts are worth reading. Most 'research' material goes straight in the bin, and one very large financial institution has a gigantic wheeled tub that goes round the investment department once a week to collect brokers' circulars for the bonfire.

Much of what you read about the City falls into place if you bear in mind a few simple facts. Most financial people the private individual is likely to meet are salesmen of one kind or another. Like salesmen in other fields they'll be tempted to sell you the product that pays them the highest commission or which they happen to have in stock. Like any salesmen, they are not always the best people to advise on the merits of the product.

When markets fall

They have a particular problem when markets are going down or likely to go down. 'Put your money into Bloggins — you won't lose more than half of it' is not an appealing sales message. They have to convince themselves and their clients that markets are going up for ever. Or they devise strategies like 'switching' that generate commission income but fall short of a straight 'buy' recommendation. In either case the message is likely to be wrapped up in further layers of gobbledegook.

Hence: 'Mike Puff, manager of the Duffer group of unit trusts, expects to see the equity market rise by 20 to 25 per cent over the year after a weak start, given the relative strength of the UK corporate sector'. This might translate as: 'Mike Puff has as little clue as the rest of us, but he's in the game of flogging investments'.

Or the message from a broker to clients: 'We therefore recommend a switch from Sainsbury to Tesco on income growth grounds. Our charts show that...'. The meaning here could be: 'There's damn all to choose between the two shares, but we rake in the commission each time you sell one and buy the other. We'll recommend you switch back next year'.

Finally, no review of moneyspeak is complete without a glance at that bastion of City tradition: the daily stockmarket report. How often have you seen that shares 'closed narrowly mixed in nervous trading'? The beauty of phrases of this kind is that the words can be used in almost any order with little if any change to the sense: 'closed nervously in mixed narrow trading', 'traded nervously in a narrow mixed close' and so on. Perhaps it means something to somebody. At least it fills column inches and helps to preserve the mystique of the financial markets.

Quick guide to moneyspeak

Here's a quick glossary of some common current terms and phrases you'll meet, with possible meanings.

Overdue market correction A near meltdown of the financial system.

Free market A market in which share prices can be manipulated with relative freedom from official supervision.

Self regulation Regulation of financial markets by the practitioners, for the benefit of the practitioners.

International (or **global**) **market in securities** A system for ensuring that a panic in New York or Tokyo spreads rapidly to London — or *vice-versa*.

Popular capitalism A device for selling shares in state monopolies to some of the people who already own them.

Insider dealer Investors who do not work in the City are 'outsider dealers'.

The shares are acquiring strong institutional backing This is one the boys have decided to ramp up.

Our research report suggests… In a broker's report on a new issue this may mean that what follows is a few unchecked facts gleaned from the company's own prospectus.

Following the acquisition of Muggitt a phased programme of asset disposals was put in train We got control then asset-stripped it like crazy.

Acquisitive stockmarket-orientated financial conglomerate Paper-shuffling asset stripper.

Acquisitive Antipodean financial entrepreneur Aussie or Kiwi market raider.

Colourful, usually linked with the word **entrepreneur**. It is not racist, neither does it usually imply blue blood. **Colourful entrepreneurs** are probably active stockmarket operators. While their tactics pay off they are in the pink. They attract acres of purple prose from the spivvier share tipsters and their competitors

278

go green with envy or white with rage. All too often they overstretch themselves and end deep in the red.

Mr Rudyard Sharpe regards his 18 per cent holding in Nuggins as a long-term investment Ruddy Sharpe is bidding for Nuggins next week.

On a long-term view... Looking beyond the next five minutes.

We are responding vigorously to recent consumer complaint In a company report this may mean they are stepping up their public relations budget and running an image-building TV campaign — otherwise carrying on as before.

The accounts give a true and fair view... In the auditors' report on a major bank this possibly means that the accounts give a true and fair view except that the £5bn of loans to Latin America are worthless but can't be written off because the bank hasn't the resources.

...has been freed from day-to-day responsibility so that he can concentrate on long-term development of the company Has been fired. Employees are sacked; directors leave in a company Mercedes and a flood of euphemisms. When a director resigns for reasons of health, it is not necessarily his current health that is at issue. It is what will happen to his health if he tries to stay.

***

'How to read between the lines' is reproduced by kind permission of The Independent, *in which a version of this chapter first appeared.*

Glossary and Index

1 per cent rule 139

1992. The British term for the unified market among European Community countries, meant to be ratified at the end of 1992. Perversely, in Continental Europe they tend to refer to it as 1993.

212 (*see* **section 212**)

3i (*see* **Investors in Industry**)

3 per cent rule 262

5 per cent rule (to be **3 per cent**) 139, 244

15 per cent rule 138

30 per cent rule 138

50 per cent (significance of) 34, 139

75 per cent (significance of) 34

90 per cent (significance of) 139

above the line 46, 257

accept (of bill) 175

acceptance credit 176

acceptances (bills) 176, 179

acceptances (in takeover) 139, 141

Accepting Houses. The old name for the top tier of merchant banks in the UK which used to be members of the Accepting Houses Committee. 176

account (Stock Exchange) 91-92, 260

account day 91

accountants (*see also* **auditors**) 27, 30

accounting standards 256

Accounting Standards Board 256

accounts (company) 32-80, 256-258

accrued (accumulated) income (on gilt-edged stocks) 157

accumulation units (unit trusts) 234

acquisitions (*see also* **takeovers**) 52

ACT (*see* **Advance Corporation Tax**)

acting in concert (*see also* **concert party**) 140

actuary 30

Additional Voluntary Contributions (AVCs) 230

adjust (profits, prices, earnings, dividends, etc.) 47, 123-124, 130-132

administrator, administration. The 1986 Insolvency Act introduced a new procedure known as **administration**. As an alternative to winding up (liquidating) an insolvent company, the court may (with the support of the creditors) make an **administration order**, approving the appointment of an **administrator**, if it appears that this may produce a better result in the long run. The administrator will take over the running of the company, selling off bits to repay debts as and when it appears advantageous. The hope is that the proceeds will be greater than if the company were closed down and the bits sold off immediately, and that it may even be possible for the core of the company to be preserved and to resume normal trading in the future. The procedure has some similarities with the temporary protection from creditors that American companies can claim under **Chapter 11** of their bankruptcy laws.

ADRs (*see* **American Depository Receipts**)

Advance Corporation Tax (ACT) (*see also* **unrelieved ACT**) 44-45

adversarial (relationship) 87

AFBD (*see* **Association of Futures Brokers and Dealers**)

aftermarket (*see also* **secondary market**) 115

agency broker 86, 88, 162

AGM (*see* **annual general meeting**)

agreed (takeover bid) 135

All-Share Index (*see* **FT-Actuaries All-Share Index**)

allotment, allocation (of shares, etc.) 117

allotment letters 119

alpha shares 86, **259**

alternative investments. Refers to objects owned at least partly as investments, which would not normally count as financial assets. Examples are: works of art (Sotheby's produces an index of values for paintings); Georgian silver; antique coins; **busted bonds** (q.v.), etc. Sometimes also referred to as **collectibles**.

aluminium 211

American deficit 188-189

American Depositary Receipts (ADRs). Instead of trading in shares of British companies as such, Americans may buy and sell ADRs, which confer ownership rights to the shares. The shares themselves are held on deposit with a bank. Trading in ADRs rather than the shares cuts the administrative hassle of registering changes in share ownership and avoids the need to pay stamp duty on each transaction.

American Stock Exchange. The smaller of the two Stock Exchanges in New York. The larger, on which the shares of most of the biggest corporations are traded, is the New York Stock Exchange (q.v.).

amortization (*see* **depreciation**)

amount paid up 120

AMPS (*see* **auction market preferred stock**)

analyst (*see* **investment analyst**)

annual percentage rate (APR). Organizations granting credit in the UK are required to state the real cost in terms of interest as an annual percentage rate. This is because many of the ways in which it is expressed in advertisements can be misleading without an APR. An individual who borrows £100 and pays it back in instalments over a year may be quoted a **flat rate** of, say, 12 per cent. But this means he is paying 12 per cent on the full amount for the whole year, whereas after 6 months only £50 will actually be outstanding. The real rate of interest is roughly double.

Annual General Meeting (AGM). General meeting of a company at which normally routine matters are put to the vote of shareholders: acceptance of the accounts, remuneration of auditors, re-election of directors, etc. 34, 41

annuity. A form of pension bought from an insurance company. In the simplest form the buyer pays over a lump sum in return for which he receives a stipulated income for life, consisting part of income on the money paid and part of return of the capital. Whether or not it turns out to be good value depends on how long he lives.

application form (in share issue) 114

appreciating currency 188

APR (*see* **annual percentage rate**)

arbitrage. Taking advantage of differentials in the price of a security, currency, etc., usually in two different markets. If Fastbuck Finance shares are quoted at 200p in London but at the equivalent of 205p in Amsterdam, the arbitrageur would make a profit by selling in Amsterdam and buying in London. This would tend to make the Amsterdam price fall and the London price rise, and the anomaly would be ironed out. Arbitrage in this sense is an example of the way speculators assist in the smooth running of markets. In the United States arbitrage is often associated with risk arbitrage, which has come to mean taking positions in takeover stocks. (*See* **arbitrageur** or **arb**.) 194

arbitrageurs (arbs) 140, 143

Articles of Association. A form of written constitution (technically a contract between the shareholders and the company), required of UK companies. Covers a number of (often standard) items such as borrowing powers, issue of shares, etc. Usually referred to in conjunction with the **Memorandum of Association** which contains information on the company's objects, share capital, etc. (*See also* **Companies House**.)

asset-backed securities. The result of securitizing various forms of loan. A company which provides loans via credit cards might issue floating rate notes or other forms of security to investors in the securities markets, the interest and capital repayment being provided by the payments from the credit card borrowers. The most common form of asset-backed security in the UK is **mortgage-backed securities** (q.v.).

basket (of currencies) 185
BCCI (*see* **Bank of Credit and Commerce International**)
bear (*see also* **short**) 93, 101
bear covering 101
bear market 93, 96
bear raid 101
bear squeeze 101
bear sale (short sale) 92, 101
bearer bond 197
bearer security 92, 197
bearish 93, 206
beat the index 61
bed and breakfast. Stock Exchange technique whereby an investor sells particular shares on one day and buys them back the next morning. The purpose is normally to establish a loss for capital gains tax purposes — the investor may have capital profits in that year against which the losses can be offset to reduce tax liability.
below the line 46
BES (*see* **Business Expansion Scheme**)
BES fund 147, 148
beta. A measure of the volatility of a share. A high beta share is likely to respond to stockmarket movements by rising or falling in value by more than the market average.
beta share 87, **259**
bid (*see* **takeover**)
bid basis (liquidation basis) 233
bid price 93, 209, 234
bid rate 181
bid timetable 141
Big Bang (27 October 1986) 4, 29, 81 *et seq*
Big Board. (*See* **New York Stock Exchange**)

bi-lateral credit line 256
bill of exchange 173, 175-176

black economy (cash economy). Areas of the economy where transactions go unrecorded (and therefore untaxed). If your local plumber quotes you two prices for a job — one which will include VAT if you want a receipt and a lower one if you pay cash and forego the paperwork — you are almost certainly contributing to the black economy if you pay cash.

Blue Arrow affair. More accurately described as the National Westminster Bank or County NatWest affair. A major scandal which led in July 1989 to the resignation of the chairman of the National Westminster Bank, several senior executives and various employees of County NatWest, its investment banking subsidiary, and of securities house UBS Phillips & Drew.

In August 1987 Blue Arrow, a rapidly growing employment agency group which was then advised by the corporate advice department of County NatWest, bid in cash for Manpower, a considerably larger American employment agency group. Finance was provided initially by a bridging facility from NatWest, to be replaced by the proceeds of a five-for-two rights issue by Blue Arrow of 504m shares at 166p to raise £837m. The rights issue was underwritten by County NatWest but, though this did not emerge at the time, was not fully sub-underwritten, leaving County NatWest at risk for over £200m.

Subsequently, the rights offer itself in September 1987 was only about 38 per cent subscribed by shareholders, though County NatWest and Phillips & Drew (which was broker to Blue Arrow at the time) themselves put in late applications to help to raise the 'take-up' to 48.9 per cent. With this level of take-up it was thought it would be possible to 'place' the shares that had not been subscribed, rather than leave the underwriters to take up the remainder of the issue, in which case the share price would have fallen heavily, causing losses all round.

The placing was conditional on all shares being placed. Of the 258m available, only 180m were placed with outside investors, so County NatWest and Phillips & Drew again used their own money to take up the outstanding 78m shares and the placing went ahead. As a result County NatWest ended up with a 13.4 per cent stake in Blue Arrow, then worth almost £160m.

Since stakes of over 5 per cent have to be declared under the Companies Act, this posed a problem. If the support from Count NatWest and Phillips & Drew became apparent it would probably defeat the object and result in a fall in the Blue Arrow price.

During the takeover and rights issue period, circulars recommending purchase of Blue Arrow shares emerged on several occasions from the County NatWest securities department.

To avoid the need for disclosure, the County NatWest holding was divided into three parts of under 5 per cent each, one of which was taken by the County NatWest marketmaking arm and another (under a profit and loss sharing agreement) by Phillips & Drew's parent, Union Bank of Switzerland (UBS). In October 1987 came the stockmarket crash and within three weeks the Blue Arrow share price had dropped from 167p to 80p.

News of the affair subsequently emerged and considerably later, in December 1988, inspectors were appointed to National Westminster Bank and County NatWest by the Department of Trade and Industry. Their report, published in July 1989, castigated various executives in County NatWest and Phillips & Drew for the attempt to 'mislead the market', though the inspectors considered that the arrangement with UBS was within the law as it then stood.

By December 1988, total losses to NatWest's investment banking arm from the Blue Arrow involvement were put at £65m, including £30m for the cost of the indemnity to UBS. **256**

board of directors. The men and women legally responsible for running a company. The structure of the board varies greatly between companies. Directors who are also employees of the company and have management responsibility are **executive directors**. Directors who simply provide experience and advice in board deliberations, and possibly have jobs elsewhere, are **non-executive directors**. The **chairman** presides at board meetings, but is not necessarily top dog in practice unless he combines his role with that of **chief executive**. The chief executive is responsible for the management of the company as a whole and is often the same person as **managing director**; but some companies have both, with the managing director in the subordinate role (Americans talk of the chief executive as **Chief Executive Officer** or **CEO**). Other directors may be distinguished according to their area of responsibility: **finance director**, etc. Each company also needs a **company secretary**, responsible for administration of the legally required paperwork involved in running the company. He or she may or may not also be a director. You need to know your company to know who really counts among the directors — titles can be misleading.

boiler room. Room with numerous telephones from which high-pressure salesmen attempt to sell securities direct to the public. Pejorative term. (*See also* **bucket shop**.)

bond. Forms of medium- or long-term 'IOU' issued by companies, governments, etc., usually paying interest and usually traded in a market. May be secured or unsecured. Interest may be fixed rate or floating rate (*see also* **gilt-edged stocks**, **government securities** and **industrial debentures** and **loans**). Bonds in the UK normally have a face value of £100. Fixed-interest bonds pay a fixed rate of interest on the £100 face value. But the yield or return to the investor depends on the price he pays for the bond in the market. A bond paying 11 per cent interest gives an income yield of around 12.5 per cent to someone who buys it in the market at £88.20

bond rating service (Moody's and Standard & Poor's) (*see* **credit rating**)
bondized (insurance) 235
bonds (insurance) 235
bonus issue (*see* **scrip issue**)
book (in shares) 84
book value 37, 38
book-keeping transaction 130
borrowing costs 18
borrowings, borrowed money (*see also* **debt**) 38, 42, 62, 70-72
bought deal 122, 127, **261**
brand names, brands 79
BP issue 117-118
British Venture Capital Association (BVCA) 146
broker-dealers 29, 87-88
brokers 88
bucket shop. Operation for 'pushing' (over-promoting)

particular shares to the public. The shares concerned are often of dubious quality (*see also* **boiler room**)

budget deficit 188
buffer stock (tin) 212
Building Societies Act 245
building society 25, 27, 164-165, 226, 230, 245
bull 93
bull market 93, 96
bull phase 96
bulldog bond 152, 196
bullish 93, 206
Business Expansion Scheme (BES) 148, 238, **263**
Business Expansion Scheme fund (*see* **BES fund**)
busted bonds (*see* **scripophily**)
buy-out, buy-in (*see* **management buy-out**)

call (*see* **at call**)
call option 206
cap (interest rate) 52, 179, 198
capital 9
capital account (of balance of payments) 188
capital adequacy 167
capital base 167
capital commitments 73
capital expenditure 54
capital gain 9, 10, 155-157
Capital Gains Tax (CGT). Tax payable on profits from the sale of most assets, particularly shares. Profits on sale of gilt-edged securities, however, are exempt. Investors in Britain could realize net gains of £5,000 (in 1989) before incurring a CGT liability. And in calculating liability, the base cost of the asset can be increased in line with

inflation from 1982 so that tax is payed only on 'real' profits. The part of the capital gain occurring before 1982 is not taxable.

capital loss 10
capital market 194
capital profit 78
capital ratio 167
capital reserves 78
capital shares 238
capital structure 135
capital value 10
capitalize (*see also* **market capitalization**). Used in a number of senses. Most common meaning is 'turn into capital'. Reserves are capitalized (turned into share capital) in a scrip issue. Interest on borrowings is capitalized if, instead of being charged against the profit of the year, it is added to the capital cost of the project to which the borrowings relate. Much investment is a process of capitalizing an income flow. If a building produces a rent of £10,000 a year an investor might be prepared to capitalize this income on a five per cent yield basis. This means he will pay a price for the right to receive this rent which gives him a five per cent return on his outlay. So he values the building on a multiple of 20 times the rent, or at £200,000. To capitalize a company sometimes means putting money into it in the form of share capital.
capitalization issue (*see* **scrip issue**)
capped floating-rate note 198
cash 40

cash cow. Business or part of a company that regularly generates useful flow of sales and profits, but without much in the way of growth prospects. Milk distribution in the UK is — possibly by coincidence — a prime example.

cash economy (*see* **black economy**)

cash flow 54

cash market (as opposed to futures) 152, 211

cash offer 135

cash settlement 91, 162

central banks 182

central rate (for currency) **265**

CEO (Chief Executive Officer) (*see* **board of directors**)

certificate of deposit (CD) 173, 176-177, 180

chairman (*see* **board of directors**)

Chapter 11 (of the American bankruptcy laws) (*see* **administrator, administration**)

charge (on assets) 63

chartered surveyors 30, 219

chartist 102, 108, 194

cheap long-term money 71

chief executive (*see* **board of directors**)

Chinese Walls 89

churning. An investment manager 'churns' investments he manages on behalf of clients when he switches too frequently between different shares, simply to generate commission or other benefits for himself or his associates.

City Code on Takeovers and Mergers (*see* **Takeover Code**)

City institutions 24 *et seq*

City Panel on Takeovers and Mergers (*see* **Takeover Panel**)

City of London 24 *et seq*

claims (insurance) 215

clawback 128

clean price (of gilt-edged) 157

clearing banks 28

clearing house. In a futures market, the body which reconciles sales and purchases, organizes margins and settlement and provides guarantees against default to users of the market.

close a position. The buyer of, say, a contract for a ton of metal for May delivery closes (cancels out) his position if he later sells an identical contract. He no longer has an outstanding liability to take delivery or to deliver. If the user of a futures market fails to maintain his margin, he will automatically be **closed out** by the market authorities who will buy or sell contracts on his behalf to close his original position.

close-ended 238

cocoa 212

coffee 212

cold calling 243

collar, cylinder. A combination of an interest rate **cap** and an interest rate **floor**, limiting exposure to changing interest rates within a defined range. 179

collateral. Assets pledged as security for a loan.

collectibles (*see* **alternative investments**)

coming to the market (*see also* **new issues**) 113

commercial lawyers 30

commercial paper. A form of short-term IOU issued to investors by a company or other major borrower, usually at a discount to its face value. Britain now has a commercial paper market, which was opened to a wider range of companies in the 1989 Budget. 177-178, 197, **264-265**

conversion premium 71
conversion terms 71
conversion value 71
convertible 71, 198
convertible capital bond 258
convertible loan stock 70-73, 82, 128, 152, 199, **258**
convertible preference 73, 75, 199, **256, 258**
copper 211
corporate finance 29, 30, 88
corporate bonds, loans 152
corporation loans 152
Corporation Tax 40, 44, **256**
cost of money 11 *et seq*
Council of Lloyd's 217
Council of the Stock Exchange (*see* **Stock Exchange Council**)
country brokers 29
County NatWest (*see* **Blue Arrow affair**)
coupon 20, 154
covenant. Undertaking to observe certain conditions in connection with, say, borrowing money or signing a lease. Used in writing about commercial property to mean 'standing of the tenant'. If Payola Properties lets one of its office blocks to ICI or Unilever, it has a strong covenant — the tenant is unlikely to default on rent payments.
crash (stockmarket crash of 1987) 3, 6, 96, 105, 106-112
Crawford's Directory of City Connections 31
creative accountancy 36
credit card (interest rates) 18
credit rating. Independent agencies, of which the best known are the US firms **Moody's** and **Standard and Poor's**, will assess the credit standing of long-

and short-term debt instruments issued by companies. Particularly in the United States, investors rely heavily on these ratings of the safety of bonds and commercial paper before making investment decisions. It is bad news for a company when one of the agencies **downgrades** its debt because of increasing worries about risk. The term **triple-A-rated** is used to describe the very best quality corporate debt. 201, **263**
creditors (*see also* **current liabilities**) 40, 70
crowding out. Describes the situation where the government is borrowing so much money that there is little available for commercial businesses to borrow, or the cost of funds becomes exhorbitant.
cylinder (*see* **collar**)
cum dividend 58, 157
cum rights 124
currencies (money and capital markets pages in FT) 185
currency contracts, options 193, 209
currency futures 209
currency movements (*see also* **foreign exchange**) 103, **265-267**
currency risk (hedging) 192
currency swaps 193, 201
current account (balance of payments) 183, 188
current assets 38-40
current liabilities 40
current value accounting 257
cushion (of equity) 62
cyclical stocks. Shares in companies whose business follows a cyclical pattern of

improved and diminished profitability. Share prices will tend to follow this pattern or discount it in advance. Examples in the UK are general insurance and housebuilding.

Daily Official List 94

Datastream. On-line screen-based system of information on prices (current and historic) for securities, commodities, currencies, etc. Also covers items from company accounts, economic statistics, etc. Information in the database can be searched and manipulated by the user and can be presented in text or graphic form. The graphs in this book are generated from the Datastream system.

dated (of fixed-interest stock) (*see* **redeemable**)

dawn raid 138-139

dealing 81

dealing floors 86

dealing for the account 92

debenture stock 20, 38, 70-71, 152

debt (*see also* **borrowings**) 19, 38, 70-72

debt and equity 19 *et seq*, 42, 164-165

debt convertible 198

debtors 40

deep-discounted bond. Bond issued at a price well below its face or par value of 100. May or may not pay interest (*see* **zero-rated bond**) but much if not all of the return to the investor is in the form of capital gain to redemption (*see also* **discount**) 198

deep-discounted rights issue 123, 126

default (on loan) 168

defence document 141

defended takeover 135

deferred equity 72

deferred ordinary shares 75

deferred tax 73

delta share 87

denationalization issues (*see* **privatization issues**)

Department of Trade and Industry (DTI) (*see also* **Blue Arrow affair**) 144, 234, 244, **271**

deposit protection 264

deposit-taking institution 164-165

depositors 164

deposits (*see* **retail deposits, wholesale deposits**)

depreciation (amortization) 38, 44, 54, **257**

deregulation 3 *et seq*

derivatives. Financial instruments that are a spin-off from the basic products and markets. Thus **options** and **futures** are derivatives, as they are a spin-off from shares, bonds, etc. **267**

development finance 146, 148

development of property 30, 222-223

dilute, diluted, dilution (of earnings, assets, etc.) 72-73, 79-80

direct shareholdings, ownership of shares 226-228, **254**

directors (*see* **board of directors**)

directors' report 35

directors' salaries 44

dirty, managed float 182

disclosure of shareholdings (*see also* **5 per cent rule**, etc.) 139, 244

discount. Used in many contexts. Stockmarkets discount future events by reacting to them before they happen. To buy or sell securities at a discount is to buy or sell them at a price below some standard measure of value, which depends on the context: their par value; their offer-for-sale price; their net asset value, etc. In this sense it is the opposite of a premium. To discount a financial instrument is to buy it below its face value, earning a return from the capital gain when it is repaid (bills of exchange). A **discount broker** is a broker offering a cut-price service (*see also* **at a discount**) 13, 100, 175, 237

discount houses 172-175

discount market 172-175

discount market deposits 180

discretionary. When an investment manager looks after investments for clients on a discretionary basis, the decisions are made at his discretion, not the client's. **Discretionary clients** of a broker are clients whose investments he manages in this way at his discretion.

disintermediation. Cutting out the middle-man: the intermediary. The person with spare cash, instead of depositing it with a bank, lends it direct to the end-user.

distribution. Usually a distribution of income and often used as a synonym for dividend.

diversification. A company diversifies when it extends its activities from its original business or businesses (which it presumably understands) to other business areas (which it may not understand so well). Not always a

sure-fire recipe for success (*see also* **conglomerate**)

dividend 10, 21, 41, 97

dividend cover 53

dividend per share 126

dividend stripping 157-158

dividend yield 10, 54-55

dollar (problems of) 188-189

domestic interest rates 183

double option 207

Dow Jones Industrial Average. Most frequently quoted index of the New York Stock Exchange. Covers thirty stocks, mainly industrial companies.

downside. 'The shares have downside potential' — there is plenty of scope for the price to fall.

droplock 198

DTI (*see* **Department of Trade and Industry**)

dual currency bonds 198

earning power (of company) 97

earnings per share (eps) 52, 55, 97

easier. Word beloved of market reporters. If a market eases or turns easier, prices are moving down (probably gently). (*See also* **firm**).

ECU (*see* **European Currency Unit**)

ECU bond futures 267

effective (of share price, earnings, dividend etc.) 132

effective control 138

EGM (*see* **extraordinary general meeting**)

eligible banks 176

eligible bills 176

EMS (*see* **European Monetary System**)

EMU (*see* **European Monetary Union**)

endowment assurance 229

endowment mortgages 230

Enterprise Zones. Designated areas of the country where businesses are freed from certain restraints applying elsewhere, notably planning restrictions and (for a time) the need to pay rates.

eps (*see* **earnings per share**)

equities (*see* **ordinary shares**)

equity (*see also* **debt and equity**) 19, 20, 42

equity capital (*see* **ordinary share capital**)

equity earnings 45, 52

equity finance 42

equity sweetener, kicker 77, 198

equivalent (of share price, earnings, dividend, etc.) 132

equivalent yield 222

ERM (*see* **Exchange Rate Mechanism**)

ESOP (Employee Share Ownership Plan). One of the methods of helping employees of a company to acquire a share stake in it. May have the additional benefit of making the company more difficult to take over, and is widely used for this purpose in the United States.

estate agents (*see* **chartered surveyors**)

eurobond 88, 163, 197-198

eurobond market 128, 158

eurobond market prices (table in FT) 202

eurocommercial paper 197

eurocurrency 195-197

eurocurrency interest rates (table in FT) 199

eurocurrency market (*see* **euromarket**)

eurodollars 195

eurodollar futures contract 209

euroequity issues 128, 200

euromarket 26, 163, 195-202, **267**

euronote 197

European Currency Unit (ECU) 176, 191-192, **265-267**

European Monetary System (EMS) 191-192, 254, **265-267**

European Monetary Union (EMU) 266

euroyen 195

evasion (*see* **tax evasion**)

ex-all (xa). Appearing after a share price, it means a purchaser buys without rights to whatever the company is in the process of issuing: dividend, rights issue shares, scrip issue shares, warrants, etc. (*See also* **xr, xc, xd** etc.)

ex-capitalization (*see* **xc**)

ex-dividend (*see* **xd**)

ex-rights (*see* **xr**)

Exchange Rate Mechanism (ERM) 191-192, **254, 265-267**

exceptional items 46, **257**

exchange controls 246

exchange cross rates (table in FT) 185

exchange rates 16

Exchequer stocks 154

exercize price (of option) 208

exercizing (an option) 204

exit PE ratio. The PE ratio that applies at the price at which a company is sold or taken over.

expiry (of option) 207

Export Credits Guarantee Department (ECGD). A government body assisting in the finance of overseas trade, mainly by insuring exporters against the possibility of non-payment by their overseas customers.

Extel cards. Statistical cards on companies and individual security issues, produced by the Exchange Telegraph Co and providing the figures and background information needed to undertake investment appraisals. A prime working tool of the investment analyst.

external growth 53

extraordinary general meeting (EGM). General meeting of a company at which non-routine proposals are voted on by shareholders. Examples of matters requiring an EGM would be an increase in authorized capital or changes to the company's aims and objects.

extraordinary items 46, **257**

face value. Nominal or par value of a security, rather than its market value. 20

factoring. A form of off balance sheet finance which can have the same effect as a loan. A factor will undertake to collect debts owing to a company on the company's behalf and meantime make an advance to the company of a proportion of the money it is due to receive.

fan club 140

fees (in eurobond market) 197

FIMBRA (*see* **Financial Intermediaries, Managers and Brokers Regulating Association**)

final closing date 142

final dividend 41

Finance Bill, Act. The legislation which implements the Budget proposals each year in the UK. The detailed provisions of the Finance Bill are normally debated for some months after the Chancellor has delivered his Budget statement.

finance director (*see* **board of directors**)

finance house deposits 180

finance houses. Quasi-banks, often owned by the major clearing banks. The finance houses specialize in hire purchase and other instalment credit, leasing, debt factoring, etc.

financial assets of individuals 227-228

financial consultants 228

financial crisis (1973-75) 167

financial engineering. Transforming one type of financial product into a different one to suit the needs of a particular type of borrower, lender or investor. The simplest example is an **interest rate swap** (q.v.) where a borrower may raise, say, fixed interest funds but swap them so that he has the use of floating rate money. **256**

financial futures contract 152, 204-206, 209-211

financial futures market (*see also* **LIFFE**) 26, 152, 205, 209-211, **259, 262**

financial health 36

financial institutions 25

financial instrument. A term covering most forms of short- and long-term investment traded in the money markets or the stockmarket: bank bills, certificates of deposit, shares, bonds, etc. 171, 173

financial intermediaries 27, 228

Financial Intermediaries, Managers and Brokers Regulatory Association (FIMBRA) 242, **271**

financial public relations 31

financial ratios 48 *et seq*

Financial Services Act (FSA) 241

financial services revolution 3 *et seq*

financial assistance for purchase of own shares 140

Financial Times (*see* **FT**)

financing gap 145

financing proposal (venture capital) 147

firm, firmer. When a market firms it means that prices are moving up rather than down, though the motion described is probably gentle. If interest rates firm they are also moving up rather than down, but in bond markets this means that prices of securities will be moving down. (*See also* **easier**.)

firm hands 117

first closing date 141

fiscal year. Year adopted for accounting and tax purposes. In the UK the government's fiscal year runs to 5 April. Companies can choose the year-end they wish, though end-December and end-March are common.

fixed assets 38

fixed charge (on assets) 63

fixed-interest market 82, 152

fixed-interest securities 12-13, 150-163

fixed-price offer (stockmarket) 115

fixed-price offer (unit trust) 234

fixed rate (*see also* **variable rate, floating rate**) 20, 51

flat rate (*see* **annual percentage rate**)

float 115

floating charge 63

floating exchange rates 182

floating-rate bonds, notes (FRNs) 181, 198

floating rate of interest (*see also* **variable rate, fixed rate**) 20, 51

floor (interest rate) 179, 198

Footsie Index (*see* **FT-SE Index**)

forecast (*see also* **profit, dividend, prospectus forecast**) 115

forecast dividend 57

foreign banks 29

foreign exchange 88, 182-194, **265-267**

foreign exchange brokers 193

foreign exchange market 15, 26, 171, 182-194

foreign exchange reserves 183, 186

forex (*see* **foreign exchange**)

formal documents (in bid) 141

forward exchange rate 192-193

forward market 192

forward rate agreement (FRA). A form of interest rate hedge which allows a prospective borrower to fix the cost of money he knows he will need to borrow in, say, three months' time. He is thus protected from adverse interest rate movements in the interim, which could otherwise have made the money more expensive when he needed it.

FRA (*see* **forward rate agreement**)

Fraud Squad. An overworked

branch of the City of London police specializing in the investigation of suspected fraud (*see also* **Serious Fraud Office**).

free issue (*see* **scrip issue**)

freehold property 221

friends (of company) 140

FRN (*see* **floating rate bond, note**)

front-end loaded. Used of various forms of regular investment, including life assurance. It means that a high proportion of the charges to the investor are deducted from his early contributions rather than spread over the life of the investment scheme.

freight futures 267

FSA (*see* **Financial Services Act**)

FT. The usual abbreviation for the *Financial Times*

FT 30-Share Index, Ordinary Share Index 58-59

FT-Actuaries All-Share Index 59

FT-Actuaries 500-Share Index 59

FT-Actuaries Gilt-edged Indexes 160

FT-Actuaries Indexes 58-60

FT-Actuaries Industrial Group Index 59

FT-Actuaries World Indexes 61

FT London Interbank Fixing (table) 181

FT-SE Eurotrack Index 259, 267

FT-SE Index 60-61

FT-SE Index (as basis for options and futures) 208, 209

fully diluted (*see* **dilute**)

fully-diluted assets per share 73, 79-80

fully-diluted earnings per share 73

fully paid 119, 130

fully subscribed 116

fully valued. 'The shares are fully valued' is often a journalist's way of suggesting they might be overvalued. Certainly, he does not think they are cheap.

fund management (*see* **investment management**)

fundamentals 23, 100, 110-112, 184, 186-188

fungible. The same as and interchangable with. If a futures contract traded in Chicago is the same as one traded on LIFFE in London, they are fungible if you could buy the contract in Chicago and sell it in London, or *vice versa*.

funny money. Used to describe complex, weird and wonderful forms of security sometimes devised by companies. A 'part-convertible subordinated index-linked loan stock with warrants attached' would be funny money. 136

futures contract 204-205

futures market 152, 203, 204-206, 209-213, **267**

G5, G7 (*see* **Group of Five, Seven**)

gain to redemption 155

gamma share 87, **259**

gas oil 213

gearing (leverage) 42, 50-51, 142-143, 237-238

general fund 235

general insurance 27, 214-215

gilt-edged market 11, 150-163, **256, 263**

gilt-edged marketmakers 29, 161, **263**

gilt-edged securities (*see also*

government bonds) 9, 12, 18, 82, 91, 150-163

gilts (*see* **gilt-edged securities**)

go short 101

go-go fund. A fund which invests in special situations and highly speculative stocks and probably deals very actively in its investments.

going concern basis. The basis on which accounts of a company are normally produced and audited. It assumes the company is viable and is continuing in business. Lower values would normally be put on a company's assets if accounts were produced instead on the assumption the company was going to be broken up (**liquidation** or **break-up** basis). If an auditor feels obliged to point out that he has approved the accounts on a going concern basis, it normally means there is some doubt as to whether the company is, in fact, viable.

gold. Is bought as an investment particularly at times of financial uncertainty. The London Gold Market was traditionally operated by five merchant banks and bullion dealers who twice a day 'fix' a gold price in the light of supply and demand for the metal; but dealing has now been opened up to a wider range of marketmakers.

golden hallo 91

golden handcuffs 91

golden handshake. Lump sum payment made to compensate sacked or redundant employee for loss of office. The more exhorbitant payments normally apply in the case of company directors, who generally 'resign' rather than being dismissed.

golden parachute. Arrangements made in advance by directors of a company to provide themselves with a happy financial landing if ousted in the course of a takeover, etc. Would include long service contracts with big in-built payments on loss of office, etc.

goodwill 68, 79-80, **257**

government bonds (*see also* **gilt-edged securities**) 9, 11, 150-163

government borrowing (*see* **PSBR, PSDR**)

government guarantee (Loan Guarantee Scheme) 149

government securities (*see* **gilt-edged securities**)

Government Securities Index 160

grain futures 267

greenmail 142

grey market 119

gross 45, 162

gross borrowings 62

gross dividend per share 45, 53

gross income yield 156

gross up, grossed up 53

gross yield 235

ground rent 221

group balance sheet (*see* **consolidated balance sheet**)

Group of Five, Seven (G5, G7) 189

growth prospects 115

growth by acquisition (*see* **external growth**)

guarantee 74, 167

Guinness affair 143-144, 244, **256**

half-year 34

hammered (of broker) 245

Hang Seng index. The most

commonly quoted index of share prices in the volatile Hongkong stockmarket.

high-tech. A 'high-tech business' should describe a company operating at the frontiers of technology — and sometimes does. Many more mundane businesses try to acquire a high-tech label in the hope of a improvement in their share ratings; this can misfire, as the stockmarket is weak on understanding of technology and when one high-tech company gets into trouble, all those with the same label may see their share prices suffer.

highs and lows. Prices of securities quoted in the newspapers, showing the highest and lowest prices reached, probably over the past year. These highs and lows will have been adjusted for scrip issues, etc.

hybrid financial instruments. Financial instruments which are a cross between two or more traditional instruments. The most common example is the convertible loan, which starts life as a bond but probably turns into share capital at a later date. **256**

indexation. Adjusting in line with an index. Usually the index is the Retail Prices Index (RPI): the most commonly used measure of inflation. The UK government issues index-linked bonds and there are index-linked forms of National Savings (Granny Bonds). An indexed share portfolio is one which seeks to match as closely as possible the composition and performance of a particular stockmarket index.

industrial property 225
inflation (*see also* indexation, RPI) 9, 151, **266**
inflation accounting 47
inflation hedge 158
insider dealing, trading 140, 143, 244
insolvency. A business can go bust in two main ways: by running out of cash to pay its bills and other obligations or by having more liabilities than assets (owing more than it owns). 'Insolvent' is sometimes used to cover both cases. It is an offence for a company to trade while insolvent.
insurance (*see also* **Lloyd's of London**) 26
insurance brokers 27, 228
insurance companies 25, 26, 103, 219, 244
Insurance Companies Act 244-245
insurance company market 215
insurances (prices in FT) 232, 235, 236
insured scheme (pensions) 27, 229
intangible assets 68
inter-bank deposits 180
inter-bank market 172, 177-179, 196
inter-bank rates 181
inter-dealer brokers 161
interest 44
interest rate differential 192
interest rate swap 180, 200
interest rates 11 *et seq*, 51-52, 96, 103, 170-181, 183-184, 210-211
interest yield (*see* income yield)
interests in associated companies 46
interim (profit announcement) 35
interim (dividend) 35, 41

internal growth 53
international capital markets (page in FT) 202
international money market (*see* euromarket)
International Petroleum Exchange (IPE) 213, **267**
International Tin Council 212
intrinsic value 77, 207-208
introduction (to stockmarket) 114
investment advisers 228
investment analyst 30, 89
investment arithmetic 33, 48 *et seq*
investment bank. The closest American equivalent to the British merchant bank. Issues and underwrites the issue of securities, buys and sells securities, provides corporate advice, etc.
investment business (authorization for) 241
investment income (insurance) 214-215
investment management 29, 88, 229, 234
investment management groups 27, 234
Investment Management Regulatory Organization (IMRO) 242-243
investment market in property 219-222
investment ratios 48 *et seq*
investment research 30, 89
investment trusts 66, 237-238
investments (interests) in associated companies (*see* associated company)
investor protection 5, 240-247
Investors in Industry (3i) 146
invisible earnings. A country's overseas earnings from

dividends, etc., received from abroad and from supply of services rather than physical goods. 24, 214

irredeemable 13, 152, 155, 158, 160

ISRO 81, 242

issue a loan 20

issued capital 75, 76

issuing house. Financial institution which arranges issues of securities on a market.

Japanese government bond (futures contract) 209

jobber/broker mechanism 85, 161

jobbers 84

jobber's turn 84

junk bonds 142, 147, **255**

kerb market. Unofficial market in securities, commodities, etc., often operating alongside the official market. Once the official trading session has ended, dealers may continue trading in the kerb market, often over the telephone.

lapse (of takeover bid) 141

Latin-American debt crisis 168

launch (*see also* **new issues**) 113

launder (of money). Take dirty money (from thefts, etc.) and turn it into clean money by putting it through some process that disguises its origin. Unit trust managers tend to be suspicious of potential investors who pay with a suitcase of used fivers.

LAUTRO (*see* **Life Assurance And Unit Trust Regulatory Organization**)

LCE (*see* **London Commodity Exchange**)

LDC (*see* **less developed country**)

LDT (*see* **licensed deposit taker**)

lead 211

lead bank 196

leaseback (*see* **sale and leaseback**)

leasehold, leaseholder 221

leases (of property) 220

leasing. Rather than buy the plant and equipment they need, businesses may lease it instead. They use it as if it were their own, but it remains the property of the institution which put up the money to purchase it: often a bank or other financial institution. The user makes regular payments for its use instead of having had to find the cash to buy it at the outset. Leasing used to offer considerable tax advantages, but these have now diminished. (*See also* **off balance sheet** finance.)

left with the underwriters 117

lender of last resort 170

less developed countries (LDCs) 168

letting market (for properties) 31, 219

level playing fields 143

leverage (*see* **gearing**)

leveraged takeovers, buy-outs 142-143, 147, **254, 261-262**

LGS (*see* **Loan Guarantee Scheme**)

LIBID (*see* **London Inter-Bank Bid Rate**)

LIBOR (*see* **London Inter-Bank Offered Rate**)

licensed dealer in securities 83

licensed deposit-taker (LDT) 169

life (of loan, etc.) 71, 152-153

life assurance 226-229, 230

life assurance companies 27, 214

Life Assurance and Unit Trust Regulatory Organization (LAUTRO) 243
life funds 229
lifeboat (for banks) 167
LIFFE (*see* **London International Financial Futures Exchange**)
lighten (share holdings) 117
LIMEAN 181
limited liability 33-34
limit up, limit down. Some overseas markets in futures or securities impose a limit on the amount by which a price is allowed to move in a single day. If the price has reached the upper limit it is described as 'limit up', and as 'limit down' if it has reached the lower one.
liquid 164
liquidation (*see also* **winding up**) 30
liquidation basis (bid basis) 233
liquidator. A liquidator, normally an accountant specializing in this type of business, goes into a company to wind it up (close it down) by selling its assets and distributing the proceeds to creditors in order of preference: the tax authorities and secured creditors rank high. Ordinary shareholders get what is left after all debts have been paid. Usually (except in the case of a voluntary liquidation where a solvent company decides to wind itself up) there is nothing. (*See also* **receiver**.)
liquidity (of market) 5, 14, 16, 85, 112
liquidity ratio (of banks) 164, 166
listed, listing 82, 113
Listing Agreement 82

Lloyd's Act 216-217, 245
Lloyd's broker 216
Lloyd's of London 26, 214-218, 245, **268**
LME (*see* **London Metal Exchange**)
Loan Guarantee Scheme (LGS) 148-149
loan stock 20, 38
local authority deposits and loans 180
locals (in futures market) 209
locking in (to a price, exchange rate, etc.) 192
London Commodity Exchange (former name of **London Futures and Options Exchange**) 211
London Futures and Options Exchange (London FOX) 211-213, **267, 269**
London Inter-Bank Bid Rate (LIBID) 181
London Inter-Bank Offered Rate (LIBOR) 174, 181, 199, **264**
London International Financial Futures Exchange (LIFFE) 193, 209-211, **259, 262**
London Metal Exchange (LME) 211-212, **267**
London money rates (table in FT) 180
London recent issues (table in FT) 119, 120
London Stock Exchange (*see also* **Stock Exchange**) **259**
London Traded Options Market (*see* **Traded Options Market**)
long (of stock) 93
long-dated gilt-edged (futures contract) 209
long-dated stocks, longs 153, 158, 160
long-tail business (insurance) 215
long-term borrowings 44

longs (*see* **long-dated stocks**)
low-coupon stocks 155
low-geared company 42
low PE ratio 56
low yield, yielding 55
loyalty bonus issue 132
Ltd (limited) 33

M & A. Stands for mergers and acquisitions, one of the buzzphrases of the late 1980s. Merchant bank corporate finance departments and securities houses make much of their money from mergers and acquisitions work.
M & G Securities (investment management group) 235
M₀ (M nought) 166
M₃ (M three) 166
Macarthys cards. A form of press clipping service which picks up and categorizes press coverage of companies and of business topics. Useful for mugging up on recent company history and developments.
main market (Stock Exchange) 83, 113, **259, 260**
Mainstream Corporation Tax 45
make a book 14
managed fund 229, 235
management advisory services 30
management buy-out, buy-in 143, 145-146, **262**
management of risk 26, 179-180, 192-193, 237
managing agent (Lloyd's) 216
mandatory bid, offer 138, 139
margin. In some markets, particularly futures markets, clients are only required to put up a proportion of the cost of what they buy: a form of deposit known as margin. But this

margin will have to be topped up if it is eroded by adverse price movements. A 'margin call' is the notice that the margin needs topping up, otherwise the investor will be closed out. 206
margin (interest rate) **264**
marginal. Frequently used in the sense 'marginal tax rate'. In the UK a high-earning individual would (in 1989) pay 25 per cent income tax on the first slice of his taxable income and 40 per cent on the top slice. Under the progressive tax system this means he will also pay the top 40 per cent rate on any margin of additional income he earns, and 40 per cent is therefore his marginal rate.
market 3-5, 11-16, 22-23
market capitalization. Used of stockmarkets and of individual companies. The capitalization of the London equity market is the total market value of all the ordinary shares of all the companies listed on the market (usually excluding foreign-registered companies). The market capitalization (strictly, equity market capitalization) of Joe Bloggs Plc is the stockmarket value of all its ordinary shares: the number of shares in issue multiplied by the market price. If Bloggs has 10m share in issue and the price is 200p, Bloggs is capitalized at £20m. 82
market price mechanism 12-13, 15-16
market professionals 133
market purchases 137
market sentiment (*see* **sentiment**)
marketable 130

marketable securities. Covers most forms of security that can be bought and sold in a market: bonds, shares, certificates of deposit, etc.

marketed (of securities) 30

marketmaker 14, 29, 84, 85, 86, 87-88, 93-94, 100-101, 161, **259**

matched bargain basis 83

maturity 72, 150, 152

medium-dated gilt-edged (futures contract) 209

medium-dated stocks 153

medium- or long-term debt 41

medium-term note (MTN) 265

mediums (gilt-edged) 160

members (of a company) (*see* **shareholders**)

members' agent (Lloyd's) 216

Memorandum of Association (*see* **Articles of Association**)

merchant banks 29, 133

merger (*see also* **takeover**) 134, 135

merger accounting 134

metals (commodities) 211

middle prices 93, 154

minimum commission 84

Minimum Lending Rate (MLR) 173

minority interests, minorities or **outside interests** 46, 73

minority shareholders 46, 73, 138

MLR (*see* **minimum lending rate**)

MOF (*see* **multiple option facility**)

money creation 165-166

money markets 15, 25, 170-181, **264-265**

money market instruments. Forms of short-term investment that are traded in the money markets and easily turned into cash. Examples include **bank bills** and **certificates of deposit** (q.v.).

money supply 165-166

Monopolies Commission 139, **262**

Moody's (bond rating service) (*see also* **credit rating**) 201

moratorium. When a business defaults on a loan, creditors may sometimes agree a moratorium with the borrower. This means they agree not to insist on immediate payment, judging they might get back more in the long run by giving the business time to wind down its affairs in an orderly manner rather than insisting it is wound up immediately.

mortgage (*see also* **specialist mortgage lenders**) 25, 222, 226, 230, **270**

mortgage-backed security 199

mortgage payments 18, 230, **270**

MTN (*see* **medium-term note**)

multinational company. Company which operates in a major way in two or more countries, such as Unilever or Shell.

multiple applications (new issues) 120

multiple of (on a PE ratio of) 55

multiple of rent (property valuation) (*see also* **years' purchase**) 220

multiple option facility (MOF) 178-179, **265**

mutual 28

naked writer. A writer (creator) of options, who does not own the underlying shares against which the options are written. Naked writing is a very dangerous practice.

names (at Lloyd's) 214-218, **268**

narrow market 100

NASDAQ. Stands for National Association of Securities Dealers Automated Quotations — the computerized price information system used by dealers in the over-the-counter market in the United States. The British SEAQ system is closely modelled on it.

National Savings Stock Register 162

NatWest Bank (*see* **Blue Arrow affair**)

NAV (*see* **net asset value per share**)

nearby, nearest month, furthest month. If we are now in January and contracts in a futures market are actively traded for delivery dates in February, April, June, August and October, then the nearest month is February and the furthest is October.

negative (inverse) yield curve. Interest rates for deposits or securities of different maturity — three months, six months, a year, five years, ten years, etc. — can be plotted on a graph. When short-term interest rates are higher than longer-term ones, this line will start high and curve downwards. This is a negative or inverse yield curve. 180

negotiated commissions. Have replaced the former fixed minimum commission structure for deals in securities on the Stock Exchange in Britain. Large institutional investors (or those who operate through brokers rather than buying at net prices) are free to negotiate the level of commission they will pay, which has dropped sharply for large trades. Small private investors with little bargaining power generally pay much the same as before or sometimes more. 85

net 45, 162

net asset value 41, 66, 79

net asset value per share (**NAV**) 64-66, 223-224, 237-238

net borrowings 62

net current assets (and **liabilities**) 40

net dividend per share 45, 53

net PE ratio 56

net prices 87, 162

net profit, net profit available for ordinary shareholders 45, 46, 52

net return 156

net tangible asset value 68, 79

net working capital 41

new issues 88, 113-121, 146, **260**

new time (Stock Exchange) 92

New York Stock Exchange (**NYSE**). The main stock exchange in the United States, on which America's major corporations are listed. Also referred to as the Big Board, or Wall Street where it is located.

nickel 211

NIF (*see* **note issuance facility**)

nil paid 125

nil PE ratio 56

no par value 75

nominal value (face value, par value) 20, 75, 154

nominee (name). Shares can be held for convenience (or, often, for secrecy) under the name of a nominee rather than that of the beneficial owner. Thus Fastbuck

Nominees might hold shares on behalf of a number of the clients of Fastbuck Finance. UK companies have powers to require the identity of beneficial owners of shares held in nominee names, but the powers are of little use when the nominee is a secrecy-pledged Swiss bank. (*See also* **section 212.**) 92, 140, 246

non-bank private sector 172

non-executive director (*see* **board of directors**)

non-recourse loan. Usually arises as follows. Company C is set up by Companies A and B (perhaps to undertake a property development). But it is not a subsidiary of either. Company C borrows the funds it needs as a non-recourse loan.Because the loan is not guaranteed by Companies A or B, no mention of it appears in their accounts. The lender is lending against the success of Company C's venture and if Company C gets into trouble he has no recourse to Companies A and B to get his money back — in theory, at least. Much property development lending is undertaken on a non-recourse or limited-recourse basis.

non-voting shares. Some companies issue classes of non-voting ordinary shares, usually so that the founders (who hang on to a fair proportion of the voting shares) can control the company without needing to own over half the ordinary share capital. Others issue different classes of shares, all of which have votes but some have more votes than others. Terms like 'A Ordinary' and 'B Ordinary' are often used to distinguish the different classes.

note issuance facility (NIF) 197

notes to the accounts 35

occupational pension schemes (*see also* **pension funds**) 26, 226

off balance sheet items. Covers a range of items — usually potential liabilities — which do not appear in the balance sheet of the company concerned. Examples of off balance sheet financing are leasing (though companies are now meant to show leased assets and the corresponding obligation to make payments), factoring, sale and leaseback finance for property development, non-recourse loans in joint venture companies, etc. Can cause concern when it disguises the extent of the commitments the company has entered into. Off balance sheet risks are now a major concern in banking, where banks — instead of lending money, which would show in their accounts — provide guarantees for securities issued by businesses or agree to underwrite future issues of securities. 167

offer document 141

offer for sale 114, 118-119, 148

offer period 142

offer price 93, 209, 234

offered rate 181

Office of Fair Trading 139

office property 225

official intervention (foreign exchange) 182

official list 94
official market 119
official prices 94
offshore companies 217
offshore funds 232, 236
oil 189-191
Old Lady of Threadneedle Street.
Coy nickname for the Bank of
England, much overworked by
some banking writers.
ombudsman (for Lloyd's) 218
open-ended 238
open interest. In a futures
market, the number of
outstanding contracts that have
not been cancelled by a contract
in the other direction.
open market operations 172
open offer 128
open outcry 209, 211
opportunity cost 18
options 82, 125, 193, 203-204,
206-209, **267**
ordinary share capital 37, 74, 75
ordinary shareholders' funds 74
ordinary shares (*see also* equity)
9, 11, 18, 20, 34, 74, 82, 97, 237,
259-260
organic growth (*see* internal
growth)
OTC (*see* Over-The-Counter
markets)
out of the money (of options) 208
outside shareholders (*see*
minority interests)
Over-The-Counter markets
(OTC) 83-84
overall return 10, 17, 98, 151
overdraft 18, 38, 41
over-geared, over-borrowed 62
overhanging the market 104, 117
overseas funds 232, 236
overseas securities and property
25

overshooting 184, 187
oversubscribed 117
overtrading 64
owners of a company (*see*
shareholders)

Panel (*see* Takeover Panel)
paper. Securities of one kind or
another (shares, bonds, etc.) as
opposed to cash. Usually used in
the context of a 'paper offer' in a
takeover — the bidder offers its
own securities rather than cash.
136
paper profit or loss. A profit is a
paper profit until you take it in
cash. If you bought 100 shares at
200p each and the price rose to
300p, you would have a paper
profit of £100. But you are only
sure of an actual profit of £100 if
you sell the shares at 300p.
paperchase 136
par value (also expressed as
nominal value and **face value**) 20,
75, 129, 154
parallel money markets 172, 177-
179
parallel syndicates (Lloyd's) 217
parent company 37
parent company balance sheet 37
parities 16, 182
park (of shares). When one
company wants to hide the extent
of its shareholding in another, it
may temporarily park the shares
with a third party to avoid the
disclosure rules. (*See also*
warehousing, Blue Arrow affair.)
part-paid 119-120, 160, 198
participating preference shares 75
partnership 34
partnership finance (for
property) 223

pass (a dividend) 53
pathfinder prospectus 118
PE ratio (*see* **price-earnings ratio**)
peaks 96
penny stocks. Shares quoted in the market at prices of a few pence only — it used to be less than 10p, but the criteria have widened. The idea is that they should be a good speculation because they usually reflect companies that are down on their luck. The company could go bust, but if somebody gets a grip on it and improves its performance, the shares could rise many times in value. However, nowadays most penny stocks are ramped well above their likely worth in the hope of something of this kind happening. They may not be a bargain.
pension fund performance 30
pension funds (*see also* **occupational pension schemes**) 25, 26, 30, 103, 219
pensions 226-227, 229-230
PEP (*see* **personal equity plan**)
percentages, percentage points. A fertile ground for confusion. If Payola Properties raises a loan at 10 per cent and Fastbuck Finance raises one at 12 per cent, Fastbuck is paying two **percentage points** more for its money (the difference between 10 and 12). But Fastbuck is equally paying 20 **per cent** more for its money than Payola (because 12 is 20 per cent higher than 10). Writers often confuse the two measures. Usually the context makes the meaning clear, but one

or two monumental misunderstandings have resulted. (*See also* **basis points**.) 21, 181
performance funds. Funds which aim for above-average capital growth, usually at the expense of income and by accepting higher risks. The fund may also switch actively between investments.
permanent capital 37
permanent interest-bearing shares (PIBS). Effectively, a form of subordinated debt issued by building societies which they can count towards their capital for capital adequacy calculations. The need arises because mutual institutions do not have the option of raising equity finance in the stockmarket.
perpetual floating rate notes (perpetuals) 198
Personal Equity Plan 238-239, 270-271
personal guarantees 34
personal loans 18
personal portable pensions 230
personal sector 227
physical market. A market (in commodities, say) where deals lead to delivery of physical commodities. In other words, deals are not merely in futures contracts which are closed out by other futures contracts. 212
PIBS (*see* **permanent interest-bearing shares**)
pig futures 267
PINCs (*see* **Property Income Certificates**)
pitches (marketmakers') 84
placing 114, 122, 127
plc (*see* **public company**)
plough back 37, 54, 77

pm (premium) 125
point, basis point. If UK bonds rise in price by £1, they are described as rising by one **point**. A stockmarket index rises by one point if it climbs from 1001 to 1002. If bank base rates are 10 per cent, an overdraft at 5 **points** over base rate will cost you 15 per cent. But a **basis point** is one hundredth of one percentage point. If **LIBOR** (q.v.) is 8 per cent, a loan at 55 basis points over LIBOR will cost 8.55 per cent. (*See also* **percentages, percentage points**.) 61, 160, 181, 199
poison pill 142
polarization. A current buzz-word, brought into prominence by the Securities and Investments Board. The SIB insists on a distinction (polarization) between financial intermediaries which market the investment products of a particular organization and those which are genuinely independent advisers, marketing a range of products from different stables. This has caused considerable annoyance among, *inter alia*, banks and building societies which like to promote themselves as sources of financial advice but have their own in-house investment products to sell. 247
politics (effect on share prices) 104
poll. Votes at company meetings are normally taken initially on a show of hands. If the result is disputed, a poll can be called for — ordinary shareholders normally have one vote per share, and the number of shares voted for and against is counted. (*See also* **proxy**.)
pooled investments (*see also* **unit linked**) 232
portfolio. The collective term for an owner's holdings of shares, loans, etc. **Portfolio investment** covers investment in securities as opposed to direct investment which usually means putting money into plant, machinery, etc. 59
portfolio insurance 108
positions (in shares) 84, 85
Post Office Register (*see* **National Savings Stock Register**)
potato futures 267
pound (*see* **sterling**)
pre-emption rights 122, 128-129
pre-tax profit 44
pre-tax profit margin (*see* **profit margin**)
predators (stockmarket) 67, 134
preference shares 46, 74, 82
preferred ordinary shares 75
preliminary announcement (prelim) 35
premium (*see also* **at a premium**) 125, 149, 204
premium (insurance) 214-215
premium income 215
premium put convertible 256,258
press recommendations 100, 249-251
Prevention of Fraud (Investments) Act 244
price-earnings ratio (PE ratio) 55-56, 97, 115
price information systems 86, 161
price-sensitive information. Information (usually unpublished) that is likely to cause share prices to move. 240

primary capital 167
primary dealers 29, 161
primary market 16, 82, 197
prime properties 224-225
prime rate. Rate charged by US banks to their very best borrowers. Not the same, therefore, as UK base rates — even the best borrowers normally pay a margin over base rate for an overdraft and base rate itself is simply a yardstick.
principal 14
private client. Used of brokers' clients to denote individual private investors rather than institutional clients.
private company. In general terms, a limited company (with 'Ltd' after its name) whose securities are not traded in a market. It could, however, be an unquoted subsidiary of a **public company** (q.v.).
privatization (denationalization) 119, 132, **254**
professional advisers 30
professional fund manager 239
profit 9
profit after tax (*see* **net profit**)
profit and loss account 35, 36, 42 *et seq*
profit before tax (*see* **pre-tax profit**)
profit margin 49
profit on ordinary activities before tax (*see* **pre-tax profit**)
profit-taking 100
project finance. Finance put up for a particular project (say, a property development) and probably secured on that project rather than forming part of the general corporate borrowing of a

company. (*See also* **non-recourse.**)
programme trading 108
promissory note 12
property 25, 219-225, **269-270**
property bonds 224, 232
property companies 223-224, **269**
property development 219, 223
property futures 267, **269-270**
Property Income Certificates (PINCs) 224, **269**
property indexes 224-225
property investment companies 66, 223
property investment portfolio 30
property lending 225, **263, 269**
property market 31, 219
property performance 225
property shares 224
property traders 223, **269**
property unit trusts 224, **269**
prospective dividend 57
prospective dividend yield 57
prospective PE ratio 57
prospectus 30, 114
prospectus forecast 115
provision (for bad debts) 169, **263**
provisions (for liabilities and charges) 73
proxy. A shareholder entitled to vote at the general meeting of a company can appoint a proxy to vote on his behalf. Directors of the company will act as proxies, or the shareholder could appoint a friend. Before the meeting the shareholder receives a **proxy card** which he can fill in and sign, nominating his proxy and indicating which way he wants his votes cast on the different resolutions.
prudential ratios (for banks) 167
PSBR (*see* **public sector**

borrowing requirement)
PSDR (*see* **public sector debt repayment**)
public company. Public limited company, with 'plc' after its name. A company whose securities are traded in a market or which invites the public to subscribe for its securities must be a plc. (*See also* **private company**.)
public offering of stock (gilt-edged) 160
public relations (*see* **financial public relations**)
public sector borrowing requirement (PSBR) 150, 190, 256, 263
public sector debt repayment (PSDR) 150
puff (a share). Over-promote the merits of a share, probably in a broker's circular or a press recommendation.
pull to redemption 157-158
purchasing power 9
purchasing power parity 187
pushing (of shares). Over-promoting a particular share to investors. (*See also* **ramp**, **puff** and **bucket shop**.)
put option 206

qualifications (auditors') 35
quarterlies. Quarterly results and dividend declarations produced by American listed companies. 34
quotation. Price quoted for a security, etc., comprising a bid and offer price.
quote 113
quoted (company, share, etc.) 83

rack rent 221
ramp (a share). Over-promote a share to get the price up.
rank (for dividend) 75
ratchet 146
rating (in stockmarket) (*see also* **credit rating**) 54 *et seq*, 115, 201
re-rated 97, 99, 190
re-rated downwards 99
readily saleable assets 66
real. The word 'real' in an investment context normally means 'adjusted for inflation'. If your money is earning 10 per cent interest in a year when prices rise by 4 per cent, your **real return** is around 6 per cent.
real rate of return (*see also* **indexation, real**) 159
real terms (*see also* **indexation, real**) 96
real value 159
receiver. A receiver is put into a company to recover a specific debt or specific debts on which the company has defaulted (or sometimes comes in effectively at the request of the directors when they know the company is in trouble and likely to default). His job is to sell assets as necessary to recover the debt or debts. Occasionally he may be able to do this without its resulting in the company's closing down, in which case the company can revert to normal trading after his departure. But generally the appointment of a receiver is the beginning of the end and the company is eventually wound up.
reciprocity 143
Recognized Investment Exchanges (RIEs) 242
Recognized Professional Bodies (RPBs) 242

recovery stocks 235
recycling (of deposits) 166-167
redeem 13, 20
redeemable 152
redemption (hold to) 157
redemption date 20, 72, 153, 158
redemption yield 155
rediscount (bill of exchange) 173
redistribution of risk 203-213
regional exchanges 81
register of shareholders 92, 124
registered securities 92, 197
regulation (*see also* **investor protection**) 7, 137, 240 *et seq*
reinsurance 215
related companies 70
relationship banking 264
rent 220-223, 224
rent reviews 220, 221
rental value 220, 224
repayment mortgage 230
replacement cost accounting 47
repos (*see* **repurchase agreements**)
repurchase agreements (repos) 174
rescheduling. Rearranging the terms of a loan. Normally involves spreading interest and capital repayments over a longer period when the borrower is unable to comply with the original terms. Sometimes involves lending him further money out of which he will effectively meet the payments on the original loan — this may help the lender to postpone recognition of the fact that he has probably lost his money. 168
reserve assets 166
reserve assets ratio 166
reserves (*see also* **capital reserves, revenue reserves, share premium account, shareholders' funds**) 38,
45, 53, 77-80, 129, 169
resistance levels (chartism) 102
resolution. Used in the sense of a proposal put to the vote of shareholders at the general meeting of a company. **Ordinary resolutions** covering the more routine matters require a simple majority to succeed. **Special resolutions**, required to alter a company's **articles of association** (q.v.), require 75 per cent of the votes cast to be in favour. This can be important in a takeover. If shareholders representing more than 25 per cent of the votes refuse to accept the offer, the bidder may gain control but will have difficulty in restructuring the victim company if non-accepting shareholders vote against proposals requiring a special resolution.
restrictive practices 85
Restrictive Practices Court 85
retail banking 88
retail deposits 25, 164, 172
Retail Prices Index (RPI). Commonly used measure of inflation. Costs of goods and services are weighted in the index to approximate to a typical family spending pattern. Can be sharply affected by increase in mortgage interest rates or in taxes on expenditure (VAT, excise duties, etc). (*See also* **indexation**.) 159
retained profit (*or* retained earnings) 41, 45, 54, 77
retentions (*see* **retained profit**)
return (*see also* **overall return**) 9, 10, 11 *et seq*
return on assets 66

revaluation (of currency) **266**
revaluation (of properties) 78
revenue reserves 45, 77, 130
reverse auction 161
reverse takeover. When a small company takes over a larger one, or when the company being taken over will effectively be the dominant force in the combined group.
reverse yield gap 98, 111
reversionary properties 222
revert, reversions 221
revolving underwriting facility (RUF) 197
RIE (*see* **Recognized Investment Exchange**)
rights issue 76, 78, 122-129, **261**
rights offers (table in FT) 125
ring-dealing members 211
risk (*see* **management of risk**)
risk asset ratio 167
risk capital 21, 42
roll up. Instead of making regular interest payments on a loan, a borrower may sometimes be allowed to add the interest to the capital amount outstanding. This **rolled-up** interest is thus effectively paid at the same time as the loan is repaid.
roll over 178
RPB (*see* **Recognized Professional Body**)
RUF (*see* **revolving underwriting facility**)
rulebook (of SROs) 242
run (on a bank) 166
running yield (*see* **income yield**)

SAEF (SEAQ Automatic Execution Facility) 86, **259**
sale and leaseback 67, 222-223
sales (*see* **turnover**)

samurai (bond) 196
savers, savings 18, 25 *et seq*, 226-239
scaled down (of share applications) 117
scrip issue (**capitalization issue**) 76, 123, 129-132
scripophily. Collecting old share or bond certificates (**busted bonds**) which normally no longer have any value as securities but appeal for their historic associations or artistic merit.
SDR (*see* **Special Drawing Rights**)
SEAQ (**Stock Exchange Automated Quotation system**) 86, 162
SEC (*see* **Securities and Exchange Commission**)
second-tier market (USM) 83
secondary bank 167
secondary banking collapse 167, 269
secondary market 16, 82, 197
secondary property 225
section 212 The section of the 1985 Companies Act that gives a company powers to require shareholders hiding behind nominee names to declare their identity.
secured loan 199
securities 9, 70, 81-82
Securities Association, The (TSA) 242, **259**, **271**
Securities and Exchange Commission (SEC) 240-241
Securities and Futures Authority, The 260, **271**
Securities and Investments Board (SIB) 234, 241-243, 246-247, **271**
securities houses 4, 29, 86, 88, 127, **260**, **272**
securities markets 16

securitization. If an investor lends money to a borrower, he is simply making a loan. If, instead, he puts up the money in return for an IOU (I owe you) note which he can later sell to somebody else, the loan has been **securitized:** turned into a marketable security. (*See also* **asset-backed security, mortgage-backed security.**) 176-177, 197, 199

security (for loan) 63, 149

self-regulation 137, 240-247

Self-Regulating Organizations (SROs) 241-243, **259, 271**

sell at a discount 175

sentiment 104-105, 184

senior debt 147

Serious Fraud Office. Official department dealing with larger or more politically sensitive fraud.

service (a debt). Meet the interest payments and capital repayment schedule of a loan. 72, 168

settlement. The process of clearing the paperwork that follows the purchase or sale of stocks and shares. The client has to pay or be paid, has to deliver or receive share certificates, and purchases and sales have to be reconciled between the different marketmakers and brokers. These are **back office** operations and high share dealing volumes can bring logjams. In an attempt to speed up the settlement process and make it cheaper, a paperless electronic share registration system is proposed under which share certificates do not have to change hands each time shares are bought and sold. This would probably be based on an existing electronic settlement system used by marketmakers called **TAURUS.** 91-92, 162, **260**

settlement day 91

shakeout 102

share (*see* **equity, ordinary shares, preference shares,** etc.)

share capital 74

share certificate 92, **260**

share exchange offer 136

share ownership, share-owning democracy 254

share premium account 77-78

share prices (in newspapers) 56-61

shareholders 21, 34, **254**

shareholders' funds 41, 42, 62, 74, 129-130

shareholders' interest (*see* **shareholders' funds**)

shell company. A company, normally with a Stock Exchange quotation, which is now relatively inactive and has little by way of earnings or assets. Former plantation companies, whose estates in the Far East have now been nationalized, are a prime example. An entrepreneur with a vigorous private company will sometimes gain control of a shell company and inject his private business into it, thus gaining a ready-made stockmarket vehicle. This process is described as a **shell operation.**

shop property 225

short 92, 100, 101

short-dated gilt-edged (futures contract) 209

short end of the market (gilt-edged) 158

short sale, bear sale 92

short sellers, selling 101

short-term borrowings 44

short-term sterling interest rates (futures contract) 209

short-termism 134

shortage (in banking system) 173

shorts, short-dated (of gilt-edged) 152, 158, 160

SIB (*see* **Securities and Investments Board**)

side-by-side finance (for property) 223

signals (from Bank of England) 171

single-capacity 84

single-company PEP 270-271

sinking fund. A form of reserve in a company's accounts, to which it makes transfers of funds to cover the eventual repayment of a loan or the eventual expiry of a lease. (*See also* **wasting asset.**)

smaller companies fund 235

soft commissions. Commissions for financial services paid in kind rather than in cash. Before the Big Bang, brokers who derived large commissions from institutional clients under the fixed commission structure often gave part of the money back by providing customized research or paying for screen information systems for the use of the client. Though the competitive system following the Big Bang was meant to eliminate soft commissions, there are signs that they are creeping back.

soft commodities 211

soft loan. A loan on terms more favourable than those applying to a normal commercial borrowing. Sometimes used to assist worthy projects — business start-ups in areas of high unemployment, etc.

solicitors 27

solvency (*see* **insolvency**)

solvency ratio (of banks) 167

soya bean meal futures 267

sources and application of funds statement 35

sources of money, finance 37, 70-72

Special Drawing Rights (SDRs). A form of artificial money created by the International Monetary Fund. Countries may hold part of their official reserves in the form of SDRs which can therefore be used for payments between countries — in this sense they can be a substitute for gold. 186

special resolution (*see* **resolution**)

special situation. Usually used to describe a company whose shares could rise sharply if a particular set of circumstances comes to fruition. Sometimes used of potential takeover stocks but more commonly of **recovery situations** — companies which have been in trouble but whose shares could rise sharply in value if management succeds in turning the company round. Some funds specialize in investing in special situations.

specialist mortgage lenders. A new breed of mortgage providers for house purchase, who recoup the money they advance by floating **mortgage-backed securities** (q.v.) in the securities markets. 199

speculators. The old distinction between long-term investors and speculators has largely broken down. Many investors are speculators up to a point. Speculation normally implies taking above-average risk and often suggests short-term investment decisions. Though frequently maligned, speculators provide a useful service in most markets by taking advantage of any short-term anomalies in prices and thus preventing prices from getting out of line with each other. They may be less beneficial when they completely supplant genuine investors in a market. (*See also* **arbitrage**.)

split (share split). If a share price becomes too **heavy**, the shares may be split. Instead of having one 20p share standing in the market at 900p, the investor ends up with, say, two 10p shares worth 450p each. The effect may be similar to that of a scrip issue, but the technicalities differ. In the case of a share split, the par value is reduced, and no capitalization of reserves is involved.

split-level trust 238

sponsors (to an issue) 115

spot price, spot market 192, 205

spread (between bid and offer price) 15, 90, 93

spread (interest rate). Sometimes used to mean the margin a borrower pays above one of the benchmark interest rates. When LIBOR is 10 per cent, a borrower paying a spread of 30 basis points over LIBOR pays 10.3 per cent.

SRO (*see* **Self-Regulating Organization**)

stag, stagging 113, 115, 120

stale bull 93

stand in the books at 65, 79

stand in the market at 15

Standard and Poor's (bond rating service) (*see also* **credit rating**) 201

standby facility (*see* **committed facility**)

start-ups 147

state pension schemes 230

statutory regulation 240-247

sterling 189-191, **265-267**

sterling certificates of deposit (*see* **certificates of deposit**)

sterling index 186

stock. Used in the sense of **government stocks. A stock unit,** however, is the same as a **share** for practical purposes.

Stock Exchange, The 25, 29, 81 *et seq*, 242, **259-260**

Stock Exchange Council 245

Stock Exchange floor 81, 86

Stock Exchange money brokers 162

stockbroker 27, 84

stockmarket launch (*see* **new issue**)

stockmarket reports 95

stocks (in balance sheet) 40

stop-go pattern 96

stop-loss. An instruction (probably given to a broker) that a security should be sold if its price falls below a certain value.

straights (eurobonds) 198

striking price (in tender) 116, 161

stub equity. The very high-geared residual ordinary share capital in a company which has been financially restructured with massive debt via some form of leveraged operation: a leveraged takeover or a leveraged buy-out.

subordinated loans. Loans which rank for interest and repayment after all the other borrowings of the company. Are issued by UK banks and others, and for some purposes are treated more as share capital than as borrowings.

subscription price 77, 126

subsidiary companies, subsidiaries 37

sub-underwriters 117

sugar (commodity) 212

supervisory systems 240-247, **271**

support (for currency) 182-183

support (for share price) 136

surplus (pension fund) 229

surplus over book values 78

surveyors and estate agents (*see* **chartered surveyors**)

swap (interest rate or currency) 180, 193, 200

Swiss banks 246

switching 150

syndicate (at Lloyd's) 215-216

syndicated (venture capital finance) 146

syndicated loans 196

syndicates (of banks) 196, **264**

take-out (for financier) 146, **262**

takeover 105, 133-143, **255**, **261-262**

Takeover Panel 137-139, 245

Takeover Code 137-139

takeover activity 134

taking position in shares 84

tangible assets 68

tap stock 160

TAURUS (*see* **settlement**)

tax (*see also* **Capital Gains Tax, Corporation Tax, Income Tax**) 30, 44-45, 156, 226-227

tax advice 228

tax avoidance, evasion. Tax avoidance normally covers the lawful methods of minimizing tax liability. Tax evasion describes

the unlawful methods.

Tax Exempt Special Savings Account (TESSA) 270

tax haven. A country or area with low rates of tax where companies may register or individuals may hold their investments to minimize tax liabilities. The Bahamas, Cayman Islands and, up to a point, the Channel Islands are examples.

tax payable 41

tax shelter. A framework in which assets can be held to minimize tax liabilities. Personal equity plans (**PEPs**, q.v.) provide a tax shelter for the investments held within them.

technical analysis 100, 102, 151

technical correction 102

tender (Treasury bills) 176

tender offer 115, 116, 160

tender panel 179

term insurance 228

term loan 38, 41

TESSA (*see* **Tax Exempt Special Savings Account**)

Third Market 83, 113, 148, **259**

Third World debt 168, **263**

tick (in financial futures) 210

time value (of option) 208

times earnings (*see also* **price-earnings ratio**) 55

tin 211

tip (a share) 100, 250

tip sheets 251

tombstone advertisements 201-202

top slice (property income) 223

TOPIC (screen information system) 86

total assets less current liabilities 41

touch (of share price spread) 94

trade bill 175, 180
trade credit 40
trade creditors 40
trade investment 70
trade-weighted index (of a currency) 185-186
traded option 77, 206-209
Traded Options Market 26, 206-209, **259, 267**
traders 203
trading floor 81, **259**
trading profit 43
tranchettes (of gilt-edged stock) 160
transaction-based banking 263-264
Treasury bills 173, 176, 180
Treasury stocks 154
trigger points (for disclosure, etc.) (*see also* **disclosure**) 138-140, 262
triple-A-rated (credit rating of a borrower) (*see also* **credit rating**) 201
troughs 96
true and fair view 35
turn (marketmaker's, jobber's) 93
turnover (of gilt-edged stocks) 150
turnover (of shares, etc.) 82
turnover (sales) 43

unauthorized property unit trust 234
unauthorized unit trust 234
unbundling. Euphemism for breaking up a company into its constituent businesses, which are probably sold individually. Sometimes not vastly different from **asset stripping**.
unconditional (of takeover offer) 139-142

undated stocks (*see* **irredeemable**)
undercapitalized 85
undersubscribed (*see also* **Blue Arrow affair**) 117
undervalued 99
underwriters (of shares) 104
underwriting (insurance) 214-216
underwriting (of share issue) 88, 117, 125-126, 136
underwriting agent (Lloyd's) 216, 217
underwriting commitment 167
underwriting fees 117, 126
underwriting profit 214-215
underwritten 125
underwritten cash value 136
unit-linked insurance 231-237
unit-linked investment vehicles 231-237
unit trusts 25, 27, 228, 231-237, **271**
United States (takeover tactics) 142-143
unitization 232, 238
unitize (an investment trust) 238
unitized property 224, **269**
Unlisted Securities Market (USM) 83, 113, **259, 260**
unrelieved ACT. The **advance corporation tax (ACT)** that companies pay to the Inland Revenue in respect of dividends is really a form of basic-rate income tax they deduct on behalf of the shareholder. It is called **advance corporation tax** because companies can offset the amount deducted against the corporation tax they are due to pay on their UK income. Companies with a high proportion of earnings from abroad may not pay enough UK corporation tax to be able to offset the whole of the ACT

write (an option) (*see also* **naked writer**) 204

write down, write off. Companies may need to write down the value of certain assets if these are no longer worth the figures at which they are shown in the books. A rag trade company might need to write down its stocks of miniskirts if hemlines moved down and made them difficult to sell. Any company might need to write down its debtors if it is owed money by a customer who has gone bust and is unlikely to pay. Write-offs are more severe than write-downs — the whole of the value of the asset is deducted. **Written-down value** is the value in the accounts after write-downs. 78

written-down (*see* **write down**)

xa (*see* **ex-all**)
xc 131
xd 58, 157
xr 124, 127

yankee bond 196
years' purchase (of property) 221
yield. To calculate the income yield on an investment you multiply the annual gross dividend or interest payment by 100 and divide by the market price. If the gross dividend on a share is 10p and the market price is 200p, the yield is 10 X 100/200, or 5 per cent. 10, 17, 54 *et seq*, 97, 115

yield curve (*see also* **negative yield curve**) 180

zero-coupon bonds. These are rather like a long-term version of a bill of exchange (q.v.). Instead of paying a rate of interest, they are issued at a price well below their face value and the investor's return comes in the form of a capital gain when they are redeemed. Apportioned over the life of the bond, this gain can be expressed as a compound annual rate of interest. For example, a bond issued at £50 and redeemable in seven years at £100 offers a compound annual rate of return of around 10.4 per cent to anyone who holds it to redemption. In other words, at a compound interest rate of around 10.4 per cent, £50 would increase to £100 in seven years. 198

zinc 211